US History for Teens

An Enthralling Guide to the Key Events and Figures That Shaped the United States of America

© Copyright 2025 - All rights reserved.

The content contained within this book may not be reproduced, duplicated, or transmitted without direct written permission from the author or the publisher.

Under no circumstances will any blame or legal responsibility be held against the publisher, or author, for any damages, reparation, or monetary loss due to the information contained within this book, either directly or indirectly.

Legal Notice:

This book is copyright protected. It is only for personal use. You cannot amend, distribute, sell, use, quote, or paraphrase any part, or the content within this book, without the consent of the author or publisher.

Disclaimer Notice:

Please note the information contained within this document is for educational and entertainment purposes only. All effort has been executed to present accurate, up-to-date, reliable, and complete information. No warranties of any kind are declared or implied. Readers acknowledge that the author is not engaging in the rendering of legal, financial, medical, or professional advice. The content within this book has been derived from various sources. Please consult a licensed professional before attempting any techniques outlined in this book.

By reading this document, the reader agrees that under no circumstances is the author responsible for any losses, direct or indirect, that are incurred as a result of the use of the information contained within this document, including, but not limited to, errors, omissions, or inaccuracies.

Free limited time bonus

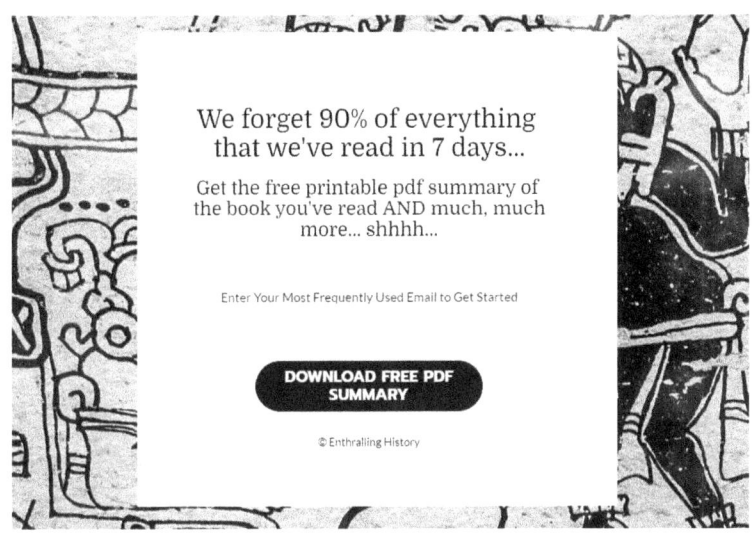

Stop for a moment. We have a free bonus set up for you. The problem is this: we forget 90% of everything that we read after 7 days. Crazy fact, right? Here's the solution: we've created a printable, 1-page pdf summary for this book that you're reading now. All you have to do to get your free pdf summary is to go to the following website: https://livetolearn.lpages.co/enthrallinghistory/

Or, Scan the QR code!

Once you do, it will be intuitive. Enjoy, and thank you!

Table of Contents

PART 1: AMERICAN HISTORY FOR TEENS 1
   INTRODUCTION 2
   CHAPTER 1: FOUNDATIONS 4
   CHAPTER 2: THE COLONIAL PERIOD (1605-1760) 16
   CHAPTER 3: REVOLUTION 28
   CHAPTER 4: CIVIL WAR 40
   CHAPTER 5: CIVIL RIGHTS 51
   CHAPTER 6: THE WAR AGAINST THE WORLD 63
   CHAPTER 7: THE SPACE RACE AND THE CUBAN ISSUE 77
   CHAPTER 8: THE WAR ON TERROR 87
   CHAPTER 9: PRESIDENTIAL PROGRESS 98
   CHAPTER 10: STAR-SPANGLED HEROES AND VILLAINS 110
   ANSWERS TO ROUNDUP QUESTIONS 121
PART 2: THE CIVIL WAR FOR TEENS 127
   INTRODUCTION 128
   CHAPTER 1: THE LAY OF THE LAND 129
   CHAPTER 2: A HISTORY OF SLAVERY IN AMERICA 143
   CHAPTER 3: A GOVERNMENT IN TURMOIL 157
   CHAPTER 4: SECESSION SPARKS THE WAR 168
   CHAPTER 5: THE EASTERN THEATER 176
   CHAPTER 6: THE WESTERN THEATER 196
   CHAPTER 7: THE WAR'S LAST GASP 210
   CHAPTER 8: BEYOND THE BATTLEFIELD 221

CHAPTER 9: THE FACES OF THE WAR 233
CHAPTER 10: HONORING THE PAST 246
HERE'S ANOTHER BOOK BY ENTHRALLING HISTORY THAT YOU
MIGHT LIKE 257
FREE LIMITED TIME BONUS 258
BIBLIOGRAPHY 259
IMAGE SOURCES 265

Part 1: American History for Teens

An Enthralling Guide to Major Events and Figures in the History of the United States of America

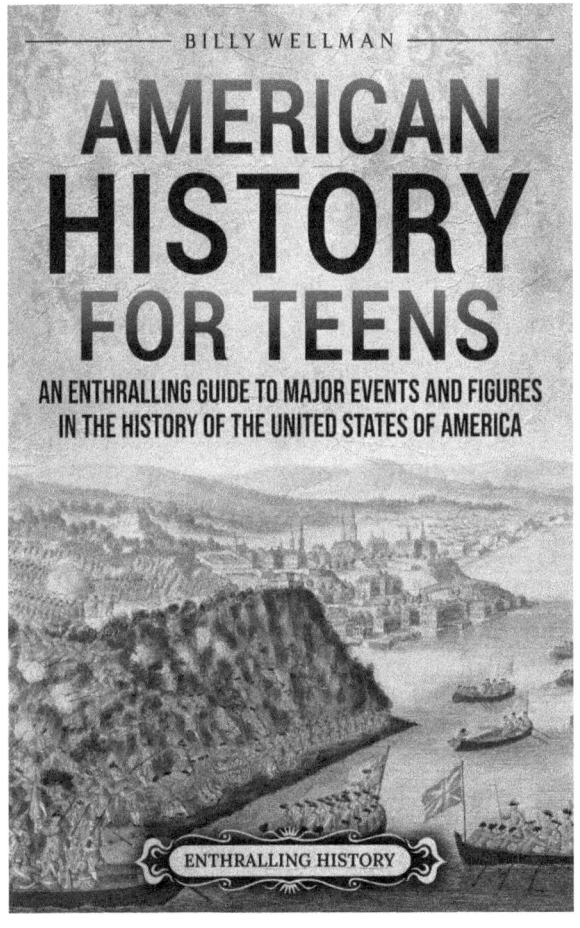

Introduction

America's history is like no other nation's. Its people came (and continue to come) from every corner of Earth. This diversity created an exciting blend of culture and new ways of doing things. Through hard work and fresh ideas, ordinary people still achieve the "American dream." The United States Constitution has protected people's rights and personal freedoms for over two hundred years.

Of course, it hasn't all been sunshine and rainbows. Many people came to America to escape oppression. They wanted a better life with bright opportunities. Yet, they displaced the people who were already in America. As the Native Americans curiously watched the colonists' ships appear on the horizon, did they have a clue that their way of life would soon end? Many ships arrived in colonial America with unwilling passengers. They had been ripped from their African homeland and shipped over as enslaved people.

Writing about America's history is complicated. There's so much information to pack in! What should be included? What, unfortunately, needs to be left out for lack of space? Should history focus only on famous people? What about all the ordinary people who made America what it is today?

This book will highlight the key events that shaped the United States of America and unwrap the stories of the resilient and brilliant people that made it happen. How did these people of the past think, feel, and act in their social and historical context? More than anything, America is a story of diverse people uniting to achieve exciting and exceptional goals. We'll explore the stories of "regular" people as well as the famous movers and shakers.

This history of America explains how we got where we are today. How did decisions made centuries ago impact how America's history unfolds? This is a key reason for diving into history. The past continues to influence the present. We'll investigate how some ideas were splendid successes. We'll also analyze the mistakes of the past that we want to avoid repeating.

America's history is an inspiring yet imperfect success story. Conflict and exploitation reared their ugly heads, and they still do. We cannot ignore or excuse the disturbing side of history, yet we can put it into perspective. America's founders were in uncharted territory. They were making it up as they went along while facing unimaginable challenges.

America's people have left an inspiring legacy. They had dreams and the tenacity, creativity, and competence to make them happen. America's founders set the course for the nation's government, economic system, and unique culture. Today, the United States of America is the most influential country on the planet. It has the world's largest economy and military and is the world leader in technology, innovation, and medical science. We have much to learn from America's mistakes and triumphs as its people overcame obstacles and forged an exceptional nation.

Chapter 1: Foundations

The first Americans were not the folks who stepped off the *Mayflower*. The Indigenous Americans had arrived thousands of years earlier. By the time the first European explorers and colonizers arrived from Spain and France, around ten million Indigenous Americans lived in what is now the United States.

How did the clash between the Indigenous Americans and colonizers play out? This chapter will unwrap the history of America's first people.

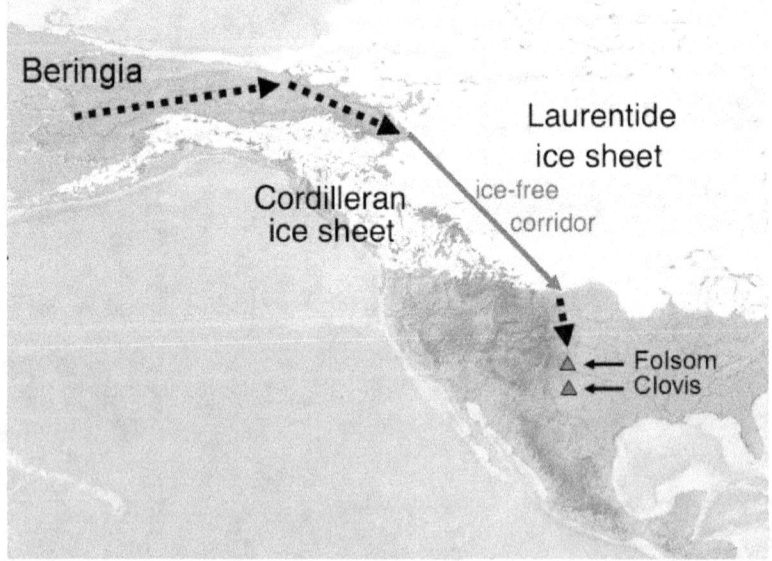

Beringia, the land bridge from Asia to America [1]

Who Were the Earliest Americans?

During the last ice age (the *Last Glacial Maximum*), people began migrating from Asia to North America. Dramatically lower sea levels uncovered a land area between Siberia and Alaska called *Beringia*. It was huge—twice as big as Texas! People and animals settled in Beringia. Some people crossed this land bridge into Alaska, following herds of woolly mammoths. As the ice age ended, the melting ice raised sea levels again. Beringia sank below the Bering Strait, so no one could walk into North America anymore.

The Clovis people were among the first tribes to enter North America and spread through the western United States. They were wandering nomads, following the mammoth, bison, and camel herds. Yes, America once had camels! These "camelops" had smaller humps and became extinct around eleven thousand years ago.

In Montana, construction workers accidentally uncovered the skulls and some bones of two little boys. One was two years old, and the other was around seven. According to radiocarbon testing, the Clovis people buried the toddler about twelve thousand years ago. His bones are the oldest human remains in the United States. Scientists named him Anzick after the family who owned the land. A nuclear genome study showed he came from Siberia, but baby Anzick's genes were closer to those of Indigenous Central and South Americans than North Americans. His tribe probably continued migrating south rather than settling down.

Later, another tribe passed through the area. They must have recognized it as a burial site. Baby Anzick was covered with red ochre, an iron oxide used in ancient burials worldwide. Tools and heirloom elk antlers surrounded him. The new tribe buried a seven-year-old boy twenty feet from Anzick. Because the burials were so close, archaeologists initially thought they were from the same era. However, radiocarbon dating puts them about three thousand years apart.

The earliest Americans spread throughout North America. Hundreds of tribes emerged with different languages, religions, housing styles, and government systems. At first, they hunted mammoths and giant armadillos called glyptodonts, the size of a small car.

The largest animals soon became extinct, probably from global warming and overhunting. The Indigenous Americans had to find other food sources. They fished, hunted smaller animals, and gathered berries and nuts. Eventually, they began farming. The Guilá Naquitz Cave in Mexico has evidence that Indigenous Americans were growing acorn squash by 6000 BCE. They soon began farming beans and maize (corn).

The Three Sisters planting system *

They grew these three crops in the "*Three Sisters*" planting system. The corn stalks were a trellis for the beans, and the beans fertilized the soil with nitrogen. The vines from the squash, grown between the corn stalks, shaded the ground, keeping it from drying out.

The Three Sisters planting system spread throughout North America. When the Europeans arrived, the Indigenous Americans taught them how to do it. The Native Americans also grew tobacco (for smoking in sacred ceremonies) and sunflowers (grinding the seeds into flour and making dye from the flowers).

Some of the Native Americans built cities. Cahokia (on the Mississippi River in Illinois) thrived in the 1100s CE. Its population of forty thousand people sprawled over six square miles, making it the largest city north of Mexico. It had 120 flat-topped mounds about 100 feet high with huge wooden temples at the top. Cahokia had a fifty-acre Grand Plaza for playing chunkey—a game in which a person threw a spear at a disk-shaped stone rolled over the ground.

A chunkey player *

Chaco Canyon in New Mexico housed thousands of people in tiered apartment buildings up to six stories high, built around 850 CE. These were the largest structures in North America for the next thousand years. One building, Pueblo Bonito, had 650 rooms. The Pueblo people built their apartments with three-foot thick walls using sandstone blocks and timber. Incredible networks of irrigation canals watered large farms outside the city.

The Indigenous Americans developed sophisticated political systems. Some used an early form of democracy, debating issues and making decisions as a group. However, they didn't emphasize individual freedoms as much as rule by the people as a whole.

The Huron (Wendat) Confederacy and Iroquois (Haudenosaunee) Confederacy formed alliances governed by clans. Membership in the clans passed from mother to child (and still does). Both men and women participated in government but in separate council meetings. The senior women advised on military and foreign policy issues. The councils decided things through negotiation and mutual agreement.

What Did the First European Explorers Discover?

The Norse Vikings were the first Europeans to sail to North America. Icelandic sagas said Leif Erikson led an expedition from Greenland to "Vinland" (Newfoundland). He had heard of the new land from other Vikings whose ship had been blown off course. They had sailed along the new land's coastline but headed back to Greenland without going to shore. Radiocarbon dating confirms Erikson briefly settled in Newfoundland around 1021 CE. Erikson wrote that they spent the winter there and returned to Greenland in the spring. Other Vikings continued to sail to Newfoundland for several decades but never established a permanent settlement.

Four centuries later, Christopher Columbus was born in Italy. He became a sailor at age fourteen and immediately fell in love with the sea. He soon became a highly skilled navigator. He believed that he could reach East Asia by crossing the Atlantic Ocean. He thought it would be quicker, safer, and easier than the complicated land and sea route people used in his day.

Columbus needed a sponsor to pay for his expedition, but Portugal and England turned him down. Finally, Queen Isabella and King Ferdinand of Spain gave him three ships. He set sail in 1492, crossing the Atlantic.

However, he thought the world was about a third smaller than it really is. Almost two thousand years earlier, the Greek mathematician Eratosthenes had calculated the circumference of the Earth and came amazingly close to today's calculations. Yet, Columbus misinterpreted the work of Eratosthenes and other early scholars.

After sailing for two months, Columbus reached an island of the Bahamas he named San Salvador. He planted a cross on its shore and led his crew in a prayer of thanksgiving. He sailed around several Caribbean islands, thinking they were in the East Indies. One of his ships, the *Santa María*, wrecked off the coast of Hispaniola (today's Haiti and the

Dominican Republic). He had to abandon the ship and left thirty-nine men behind to set up a colony.

Columbus lands in the New World.'

When Columbus returned to Spain, the king and queen made him governor of the new land. He sailed to the New World three more times. On his third voyage, he discovered South America, realizing it was a new continent. He spent his fourth voyage exploring Central America, trying to find a passage to Asia.

His attempts to govern the new land were unsuccessful. He was overly harsh to both the Indigenous people and the Spaniards he commanded. Nevertheless, his discovery of Central and South America opened the door to European colonization.

Who First Colonized the Land That Is Now the United States?

At first, the Norse Vikings of Greenland seemed interested in colonizing North America. However, they forgot about the new land as other problems distracted them. Their existence was threatened by lethal attacks by the Inuit people, climate change (it got a lot colder in an already cold country), and the plague. By 1540, the few Norse people who hadn't died abandoned Greenland.

Amazingly, it was almost two decades after Columbus died when the Spanish explorer Juan Ponce de León rediscovered North America. In

1513, Ponce de León waded ashore near today's St. Augustine, Floria, and planted the Spanish flag. Six years later, he brought fifty horses and two hundred people to establish a colony near today's Port Charlotte on Florida's southwest coast. However, fierce attacks by the Calusa people killed eighty of his men and wounded Ponce de León. The survivors retreated to Cuba.

In 1527, Pánfilo de Narváez led an expedition of six hundred men to explore Florida and set up colonies. Before even reaching Florida, a hurricane in the Caribbean sunk two of his ships. The remaining ships landed on Florida's west coast. Narváez sent three hundred men to hike up the coast, scouting out the area. Meanwhile, another one hundred men stayed on the ships sailing north. The two groups were supposed to meet at Tampa Bay, but that never happened. Narváez was confused about where he was. He thought Tampa Bay was north, but it was actually behind them, to the south.

The ships sailing up the coast looked for the land expedition but couldn't find it. Eventually, they gave up and sailed to Mexico. Led by Narváez, the land troops trudged north, dying from starvation, disease, and attacks by the Native Americans. They resorted to killing their horses and eating them. Finally, they made rafts and tried to sail to Mexico, but a storm killed all but eighty men, including Narváez. The survivors landed on Galveston Island off the Texas coast, where the Indigenous Americans enslaved them. Only four men managed to escape.

Álvar Núñez Cabeza de Vaca was one of the four escapees. It took him and his three companions eight years to make their way to the Spanish colonies in Mexico. On the way, they learned the Indigenous people's languages. The local people respected them as "children of the sun" who could pray over the sick, and they became well. These four men were the first Europeans known to explore what is now the southwestern United States.

In 1539, Spanish explorer Hernando de Soto launched an expedition to explore America's southeast. He landed at today's Tampa with three hundred horses and seven hundred men. His primary objective was finding gold, which did not pan out. His second goal was colonizing the area. He traveled north through today's Georgia, the Carolinas, and Tennessee. He kept the Indigenous Americans at bay by sending his scouts to capture their chiefs and hold them hostage. He captured and enslaved other Native Americans, put collars around their necks attached to chains, and forced them to haul supplies and grind corn to feed his men.

Hernando de Soto[5]

However, de Soto's luck ran out when he passed through Alabama in 1540. This was the land of the powerful Coosa chiefdom, which ruled over a confederation of other tribes. De Soto's men captured Tuscaloosa, the Coosa chief. When de Soto demanded supplies, Tuscaloosa told him that the nearby town of Mabila had everything they needed. De Soto marched with Tuscaloosa to Mabila and entered the town immediately with his team, not waiting for the rest of his army.

A wall of wooden poles and woven vines slathered with clay surrounded Mabila. It had several watchtowers. Tuscaloosa distracted the Spaniards by having twenty teen girls perform a dance. Yet, they were the only women around. No children could be seen either. Most of the men were fixated on the dancing girls, but one soldier peeked into a house and saw armed men crouching inside. Meanwhile, Tuscaloosa slipped away.

Suddenly, the Coosa warriors poured out of the huts like maddened bees flying out of a hive. They sent a hail of arrows toward the Spaniards, panicking the horses and instantly killing several men. In the tight space, the Spaniards could not put their horses into play. They fled out of the town gates, which the Coosa barred behind them. At that point, the rest of de Soto's men arrived. The Spaniards hurled flaming torches over the walls of Mabila, setting the houses' thatched roofs on fire. Tuscaloosa died, along with around 2,500 of his men. Twenty-two conquistadors died, and hundreds suffered arrow wounds.

De Soto led his men west, discovering the Mississippi River. They built rafts, and as they crossed the river, two thousand Aquixo warriors paddled their canoes out to greet them. The Aquixo offered gifts to de Soto, communicating friendliness, but he ordered his men to fire on them.

That winter in Arkansas was bitterly cold. De Soto had lost half his horses and one-third of his men. He died of fever in 1542, never finding the gold he wanted nor establishing a permanent colony.

In 1559, Spanish explorer Tristán de Luna y Arellano tried again to colonize Florida, leading over fifteen hundred men to Pensacola Bay. He had been a conquistador in Mexico, conquering regions and setting up colonies there. But a hurricane struck before they even unloaded the ships, sinking most of his vessels and flooding the land. The survivors fled inland to Alabama and found an abandoned Indigenous village on the Alabama River. They stayed there through the winter, but a lack of food forced them to abandon the colony.

Meanwhile, France had become interested in Florida. In 1562, the French explorer Jean Ribault explored the peninsula. In 1564, the Protestant French Huguenot, René Goulaine de Laudonnière, built Fort Caroline on the St. Johns River, near today's Jacksonville.

Spain found this threatening since their ships followed the Gulf Stream current along Florida's east coast before sailing across the Atlantic. Spanish colonizers in Mexico and Central America had finally found gold, and their ships carried treasures back to Spain.

The Spanish king, Philip II, assigned his best admiral, Don Pedro Menéndez de Avilés, to establish a colony on Florida's northeastern coast to defend against the French. In 1565, Avilés built St. Augustine with six hundred men, the first permanent colony in what would become the United States. His brilliant military maneuvers shut down the French Fort Caroline.

The Gonzalez-Alvarez House, built around 1723, the oldest surviving house in the continental United States' oldest city[6]

Once St. Augustine was established, Spain built other colonies in today's United States. In 1566, the Spanish built Santa Elena on Paris Island in South Carolina. In 1598, the Spaniards established a permanent colony in New Mexico, and in 1610, they built Santa Fe.

When Did the Slave Trade Begin?

The Indigenous Americans practiced slavery long before the European colonizers arrived. Their enslaved people were usually prisoners of war from other tribes. Slavery was especially rampant among the Aztec of Mexico, who needed a constant supply of sacrificial victims for their bloodthirsty gods. However, tribes like the Creek, Cherokee, and Iroquois used slaves for labor.

In 1415, the Portuguese began exploring West Africa's coast, looking for gold and other treasures. Although West Africa did have gold, the Portuguese developed another commodity: the sale of people. They began kidnapping Africans and selling them. In 1444, they sent 235 captured Africans to Portugal to sell as enslaved people. When the Portuguese started colonizing South America in 1500, they imported enslaved

Africans to farm their plantations. For the next three centuries, more African slaves traveled to the Americas than European colonists.

Why didn't the Portuguese enslave the Indigenous Americans? They tried. For instance, de Soto used some of them as baggage carriers. However, the Indigenous people knew the land. It was too easy for them to escape and make their way back home. Furthermore, they had contacts with nearby tribes and could act as informants. The only way the colonizers could successfully use Indigenous Americans as slaves was to capture them in one place and then sell them in a faraway colony. For instance, they might transport them from Florida to Brazil.

Another issue was that the Native Americans had no immunity to diseases brought from Europe, like smallpox, measles, and typhus. These diseases wiped out the Indigenous Americans who came in close contact with the colonizers. At least 80 percent died in the first century after Columbus arrived. In 1537, Pope Paul III forbade the enslavement of Native Americans. Although it continued to an extent, the Spanish and Portuguese colonizers began importing enslaved Africans on a large scale.

Roundup Activity

Find the words in the puzzle. Then, write a definition of each word. Check your answers in the back of the book.

Word Search: America's Early Foundations

```
V K D P F T A C J V M U K Y O
A H V S P S H L C B Y M P U W
O N U F J T Y S A U D P Q Q C
K O Z R L Z H V H X R K Z A A
D X L I O P A P O V M C B E L
D P C E C N P R K Y Q O P R U
I C A F X K S A I P O L H A S
R O M G T U S C A L O O S A A
O L E W J Y P B R Z N N B M C
Q U L D B C G S M E M I X A O
U M O B E R I N G I A Z C I O
O B P O Y C R Z T F V E D Z S
I U S C L O V I S Y U R L E A
S S D K F A E K P V M S I Q L
C N K D R G S B J M T I W J O
```

Tuscaloosa   colonizers   Beringia
Iroquois   Anzick   camelops
Cahokia   Clovis   Hurons
Coosa   Columbus   Calusa
maize

Image source[7]

Chapter 2: The Colonial Period (1605-1760)

For several centuries, the British and others colonized the land that became the United States. This chapter dives into some key events and influences in this pivotal period. What challenges did the early colonists face? How did their values shape America? What transformed America's colonies?

How Did the Reformation Influence America's Colonization?

On October 31, 1517, a monk named Martin Luther nailed his *Ninety-five Theses* to Wittenberg Castle's door. He firmly stated that only the Bible had authority on matters of faith. Only faith in Jesus brought salvation. Martin Luther's ideas turned Europe upside-down. Thousands left the Roman Catholic Church to form new Protestant groups, like the Church of England, the Puritans, and the Baptists. Some of these groups had a fresh philosophy about government. For instance, many believed religion and government should be separate. The early Reformers suffered persecution in Europe for their beliefs. They were looking for a place to be free to practice what they believed were Biblical teachings on daily life, government, economics, and more.

The new colonies in America were remarkably progressive compared to the European countries they left. The colonists considered Europe's governments to be tyrannical. They felt that the abuses and corruption in the church made it a shadow of what it was meant to be. The colonies became a haven for groups escaping religious persecution. Of course, they didn't always do it perfectly, and disagreements on how things should be done led to messy situations.

The Jews also suffered under the Inquisition in Portugal and Spain. Muslims and Jews had to convert to Christianity or be burned at the stake. Thousands did convert, but then the rulers of Spain and Portugal suspected their conversions were fake. To escape this horrific treatment, about three thousand Jews immigrated to America in the colonial period. Many Muslims fled to North Africa, where they could legally practice Islam.

What Happened to the "Lost Colony?" (1585–90)

In 1585, Sir Walter Raleigh established America's first British colony on North Carolina's Outer Banks. After a failed first start, Sir Raleigh tried again. In 1587, 115 men, women, and children arrived on Roanoke Island. Their governor was John White. His pregnant daughter, Elizabeth Dare, gave birth in August 1987 to Virginia Dare, the first English child born in America. Shortly after, Governor White returned to England to organize more supplies.

A war between England and Spain delayed his return. When White returned to his colony three years later, no one was left on Roanoke Island. They found fresh tracks but no people. The word "Croatoan" was carved into a post. White assumed the colony had fled to nearby Croatoan Island after a hostile attack by the Indigenous people. However, expeditions to find the missing colonists turned up nothing.

The Lost Colony, painted by colonist John White[9]

Who Settled Jamestown, the First Permanent English Colony? (1607)

The Virginia Colony was America's first successful English colony. Three ships holding 149 men and boys arrived in today's Virginia in 1607. One of their council leaders was John Smith, who was once a pirate and a slave. How did that happen? He was shipwrecked off the coast of France and then rescued by pirates, whom he joined for a time. Later, he was captured in battle while helping Austria fight the Turks. The Turks took him to Constantinople (today's Istanbul) as an enslaved person, shaved his head, put an iron ring around his neck, and often beat him. He finally escaped, returned to England, and joined the colonists heading to Virginia.

The colonists settled their new town on the James River. They named it Jamestown after King James I (the same king who commissioned the King James Bible). Two weeks after the colonists landed, the Powhatan tribe attacked, killing two Englishmen and wounding several others. More trouble ensued. The colonists needed safe drinking water and ran out of food. By September, sixty men had died.

John Smith and several other men were scouting for food and water when they ran into hunters from the Powhatan tribe. The Powhatans killed everyone but Smith and took him as their prisoner. The chief planned to kill Smith, but his ten-year-old daughter, Pocahontas, suddenly wrapped her arms around Smith's head, laid her head on his, and begged her father to spare him.

Chief Powhatan let Smith return to Jamestown and even sent food for the hungry colonists. He negotiated peace between the English and the other Indigenous tribes in the region. More ships arrived with new settlers, including the first women, but not enough food to sustain the growing settlement. Few of the colonists had been farmers in England. Some came from the upper class and were unwilling to work in the fields.

Unfortunately, a gunpowder explosion injured Smith's eye. He sailed to England for treatment, never returning to Jamestown. After he left, the settlers' relationship with the Powhatan tribe deteriorated. They demanded food from the tribespeople as if they were owed it. They kidnapped Pocahontas, using her as a bargaining chip. The Rev. Alexander Whitaker taught her English and how to read. She became a Christian and married John Rolfe, a prosperous tobacco farmer. (The Powhatans had taught the settlers how to grow and use tobacco.)

Pocahontas in British clothing, based on an engraving by Simon de Passe[9]

A group of Africans arrived in Jamestown in 1619. They had been kidnapped by the Portuguese, branded, chained, and forced into the hold of a slave ship packed so tightly that they could not move. Their ship was bound for Mexico when pirates attacked and took the enslaved people. The pirates sailed to Jamestown and exchanged around thirty Africans for food and supplies.

Slavery was not legal in England. Yet, the Jamestown colonists desperately needed workers to farm the land and build infrastructure.

They had been bringing indentured servants from England. These petty criminals and desperately poor people served for about seven years. They then became free and usually got a plot of land. The Jamestown colonists decided to make the Africans indentured servants. Two Africans, Isabella and Anthony, worked for William Tucker. They had a son named William in 1624. He was the first African child born and baptized in the English colonies of America.

What Brought the Puritans to America? (1620)

The Puritans were Christians who thought that the Church of England needed more reform. Although it had separated from the Roman Catholic Church, it still held many beliefs and practices that the Puritans thought were unbiblical. After enduring persecution in England, many Puritans headed to Holland, which had more religious freedom. They were free in Holland but felt the culture was *too* free. They worried that their children would be led astray.

The Puritans decided to immigrate to America to set up their own colony with their own values. In 1620, 102 pilgrims sailed on the *Mayflower* to America. One young man, John Howland, was on the deck when a large wave suddenly swept him overboard. He would have surely died except that a rope was trailing behind the ship. He managed to grab the rope and was pulled back to safety. He and his wife eventually had ten children, and their descendants included three presidents (Franklin Roosevelt and both Bushes) and the poets Henry Wadsworth Longfellow and Ralph Waldo Emerson.

The Puritans originally planned to settle in the northern part of the Virginia Colony. They got permission to do this, but a storm blew them off course. They finally weighed anchor much further north, off Cape Cod in Massachusetts. Since this region was outside British jurisdiction, they formed their own governmental system called ***The Mayflower Compact***. Based on the agreement of the majority, the men wrote up a set of laws they would follow. They pledged their continued loyalty to King James I; however, they made it clear they intended to self-govern as a society of equals. Forty-one men, including two indentured servants, signed the compact.

The Plymouth Colony suffered in its early days. The pilgrims arrived in November when the cold and snow had already set in. Most were sick, and only a few were strong enough to forage for food and water. Half of the colonists died in that brutal winter. The *Mayflower* had moored for the winter at Cape Cod, yet, astoundingly, when it sailed back to England in the spring, no colonist chose to return. They were committed to sticking it out.

Samoset introduces himself to the Puritans.[10]

How Did the Indigenous People Help the Puritan Colonists?

In the spring, the Puritans met the Indigenous Americans for the first time. A man named Samoset walked into their village. To their astonishment, he spoke to them in broken English. He told them he had become friends with English fishermen who came to the area in the summer. He said the fierce Patuxet people had recently lived where the Puritans had settled, but a plague had wiped them out (probably something like smallpox brought by the Europeans). Samoset was from the Abenaki tribe in Maine but was staying with the local Wampanoag people. He told them he would introduce them to the tribe.

Several days later, Samoset arrived with Chief Massasoit and several men with whom the Puritans made a peace treaty. One of the men who visited was Squanto, a Patuxet with an incredible story. An English explorer had kidnapped Squanto and twenty-six other Patuxet. He took them to Spain and sold them as enslaved people, but some Catholic friars bought the Patuxet people and freed them. Squanto traveled to England, where he worked as a shipbuilder. Because he had learned Spanish, English, and several Native American languages, he became an interpreter on a trade ship to get passage back home.

When Squanto reached Massachusetts, he discovered the plague had wiped out his tribe. Like Samoset, he found a home with the Wampanoag people. Squanto joined the Puritans and was invaluable. He taught them how to fish, hunt, and farm like the Native Americans. He also taught them how to live peacefully with the neighboring Indigenous people. For instance, the Puritans habitually purchased the land for their colonies from the local tribes.

The Puritans starved in their first winter. However, as the second winter approached, they had adequate food stores thanks to their Indigenous friends, especially Squanto. Governor William Bradford announced a day of thanksgiving to celebrate a good harvest and their freedom to live and worship as they chose. They invited the Wampanoag to join them, and ninety came to the feast of turkey, deer, lobster, eel, cornbread, and pies. Their Wampanoag friends stayed three days, and everyone enjoyed races, wrestling contests, and shooting competitions.

The Puritans and Wampanoag enjoy a thanksgiving feast[11]

At this time, the colony had twenty-two men, four women, fourteen teens, and thirteen small children. In the late fall, thirty-five more colonists arrived, to everyone's happy surprise. Unfortunately, they had not brought any extra food or supplies, so the Puritans had to divide up what they had.

With hard work and Squanto's help, the Puritans made it through the second winter.

How Did the Puritans Shape American Values?

A problem Jamestown experienced was that some of the colonists were unwilling to put in the challenging work of farming and building. The Puritans also experienced some lazy colonists at first. However, they applied this biblical teaching: "But if any provide not for his own, and specially for those of his own house, he hath denied the faith, and is worse than an infidel" (I Timothy 5:8, KJV). The value of hard work and self-reliance became core American values.

The Puritans also had a spirit of toughness in the face of adversity. Their problems engendered innovation, as the Puritans had to learn how to survive in a completely different world. Other Puritan values that influenced America were individual freedom, self-government, self-improvement, and building wealth through free enterprise. They believed that anyone could be successful if they applied themselves.

The Puritans were dedicated to quality education from primary school through college. They believed that boys and girls needed to be literate so they could read the Bible for themselves. They paid for schools through public money and required all children to attend. The literacy rate of Puritan colonies was much higher than that of the colonies to the south. The Puritans founded Harvard College in 1636 and Yale in 1701.

What Were Other Early Colonies?

The Puritans established colonies in Connecticut, Massachusetts, New Hampshire, and Rhode Island. British Catholics established Maryland as a tobacco-growing colony in 1634. The Dutch founded New Netherland in 1624, which became New York. Sweden settled Delaware in 1638, and the Swedes and Dutch settled New Jersey. In 1661, England took over all these colonies, and in 1663, they took the Carolinas. In 1681, a Quaker named William Penn colonized Pennsylvania and absorbed Delaware, although it was still a separate state. The British colonized Georgia in 1733. These colonies, along with Virginia, were all under British control by the mid-1700s.

How Did St. Augustine Become the First "Underground Railroad?"

Although slavery never became legal in England, the British colonies in America got involved in slavery. In the early days, the colonies used indentured servants to help farm their plantations. Half of the immigrants from England to Virginia were indentured servants. To the south, Spain and Portugal were importing thousands of enslaved Africans for the plantations in Brazil, the Caribbean, and Mexico.

Jamestown was the first to use Africans as indentured servants. They were supposed to release them after they completed their indenture. However, in 1640, an African indentured servant named John Punch ran away from his plantation with two White indentured servants. They were all captured, and the White men got a year added to their indenture as punishment for running away. However, John Punch received lifelong slavery as his penalty for the same thing. Within a year, Massachusetts became the first colony to legalize slavery, and the other colonies quickly followed. By 1700, the British colonies had close to 16,000 enslaved people.

Meanwhile, the Spanish colonists in Florida had been importing enslaved people since establishing St. Augustine in 1565. However, the Spanish king granted freedom to any slaves who escaped the British colonies and came to Florida. All they had to do was become Catholic and serve in the military for four years. The idea was to cripple the British colonies by reducing their labor force while building up Florida's military. The Spaniards settled the freed slaves at Fort Mose, just north of St. Augustine. Ironically, the Spaniards in Florida did not free their own slaves.

What Was the Great Awakening? (1730s–70s)

The Great Awakening was an extraordinary surge in Christian faith and enthusiasm that left a lasting impact on Britain and America. Thousands became Christians, and thousands more renewed their Christian faith. Benjamin Franklin wrote, "One could not walk through the town in an evening without hearing Psalms sung in different families of every street."

Jonathan Edwards was a Congregationalist pastor invited to speak in Enfield, Connecticut, a congregation with little interest in spiritual things. Edwards dusted off a sermon he'd already preached in his church in

Northampton. He was not an electrifying, Bible-thumping preacher. He read his sermon, *Sinners in the Hands of an Angry God,* in a monotone without looking out at the congregation.

Jonathan Edwards, engraved by R. Babson & J. Andrews [12]

Yet, as Edwards preached, the atmosphere in the church changed. People began shrieking and weeping as they recognized their sin. Edwards paused, waiting for people to regain their composure. As they quieted, he assured them that Jesus had "flung the door of mercy wide open and [stood] in the door crying and calling with a loud voice to poor sinners."

Another great preacher of the Great Awakening was the British minister George Whitfield. He was a friend of John and Charles Wesley, who were stirring up revival in England. Whitfield traveled through America's colonies, preaching to large outdoor crowds.

Some Christians began to question infant baptism, saying it wasn't anywhere in the Bible. These "Separatists" broke off to form new churches, especially Baptists and Methodists. It was the birth of evangelical Christianity.

The Great Awakening doubled church membership in New England. Edwards, Whitfield, and other preachers emphasized a personal conversion experience and intimacy with the Holy Spirit. As people gathered in churches and homes, emotionally singing and praying, some spoke in unknown tongues and experienced physical healing.

Roundup Activity: Fill in the Blank

Place the correct words and phrases from the list below in the chapter summary. Check your answers in the back of the book.

Carolina	Fort Mose	George Whitfield	Holland	literate
John Smith	Jonathan Edwards	Protestant		Squanto

Most of the colonists in Virginia and New England came from _____ groups. The Lost Colony disappeared from _____'s Outer Banks. Among Jamestown's early leaders, _____ _____ was a former pirate and slave. After leaving England, the Puritans first went to _____ before sailing to America. _____, a Patuxet man, taught the Puritans to farm, hunt, and fish. The Puritans believed all children needed to be _____. The Spaniards in Florida offered freedom to slaves who escaped the British colonies and settled them at _____ _____. _____ and _____ were two ministers who helped spark the Great Awakening.

Chapter 3: Revolution

Twelve years before the American Revolution, the British won an astounding victory in the French and Indian War, quadrupling the size of its American colonies. Patriotism was at an all-time high among the colonists. How did it all come crashing down? What were the seeds of the revolution? Why was the American Revolutionary War arguably among the most critical events in world history? Let's explore!

How Did the French and Indian War Change the Colonies? (1754–63)

In 1754, conflict erupted between America's British, Spanish, and French colonies. It started in Pennsylvania when the French and British both claimed an area in the Allegheny Mountains. George Washington, twenty-two at the time, outwitted a French ambush with his Seneca allies. However, while Washington was negotiating peace terms with the French commander, the Seneca chief suddenly planted his hatchet in the Frenchman's head. Negotiations fell apart, and the war began.

At this point, Britain controlled the colonies stretching from New Hampshire to Georgia. The French territory reached from Canada through the Midwest and down to Alabama, Mississippi, and Louisiana. Spain controlled Florida and the Southwest. France and Britain argued over who owned the Ohio River Valley of southwestern New York, western Pennsylvania, Ohio, West Virginia, Indiana, Kentucky, and Tennessee.

Some Indigenous American tribes allied with the French, and some with the British. The Iroquois Nation and Cherokees supported the British. This war was part of a global conflict—the *Seven Years' War*—that pitted Great Britain and Prussia against France, Spain, Russia, Sweden, and Saxony. The 1763 *Treaty of Paris* ended both wars. The British added everything east of the Mississippi to its territories. Britain also gave Cuba to Spain in exchange for Florida. Spain got most of France's territory west of the Mississippi.

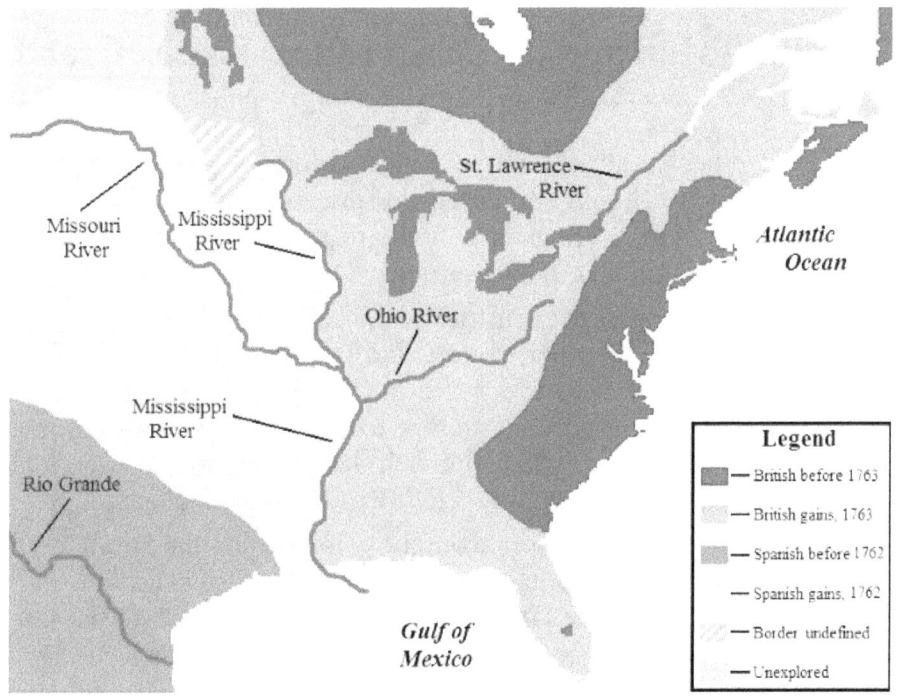

Territory at the end of the French and Indian War [18]

How Did the "Enlightenment" Influence the Colonies?

The Enlightenment was an intellectual trend in the seventeenth and eighteenth centuries that placed reason over faith and tradition. In Europe, many Enlightenment thinkers were also agnostic or atheist, believing one could not be both an intellectual and a Christian. However, many American Enlightenment thinkers still believed in God. Nevertheless, they thought philosophy and science were the answers to their problems.

A key American Enlightenment figure was Benjamin Franklin. He came from a profoundly religious Puritan family. Yet, as a teen, he embraced deism, which says that God created the world but then left it to run itself. Franklin believed religion was valuable because it taught moral behavior, which an orderly society needed. That's why he approved of the Great Awakening, although some folks said it was "anti-intellectual." Both the Enlightenment and the Great Awakening led to a change in thinking. People began to question tradition and governmental authority.

How Did Mercantilism and Other Issues Create Unrest?

Britain (and other countries) had colonies to increase their wealth and access to resources. Britain controlled the price of cotton, tobacco, and gold from the colonies. England's trade regulations discouraged their colonies from trading with other countries.

England also discouraged industries in the colonies. They wanted them to send raw goods, like timber, cotton, and precious metals, to England. The colonists then had to buy things from England made from raw goods. This is called **mercantilism**—the attempt to build power and prosperity through one-sided trade. This approach led to tension between the colonies and England as the colonists felt Britain was exploiting them.

Britain began to demand more from the colonies after the Seven Years' War, which had emptied Britain's treasury and sunk it deep into debt. Britain's young King George III felt it was fair for the colonists to pay taxes on things like coffee, sugar, and wine to help pay the debt. In 1765, Parliament introduced the **Stamp Act**, a tax on documents in the colonies. Almost all documents, even the newspapers, were printed on stamped paper, so they had to be taxed.

Benjamin Franklin thought the taxes were reasonable. However, many colonists grumbled, "We have no American seats in the Parliament. How can we be taxed when no one speaks for us?"

The British leaders replied, "You are *virtually* represented! You are right—you can't vote for members of Parliament, but neither can women or poor people here. Nevertheless, we're looking out for their best interests, just like we're looking out for yours."

Benjamin Franklin by Joseph-Siffred Duplessis, circa 1778 [14]

A young lawyer named Patrick Henry published a list of reasons why the Stamp Act was illegal. Britain began having second thoughts. They called Benjamin Franklin over to testify before Parliament. Although Franklin didn't personally object to the Stamp Act, he was brutally honest with Parliament on its impact on American morale.

"What was the temper of America toward Great Britain before the year 1763?"

"The best in the world!" Franklin answered. "They submitted willingly to the government of the Crown."

"And what is their temper now?"

"O, very much altered."

The Parliament asked Franklin if the colonists would submit to the Stamp Act if they removed the obnoxious parts. He shook his head. "No, they will never submit to it."[1]

---

[1] Thomas Kidd, *American History, Combined Edition: 1492-Present* (B&H Academic, 2019).

What Led up to the Boston Tea Party?

Parliament repealed the Stamp Act in 1766, but they passed the *Townshend Acts* the following year—more taxes and regulations. The first act punished New York for not supporting the British soldiers in their colony. The second act taxed glass, lead, paint, paper, and tea shipped from Britain to America. The third act was a system to collect taxes, and the fourth act removed shipping fees for the British sending tea to America.

The indignant colonists sputtered, "Well, in that case, we won't import goods from Britain!"

In 1768, four thousand British soldiers were stationed in Boston.

"Why did they send so many soldiers?" people anxiously wondered. "We have only 16,000 people in Boston, including women and children!"

In 1770, an unruly crowd gathered in Boston, heckling the British soldiers and throwing snowballs at them. The British shot into the crowd, killing five colonists and wounding six others. After this, the British repealed most of the Townshend Acts. Yet, they kept the tax on tea. "We still have sovereign authority to tax the colonies!"

In response, the American colonists stopped buying tea. They began growing their own herbal teas or drinking coffee. Drinking regular tea became "un-American."

Losing the American market devastated the British-owned East India Company. The British tried to fix the problem with a new bill in 1773 that reduced the tea tax. However, it only allowed a few colonists loyal to the Crown to act as tea agents.

"Send it back!" the American patriots roared, blocking tea shipments into New York and Philadelphia.

In Boston, a group of patriots disguised themselves by rubbing soot on their faces and dressing as Native Americans. They boarded the tea ships, broke 342 crates open, and dumped the tea into Boston Harbor. The "Boston Tea Party" enraged the British Parliament. Britain closed Boston Harbor to all merchant ships. It also reworked Massachusetts' government, giving power to royal appointees.

The colonists were appalled. "Massachusetts had a legally elected government! How could the British shut it down? What will happen to our other colonies? We must get all the colonies together and discuss our next actions!"

What Did the First Continental Congress Decide? (1774)

Delegates from every colony except Georgia gathered in Philadelphia for the *First Continental Congress*. Leaders in the group included George Washington, Patrick Henry, and Samuel Adams. Adams was a radical who wanted to escalate the resistance movement. Others want to avoid goading Britain any further. Paul Revere brought the "Suffolk Resolves" from Massachusetts, demanding that the colonists resist any further actions of Britain to "enslave America."

"We must prepare a military for self-defense and end all commerce with Britain!"

The Continental Congress adopted a *Declaration of Rights*, which said the colonists were "entitled to life, liberty, and property."

"We should have the same rights and freedoms as the people living in England!"

The Congress also formed an association of seven thousand men to enforce a ban on British trade with America. Patriotic women formed groups to educate other women about substitutes for British goods. They shamed anyone they found out was using them. Conversations among patriotic women often sounded something like this:

"Ladies, did you hear that Mrs. Appleton is still drinking tea?"

A collective gasp rose from the women bending over their needlework.

One woman cleared her throat. "We must explain to her that coffee is patriotic. It's the American way!"

"Hear! Hear!" the other ladies murmured.

"Give Me Liberty or Give Me Death!"

In March 1775, Patriot Patrick Henry was a delegate to the Second Virginia Convention, which discussed an independent militia. Thomas Jefferson and George Washington attended. Patrick Henry defended the need for an American army: "The war is inevitable, and let it come! ... Is life so dear, or peace so sweet, as to be purchased at the price of chains and slavery? Forbid it, Almighty God! I know not what course others may take; but as for me, give me liberty or give me death!"[i]

---

[i] Thomas S. Kidd, *Patrick Henry: First Among Patriots* (Basic Books, 2011), 52.

"The Shot Heard Round the World"

No one technically declared war, but it began anyway. The British heard that the colonists had a cache of weapons in Concord, Massachusetts. On April 18, 1775, the British "Redcoats" marched on Concord by night. The "Sons of Liberty," a clandestine patriot group, had an alert system set up using lanterns and horseback riders. Paul Revere and William Dawes raced by horseback to Lexington, alerting their riders on the way.

Paul Revere's Ride[15]

The Massachusetts colonists quickly mobilized to fight the British in the Battles of Lexington and Concord. It began with "the shot heard round the world" in Lexington. No one was sure where the first shot came from. Was it a British or American soldier? Yet, once that shot rang out, the bullets flew. The British shot eight Americans and headed to Concord, where they faced a formidable defense. It was a swift victory for the colonists, who chased the Redcoats back to Boston. Ralph Waldo Emerson immortalized the first gunshot in his 1837 poem "Concord Hymn."

Three weeks later, the Green Mountain Boys, a Vermont militia, attacked Fort Ticonderoga on Lake Champlain. Their dawn attack surprised and quickly overcame the sleeping British. After the Green Mountain Boys' victory, they sent the fort's cannons to the American forces outside Boston to use in their siege against the city.

The Battle of Bunker (Breed's) Hill (June 1775)

On June 14, 1775, the Second Continental Congress authorized a Continental Army commanded by George Washington. On June 17, the British and the Americans clashed in the Battle of Bunker Hill outside Boston. Technically, the British won, as the Americans retreated. However, 1,054 British were killed or wounded compared to 450 Americans who were killed, captured, or injured. The inexperienced American militia proved they had what it took to fight the British army.

The Boston Siege (1776)

In the spring of 1776, George Washington's troops attacked Boston again. With the Americans surrounding Boston, the British could only get supplies or reinforcements by sea. However, Washington commissioned local fishing boats to interfere with these shipments. Over the winter, the Americans had dragged the canons from Ticonderoga on sleds over the snow to Boston's outskirts. They set their canons up at high spots around Boston and began bombarding the British on March 2. The British shot back, but their smaller cannons were out of range. On March 17, about ten thousand British troops fled Boston by ship.

The Declaration of Independence (July 4, 1776)

Heady with their early victories, the Continental Congress met in Philadelphia to formally declare that the thirteen colonies were independent. The Declaration of Independence stated: "We hold these truths to be self-evident, that all men are created equal, that they are endowed by their Creator with certain unalienable Rights, that among these are Life, Liberty and the pursuit of Happiness."

The declaration explained that when a government becomes destructive, it is the people's right to change or end it. It then listed King George's tyrannical acts against the Americans. The declaration dissolved America's political connection to Britain.

Crossing the Delaware by Emanuel Leutz [16]

Battle of Trenton (Christmas 1776)

The euphoria from the spring victory melted away in the fall when the Americans lost three battles in New York and New Jersey. The loss at Manhattan was especially disastrous. The Americans had quickly built Fort Washington overlooking the harbor, and General Nathanael Greene was busy sinking British ships. That's when British General William Howe decided to take out the American fort with his 8,000 British forces. General Washington was on the other side of the Hudson, unable to help the men in Manhattan. The Americans fought bravely but ultimately surrendered on November 16, 1776.

Washington and his demoralized men fled to Pennsylvania, where they camped by the Delaware River. Copies of Thomas Paine's booklet *Common Sense* circulated through the troops, giving them fresh encouragement: "The cause of America is in a great measure the cause of all mankind." Paine criticized the kingship system: "'Tis a form of government which the word of God bears testimony against, and blood will attend it." Paine laid out what an ideal government might look like, led by a president, with each colony represented by delegates. Paine challenged his readers, "A government of our own is a natural right."

With their resolve strengthened, Washington's men rowed over the Delaware on a dark and icy Christmas Eve. They marched to Trenton, arriving at dawn and surprising the Hessian soldiers (Germans hired by the British). Some of the Hessians escaped, but after their leader, Colonel Johann Rall, died from a gunshot, the rest surrendered. The Battle of Trenton brought a welcome victory on Christmas Day with captured food and supplies. With emboldened troops and restored morale, Washington scored another stunning triumph a week later at Princeton.

Battle of Saratoga (September–October 1777)

This pivotal battle took place just north of today's Albany, New York. Eight thousand British troops were marching south from Canada, led by General John Burgoyne. Thirteen thousand Americans, led by General Horatio Gates, wanted to block them from the Hudson River Valley. With greater numbers and assistance from French cannons, the Americans prevailed. The victory helped convince France to throw its support firmly behind the Americans.

The Battle of Yorktown Ends the War (September–October 1781)

The war had been dragging on for six years. Everyone was weary. The Americans were low on food and deep in war debt. Britain was simultaneously fighting France and Spain. General Washington had to decide: should he make another strike on New York City and wrap things up there, or should he march south and face off against General Cornwallis in Virginia? Washington gambled on Virginia.

His French ally, Lt. Gen. Comte de Rochambeau, promised the French forces would support the Americans. Washington had almost twenty thousand French and American troops, yet the British only had nine thousand in Virginia. Most of their army was in New York, where they expected Washington to attack. As Washington marched south, the French Navy blocked the British Royal Navy from entering Chesapeake Bay.

On September 28, the American army arrived at Yorktown and began digging trenches around the city. The British tried firing on the ditch diggers but were low on ammunition. The serious fighting began on October 9. Washington's canons pummeled the British for five days. Clouds covered the moon on October 14, and under cover of darkness, the Americans launched a surprise attack on the British fortifications outside the city.

On October 17, the Americans saw a drummer boy on a parapet, beating the rhythm to "Parley" (discussion of terms). Next to him stood a British officer waving a white handkerchief. The British had lost about 8,500 men compared to under 400 Americans and French. The British war machine had collapsed. When word reached Britain, Prime Minister North sighed, "Oh God. It is all over. It is all over."

The Peace of Paris (1783)

Several months later, Parliament authorized peace terms with America. It took two years of diplomatic negotiations to hash out the terms. The *Peace of Paris*, signed on September 3, 1783, officially ended the war. It recognized the United States as an independent nation with the Mississippi River as its western boundary. Britain gave Florida back to Spain.

How Did the Constitution and the Bill of Rights Shape the New Nation?

Written in 1787 and put into action in 1789, the United States Constitution created America's government. It separated the government into three branches: legislative, executive, and judicial. The legislative branch (Congress) makes the laws. The executive branch carries out the laws. It includes the president and his or her Cabinet and federal agencies. The judicial branch (the Supreme Court and lesser courts) evaluates and interprets laws. On April 30, 1789, George Washington became the United States' first president.

Within two years, the new American leaders realized they had forgotten to include

George Washington by James Peale, circa 1782 [17]

fundamental human rights in the Constitution. So, they added the **Bill of Rights** as the first ten amendments to the Constitution. They provided for the protection of private property, protection from unreasonable searches and cruel punishment, and the right to free speech, carry arms, gather peacefully, practice one's religion, and have a speedy and fair trial.

Roundup Activity: True or False?

Mark each question "T" or "F." Check your answers in the back of the book.

( ) 1. The 1763 Treaty of Paris gave the French all the colonies east of the Mississippi River.

( ) 2. The Enlightenment thinkers preferred intellectual reason over faith and tradition.

( ) 3. The British trade policies with the American colonists were fair and profitable for all.

( ) 4. The Boston Tea Party led to the British closing Boston Harbor.

( ) 5. The Green Mountain Boys sent the canons from Fort Ticonderoga to Boston.

( ) 6. The Continental Congress wrote the Declaration of Independence at the war's end.

( ) 7. Thomas Paine's booklet *Common Sense* strengthened the resolve of the Americans.

( ) 8. Washington's troops won the Battle of Trenton on Christmas Day.

( ) 9. The Treaty of Paris recognized American independence and gave Florida back to Spain.

( ) 10. The Bill of Rights included freedom of speech and religion.

Chapter 4: Civil War

The Revolutionary War created the United States of America yet left unfinished business. The Declaration of Independence says all people are created equal. They have God-given rights to liberty and the pursuit of happiness. Was everyone in America truly equal in 1776? The half-million enslaved people were not. They did not have freedom and could not pursue happiness. In less than a century, the number of slaves morphed to four million!

The Civil War (1861-65) freed the enslaved people, which was the fundamental cause of the war. Yet the war also tackled another question: Could states just *secede* (drop out) if they were unhappy with the central government? Could the United States split up, or was it an indivisible nation?

When the North won the war, it settled the slavery and secession issues. Yes, the United States *is* one nation. It cannot be divided. States cannot pull out because they dislike how the White House runs things. The war settled the matters—but at a horrific cost. It killed at least 625,000 people. The war destroyed the South's infrastructure and economy, and it left the country drowning in debt.

How Were the Early Abolitionists Agents of Change?

The abolitionist movement was a group of people who worked to change how folks thought about slavery. In colonial days, many Americans considered it a "necessary evil." The abolitionists tried to educate Americans about the horrors of slavery. No evil is necessary. There is always another path.

- **Thomas Jefferson (1743-1826)** wrote the Declaration of Independence and was America's third president. He expressed "radical" views about slavery even before the American Revolution: "It's moral depravity and a hideous blot on our nation!" "It's contrary to the laws of nature! Everyone has the right to personal freedom." "Slavery is the greatest threat to America's survival."

Unfortunately, Jefferson did not practice what he preached. He owned over six hundred enslaved people. After his wife died, Jefferson began a sexual relationship with his slave, Sally Hemmings, when she was about sixteen. Sally was his wife's half-sister. They had the same father, but Sally's mother was enslaved. Jefferson was the father of Sally's seven children. He freed some of them in his lifetime and left instructions in his will to free the rest after he died.

To his credit, Jefferson legally ended slave traders bringing new enslaved people to America. In 1807, when Jefferson was president, Congress passed a national ban on importing slaves. (They still got smuggled in illegally.) But what about the enslaved people already in America? Jefferson recommended all slaves should be educated, released as adults, and sent to a colony in Africa.

- **Ralph Waldo Emerson (1803-82)** was a philosopher and poet in the transcendentalist movement popular in the 1800s. This movement taught that people and nature are good at their core but corrupted by society. They believed that one's intuition or gut feelings are more important than what one sees and experiences in real life.

Emerson gave lectures opposing slavery and spoke out against the **Fugitive Slave Law**, which said that an enslaved person who escaped and traveled to another state had to be returned. In his 1860 essay collection, *The Conduct of Life*, Emerson said that civil war might be the only way to end slavery. He roared out in a speech, "The South calls slavery an institution ... I call it destitution."

Although he influenced people against slavery in his speeches and essays, Emerson believed in a hierarchy of races (common at that time and eventually part of Nazi philosophy). He believed those of European descent were better than Africans, and, among Europeans, the Saxons (Germanic people in England and Germany) were superior.

Frederick Douglass [18]

- **Frederick Douglass (1818-95)** was an enslaved Black person in Maryland who escaped to New York when he was about twenty. "A new world had opened upon me. If life is more than breath and the 'quick round of blood,' I lived more in one day than in a year of my slave life. It was a time of joyous excitement which words can but tamely describe."

  Douglass had learned to read and write while an enslaved person and taught other enslaved men to read. When he escaped slavery, he became a preacher. Once, while speaking against slavery in Indiana, a mob attacked him and broke his hand. Douglass changed his name after escaping slavery but was always looking over his shoulder, wondering if his former owner would hunt him down. He traveled to Ireland and England, speaking in churches. Some British friends legally bought his freedom from his owner.

Douglass returned to New York state and began publishing an anti-slavery newspaper, *North Star*. He and his wife also worked with the Underground Railroad, assisting escaped slaves on their way to freedom in Canada. Although the Northern states did not have slaves, the Fugitive Slave Law required the Northern states to return slaves to their masters in the Southern states.

After the Civil War, Douglass strongly advocated for Black men to have the right to vote. (Neither White nor Black women could vote until 1919.) He started the first Black labor union in the United States: the *American League of Colored Laborers*.

How Did the Second Great Awakening Influence the Abolition Movement?

In 1803, the Louisiana Purchase doubled America's land area. The United States bought 828,000 square miles of land west of the Mississippi from France. A surge of nearly one million pioneers poured into the new frontier. Several years before this happened, Christian ministers had been moaning about the spiritual need in Kentucky and Tennessee, where many of these pioneers came from. They said, "Most of them have never seen a Bible, much less read one. Thousands out here have never been baptized or heard a sermon! They've never heard the name of Christ except in curses."

New territory from the Louisiana Purchase[19]

The spiritual condition of the settlers seemed hopeless until reports began filtering in of "times of refreshing." It started with several Presbyterian ministers in Kentucky and Tennessee, led by Rev. James McGready, who began holding camp meetings. As the ministers preached, many people fell to the ground, shrieking in anguish, "How can I be saved?" God's love and goodness overwhelmed them as they responded to the call for salvation.

The revival spread from Kentucky and Tennessee into Indiana and Ohio, and the Methodist and Baptist churches joined in. Renewed faith followed the pioneers into the Midwest. In the Northeast, a revival occurred at Yale University, under its new president, Timothy Dwight (Jonathan Edwards' grandson), and spread through the New England colleges.

Some pastors had already been preaching against slavery. The Quakers had always spoken out against the unjust system. Now, the new religious fervor among evangelicals amplified the message: "All people bear the image of our Creator! That means we are all equal."

Renewed faith led to a desire to cure problems in society, like alcoholism, prostitution, and child labor. Devout men and women took up the cause of slavery. Most abolitionists were in the Northern states, which had already outlawed slavery. They shamed the Southern churchgoers, "It's hypocritical to say you're a Christian when you own slaves!"

What Part Did the Democrat and Republican Parties Play?

A question arose about the territory from the Louisiana Purchase. Would slavery be allowed in the new Midwestern states? The Democratic Party was formed in 1828 as a pro-slavery party. The Republican Party was established in 1854 and opposed expanding slavery to new territories. The two parties clashed over the **Kansas-Nebraska Act** of 1854, which the Democrats drafted and President Franklin Pierce signed.

The Kansas-Nebraska Act permitted the opening of new land for American settlers and the building of a transcontinental railroad through it. However, in politics, it's always a game of "If you sign my bill, I promise I'll do such and such for you." To get the Southern Democrats to support the Kansas-Nebraska Act, the backers promised to repeal the **Missouri**

Compromise of 1820.

The Missouri Compromise did three things. It admitted Maine and Missouri into the US as new states. It said that Maine was a free state but that Missouri could have slaves. However, aside from Missouri, the bill said there could be no new slave states north of latitude 36°30' north. The backers of the Kansas-Nebraska Act got the Missouri Compromise overturned. Now, the Northern states in the new territory could have slaves.

How Did Abraham Lincoln's Election Shake Things Up?

For the 1860 presidential elections, the Republicans chose Abraham Lincoln as their candidate. He made a campaign promise that the new territories would not have slavery. Lincoln won the election, becoming America's first Republican president. At that point, seven Southern states seceded from the United States. South Carolina left the Union first. Alabama, Florida, Georgia, Louisiana, Mississippi, and Texas withdrew two months later. The seven states formed a new country: the Confederate States of America. Arkansas, North Carolina, Tennessee, and Virginia seceded within several months. In February, the Confederates elected Jefferson Davis as their president. He had been secretary of war and a United States senator.

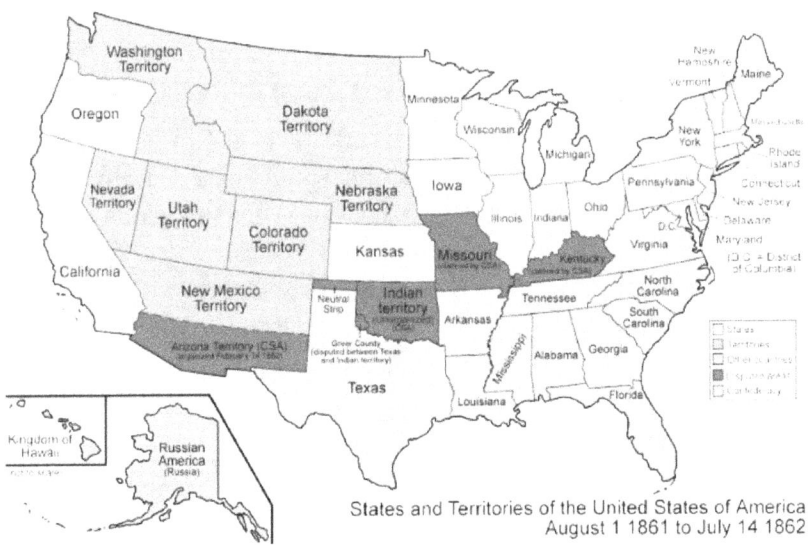

At the beginning of the Civil War [30]

Lincoln's government and the Northern states refused to recognize the Confederate States. On April 12, 1861, events at Fort Sumter near Charleston triggered war. The Confederates took control of the fort and lowered the American flag. Insurrection! President Lincoln called out for his army. Over the next four years, almost three million soldiers confronted each other in battle. Families were split, with some men fighting for the North and other brothers or sons for the South.

What Resources and Leadership Did Each Side Have?

At the beginning of the war, the population in the North (around 22 million) was more than twice that of the South. Of the South's nine million people, four million were enslaved. The North also had more resources, like food, money, and factories. Yet, the Confederates held a vast swathe of land with excellent ports. Making headway in the Southern states spread the Union army thin.

Two important generals were Robert E. Lee and Ulysses S. Grant. Both graduated from the United States Military Academy at West Point. Lee came from one of Virginia's founding families and became the Confederates' lead commander. Grant commanded the Northern troops and was elected President of the United States after the war. The two men had different leadership styles but became seasoned and stellar commanders as the war continued.

Battle of Bull Run, Virginia, July 1861

The first major confrontation was the Battle of Bull Run, only twenty-five miles from Washington, D.C. Before the battle started, both sides were confident that they would win the war quickly. After the brutal and bloody encounter of more than sixty thousand men, both sides realized there would be no quick and easy win. Nevertheless, no one imagined the struggle would last four years.

The battle began at dawn when Union General Irvin McDowell led his troops up Bull Run Creek. He hoped to cross behind General P. G. T. Beauregard's rebel forces. However, the Confederate scouts spotted them, and McDowell lost the element of surprise. Nevertheless, his men successfully pushed the rebels into retreat. But then, Brig. Gen. Thomas J. Jackson arrived with a Virginia brigade.

Jackson earned the nickname "Stonewall" that day. His men hid in the tall grass on a hill. Not knowing they were there, McDowell positioned his rifled artillery batteries just three hundred yards away. They were sitting ducks for Stonewall's men. Jackson's men held the line like a "stone wall" until Confederate reinforcements arrived and chased the Union soldiers down the hill.

Crowds of spectators had come from D.C. to watch the battle, confident the Union would crush the rebels. As the Union soldiers rushed in full retreat, they collided with the spectators. Almost three thousand Union soldiers were killed, wounded, or captured compared to about two thousand Confederates.

The Thai King Offers His War Elephants

In early 1861, Rama IV of Siam offered to ship some war elephants to America. "I heard you have no elephants! I would like to send you several pairs. You can set them loose in your forests to breed and build up large herds. With their enormous size and strength, they can easily travel through uncleared woods and matted jungles." Abraham Lincoln wrote back, politely thanking the king for his kind offer but explaining that America's climate and geography did not favor breeding elephants.

Battle of Antietam, September 1862

This battle had horrifying casualties (22,000). And yet, the blood bath had no clear winner. Lincoln declared a Union win, but the North lost more men. What's worse, Union General George B. McClellan dropped the ball tactically. He wasn't aggressive enough, allowing General Robert E. Lee to move his men around and fend off the Union attacks.

Lee marched into Maryland, intending to move the war to the North. He even hoped to capture Washington, D.C. Stonewall Jackson had just scored an astounding victory at Harper's Ferry, where all thirteen thousand Union soldiers surrendered. Lee lined his men up at Antietam Creek. It was too deep and swift to cross except by bridge. His men could fire on the Union soldiers without worrying about a charge.

However, General McClellan sent part of his Union army downstream to cross over a bridge. They hiked back on the other side of the river and attacked the Confederates' left flank in a cornfield. However, Jackson's men mowed down the Union soldiers in the field and held the line. Other Union soldiers crossed the creek and attacked the center forces, yet they could not hold the charge. They retreated. The Union General Ambrose Burnside crossed another bridge under heavy fire. He attacked the Confederate right flank and would have won, except more Confederate men arrived from Harper's Ferry and saved the day.

So many men suffered horrific injuries that the battlefield doctors were overwhelmed. Nurse Clara Barton (who later founded the Red Cross) arrived with a wagon full of bandages and other medical supplies. The "Angel of the Battlefield" assisted the surgeons in caring for the injured and dying men as the bullets were still flying.

Clara Barton, Founder of the Red Cross [21]

Emancipation Proclamation, 1863

On New Year's Day, 1863, Abraham Lincoln's Emancipation Proclamation took effect. It freed the enslaved people in the "rebellious states" but not those in the Union. Four states in the Union —Delaware, Kentucky, Maryland, and Missouri—still had slaves. They were the border states between the North and South. Lincoln was afraid that if he made them give up their slaves, they would go over to the Confederate side.

What was the point of the Emancipation Proclamation? If the enslaved people in the Confederate states could escape to the North, they were officially free. About one-half million did, but three million stayed in the South. If enslaved men could flee to a Union army that was fighting in the

South, they were considered free and could join the army. About 180,000 Black men served in the Union Army, but some had been free before the war started.

Battle of Gettysburg, Pennsylvania, July 1863

The Battle of Gettysburg turned the tide for a Union victory. Robert E. Lee made a second attempt to invade the North, hoping to score a win for the Confederates. He made it to Pennsylvania. However, losing over one-third of his men (killed, injured, or captured) dashed his hopes.

The battle began when the Union army launched a surprise attack on Confederate forces marching to Gettysburg to snatch supplies. The Confederates fended off the Union soldiers, but the following day, the Union line blocked access to Gettysburg. General Lee had more men than the Union, so he outflanked the Union army.

The South prevailed on the second day, but disaster loomed on the third day. The Confederate soldiers daringly launched a charge toward a small ridge. They reached the top and held it temporarily but lost over half their men. Lee's forces withdrew and plodded south through the rain. Inexplicably, Union General George Meade did not chase them, to President Lincoln's despair. "We had only to stretch forth our hands, and they were ours."

The War Grinds to an End

The war raged on for two more years, with around a hundred more battles and skirmishes. Both sides used submarines—or at least tried to. The Union had a submarine called the *Alligator* with compressed air and a diver lock. However, before it was used in war, it sank in a storm off Cape Hatteras. In February 1864, the Confederate *H. L. Hunley* sank the USS *Housatonic*, the first time a submarine sank a warship. Nevertheless, the blast also killed the crew members on the *Hunley*, and it sank to the bottom of the Atlantic Ocean outside Charleston Harbor.

In May 1864, General William Sherman penetrated the Confederate heartland. For two months, he battled his way closer and closer to Atlanta. When he reached the outskirts, part of his army pummeled Atlanta with cannon fire while the rest severed the railroad lines around the city, cutting off supplies. In September, Atlanta surrendered. Sherman left Atlanta in ashes and marched from there to Savannah, leaving a swathe of destruction in his wake.

On April 9, 1865, General Lee surrendered to General Grant at the Appomattox Court House in Virginia. The war was over, although it took a few weeks for the other Confederate armies and states to surrender.

On April 14, 1865, President Lincoln was assassinated, and his vice president, Andrew Johnson, became president. Johnson granted amnesty to most of the Confederate leaders and soldiers. By December 1865, the Thirteenth Amendment passed, which ended slavery in the United States.

Roundup Activity: Essay

Choose a vital aspect of the Civil War, such as a significant battle, the abolition movement, or the results of the war. Write a half-page essay highlighting why it was important in changing American history.

Chapter 5: Civil Rights

Perhaps you are wondering why this chapter appears in the middle of the book. Wasn't the civil rights movement a 1960s thing? Yes, it was, but the struggle did not begin then. The Thirteenth Amendment ended slavery, but people of color still had limited rights. How did the struggle for equality unfold? How did civil rights heroes shatter the strongholds of segregation and discrimination? Let's explore this important topic.

What Is Racism?

Racism is the belief that a person's genetics determines their morality, intelligence, and abilities. Many people of European ancestry justified slavery because they thought Africans and Indigenous Americans were racially inferior. Did they really believe that—in their heart of hearts? For some slave owners, labeling non-Whites as "lesser" people helped them avoid a guilty conscience. Other Americans and Europeans sincerely believed the White race was superior and had every right to dominate the world.

How Did Abraham Lincoln Weigh In?

Abraham Lincoln clarified his views in his debate with Stephen A. Douglas in 1858:

"I am not, nor ever have been, in favor of bringing about in any way the social and political equality of the white and black races ... I am not nor ever have been in favor of making voters or jurors of negroes, nor of qualifying them to hold office, nor to intermarry with white people. I will say, in addition to this, that there is a physical difference between the white and black races, which I believe will forever forbid the two races living together on terms of social and political equality. And inasmuch as they cannot so live, while they do remain together, there must be the position of superior and inferior, and I as much as any other man am in favor of having the superior position assigned to the white race."[i]

However, Lincoln's views on race are complex and hotly debated. There is evidence that his views shifted over time.

How Did Charles Darwin Contribute to Racist Ideology?

In the mid-1800s, Darwin wrote about his theory of evolution. Because evolution was an ongoing process, he said that those of European descent were more evolved than those from Africa. Thus, Darwin believed that a racial hierarchy was natural. Whites should run the show because they evolved earlier and had more abilities. He even suggested in *The Descent of Man* (1871) that "the civilized races of man will almost certainly exterminate and replace the savage races throughout the world."[ii]

What Happened in the Reconstruction Period? (1863–77)

Reconstruction was the rebuilding and reshaping of the nation at the end of the Civil War. The formerly enslaved Black people were free, but what did freedom look like? What rights did they have?

President Lincoln was shot just five days after General Lee surrendered to General Grant. Before Lincoln died, the Republicans were pushing for equal rights for the freed slaves. They wanted to make that a condition for states returning to the Union. Several days before his murder, Lincoln talked about allowing some Black Americans the right to vote—if they had served in the Union Army and if they were "very intelligent."

---

[i] Neely, Mark E. Jr., *The Abraham Lincoln Encyclopedia* (Da Capo Press, Inc., 1982), "Fourth Debate: Charleston, Illinois, September 18, 1858," National Park Service. https://www.nps.gov/liho/learn/historyculture/debate4.htm.

[ii] Charles Darwin, *The Descent of Man and Selection in Relation to Sex* (Classic Literature Library, 1871), 105. https://charles-darwin.classic-literature.co.uk/the-descent-of-man/ebook-page-105.asp.

Weeks after unexpectedly becoming president, Andrew Johnson announced the "Reconstruction Act." It spelled out how the Southern states would be readmitted into the United States.

Three new laws stated what rights the newly freed Black Americans had. The Thirteenth Amendment (December 1865) freed the enslaved people. The Fourteenth Amendment (July 1868) said everyone born in America had United States citizenship. The citizenship of African Americans had been controversial, as illustrated in the "Dred Scott Case."

Dred Scott by Louis Schultze, circa 1888 [z]

Dred Scott and his wife Harriet were enslaved African Americans. Their owner, John Emerson, moved several times. They started in Missouri, a slave state. But then, Emerson moved to Illinois (a free state) and Wisconsin Territory (also free). Finally, Emerson moved back to Missouri with the Scotts. Emerson died, and the Scotts tried to buy their freedom from his wife, but she refused.

The Scotts then filed lawsuits for freedom. Technically, they were free when they lived in Illinois and Wisconsin, and the courts usually followed a "once free, always free" rule. Yet, the courts turned down the Scotts' lawsuits. The US Supreme Court said in 1857 that Dred Scott was not a citizen and that slaves were "inferior" and had no rights. One year later, the Blow family bought the Scotts from Mrs. Emerson and promptly set them free. Dred only lived a year in freedom before dying of tuberculosis, but Harriet lived until 1876.

The Fourteenth Amendment also said that the US government and the local state governments could not take away a person's life, freedom, or property without legal due process. Everyone (including formerly enslaved people) had to be equally protected by the federal and state laws. The Fifteenth Amendment (February 1870) gave Black men the right to vote.

Most Southerners were pardoned. Johnson allowed the Southern states to govern as they chose as long as they got rid of slavery and paid off their war debt. As expected, the Southern states only elected White men as leaders. They passed **Black Codes**. These laws said Black Americans had to sign annual labor contracts. Any Black people without a job were "vagrants" who could be forced to work for the White plantation owners. Life had not changed much for Southern African Americans.

What Was the Memphis Massacre? (May 1866)

Tensions were high during the Reconstruction period. After getting freed, many Black people in Tennessee left the rural plantations and moved to Memphis. The city's Black population swelled to about twenty thousand. Some Black men were already there. They had fought in the 3rd US Colored Artillery Regiment of the Union Army and now lived in and around Fort Pickering, just outside Memphis.

Many Irish people had immigrated to Memphis after the 1840s Great Famine in Ireland. The recently-arrived Irish took most of the police and firefighter jobs. The freed Africans competed with the Irish population for craftsmen and labor jobs. Tensions flared between the two groups. On May 1, 1866, the African American Veterans held a street party celebrating the war's end by shooting their guns in the air. The (mostly Irish) police tried to break up the party, but the African Americans refused because they were outside Memphis police jurisdiction.

SCENES IN MEMPHIS, TENNESSEE, DURING THE RIOT—BURNING A FREEDMEN'S SCHOOL-HOUSE.
[SKETCHED BY A. R. W.]

Freedmen's Schoolhouse burns in the 1866 Memphis Riot in this illustration by Alfred Rudolph Waud, Harper's Weekly.[35]

A police officer reached for his gun but accidentally shot himself in the leg. His companions thought the Black soldiers had shot him. In the chaos, bullets flew, and a police officer was killed. As a mob formed, General Stoneman sent two units of soldiers to disperse the mob and ordered the Black veterans to come inside the fort. By 11 p.m., everything was quiet around Fort Pickering.

Yet, the mob (which was one-third policemen and firefighters) wanted revenge. They couldn't get to the Black soldiers, so they turned on the African American neighborhoods in Memphis. They burned down Black schools, twelve churches, and ninety-one homes, some with people still in them. They killed forty-six Black people and injured countless others.

The New Orleans Massacre, July 1866

Three months after the Memphis atrocities, another bloodbath ensued in New Orleans. The Democrats were trying to regain power and keep the Black people "in their place." The Republicans were holding their local convention at the New Orleans Mechanics Institute, promoting the right of Black people to vote. About two hundred unarmed Black veterans marched in a parade to the convention.

Suddenly, a horde of police officers, firemen, and armed Democrats descended on the parade. They kicked and clubbed the African Americans, then turned on the Republicans in the institute, firing into the windows. The unarmed people inside desperately tried to escape, slipping on the blood-covered floor. Thirty-seven unarmed people died, and over one hundred suffered severe injuries.

How Did "Redemption" Impact Black Americans?

"The slave went free, stood a brief moment in the sun, then moved back again toward slavery."[i]

The "Redeemers" were Southern White Democrats retaliating against the gains made on behalf of formerly enslaved Americans. The Redeemers called any White people who advocated for Black Americans "Scalawags." Former Confederate soldiers created the Ku Klux Klan, a terrorist group targeting Black Americans, Jews, and Catholics. Wearing hooded white robes, they burned crosses in front of Black leaders' homes. They lynched (murdered by hanging) over three thousand Black people and more than one thousand White people who supported civil rights.

A Ku Klux Klan demonstration in Tampa, Florida, 1939[ii]

---

[i] W. E. B. Du Bois, an African American historian and civil rights activist. https://duboiscenter.library.umass.edu/du-bois-quotes/.

The Southern Democrats worked to overturn Black people's right to vote despite it now being constitutional. People who registered to vote had to pay poll taxes, which many African Americans could not afford. Another requirement was a literacy test. For instance, a person might have to read a paragraph of the state constitution and interpret it. Many enslaved people had never learned to read. Even if they could read, the registration officials subjectively decided whether or not they passed. The poll tax and literacy requirements cut the Black voters by more than half.

"Jim Crow" laws lasting into the 1970s were another method of "keeping down" Black people in the South. Many restaurants made Black patrons eat outside. Blacks and Whites had separate schools, railroad cars, hospitals, water fountains, restrooms, and parks. African Americans had to sit at the back of the bus.

How Did the "Great Migration" Shift America's Black Population? (1916-70)

Life was nearly unbearable for Black people in the South. They had few opportunities to get ahead in life. More than six million Black Americans moved to the West, Midwest, and especially to the North in the early and mid-1900s. Industry was taking off in the North, and recruiters passed through Southern towns, offering good pay for work in Northern factories.

Even in the North, African Americans encountered racism. City maps had "red lines" that marked Black neighborhoods. These were the only places where African Americans could get a home loan. It meant that schools were essentially segregated. This practice continued well into the 1960s. However, the African Americans who moved north could register to vote without the nonsense of poll taxes and reading tests. This gave them a political voice and elevated many Black people into leadership positions.

Antisemitism in America

Black Americans were not the only victims of racism. As deadly antisemitism ramped up in Europe in the late 1800s and early 1900s, millions of Jews immigrated to America. Even in America, Jews experienced racist policies. For instance, schools like Harvard, Yale, and Princeton had quotas for how many Jewish students could enroll. Some colleges banned Jews altogether.

The American industrialist Henry Ford published a newspaper called the *Dearborn*, which was full of antisemitic propaganda. He and many other Americans feared the Jews would use their business genius to take over the world. Of course, Hitler's manifesto, *Mein Kampf*, fueled the fire. American radio stations freely aired Nazi ideas and hatred against Jews. Vandals painted swastikas on Jewish businesses.

The American government had quotas on how many Jewish immigrants were allowed. They sent hundreds back to Germany and the Holocaust, which killed six million Jews.

After World War II, the atrocities observed and photographed in Hitler's concentration camps by American troops jarred the American public. Americans began to sympathize with the plight of the Jews. Restrictions and quotas faded away. As they were permitted to move ahead in life, Jewish Americans won an astounding number of Nobel prizes. Yet, even today, antisemitism continues, especially on America's college campuses.

Rosa Parks and the Montgomery Bus Boycott (1955-56)

In 1955, Mrs. Rosa Parks got on the bus to go home. She was weary after a long day at work. In Montgomery, Alabama, the Jim Crow laws said Black folks had to sit in the back of the bus. Mrs. Parks sat down in the first row of the Black people's section. However, the White people's section in the front filled up. The bus driver told Rosa to move further back so White people could sit in her seat.

However, Mrs. Rosa Parks was tired of all the rules Black people had to endure to "keep them in their place." Earlier that week, she had attended a meeting at Dexter Avenue Baptist Church, pastored by Rev. Martin Luther King, Jr. Everyone was talking about Emmett Till, a fourteen-year-old in Mississippi. Someone said he had flirted with a White woman. He'd been kidnapped, blinded, beaten, shot, and thrown into the Tallahatchie River. The all-White jury said his murderers were "not guilty," and they walked free.

The bus driver cleared his throat. "Move to the back!"

Rosa quietly said, "No."

As his face turned red, the driver had Mrs. Parks arrested. Reverend King helped bail her out, and then he and his friend, Ralph Abernathy, planned a bus boycott. They spread leaflets from door to door in the Black community and churches that read "Don't ride the bus on Monday!" Most African Americans in the South did not own cars. The leaflets suggested they walk to work, share rides, or take a cab.

Rosa Parks arrested a second time in 1956 for helping organize the bus boycott [25]

That Monday, it rained. Nevertheless, only eight Black people rode the bus. Everyone else carpooled, biked, took a cab, or walked. And not just Monday—they boycotted Montgomery's bus system for an entire year! Since at least half of Montgomery's bus riders were African Americans, the bus company went bankrupt. The police arrested Reverend King and even the carpool drivers for "interfering with a business." Racist thugs bombed four African American churches and Reverend King's house.

Many angry Black Americans wanted to strike back. Some civil rights activists, like Malcolm X, advocated for a violent revolution. But Reverend King insisted, "We meet violence with non-violence. We meet hate with love. Jesus told us to love our enemies and pray for them."

Finally, victory was achieved! The courts said it was unconstitutional to segregate the buses. The state appealed, and it went to the Supreme Court, which ruled that buses could not be segregated.

Martin Luther King Jr.

After winning the case against segregated buses, Rev. Martin Luther King Jr. continued advocating for equality for African Americans. In 1963, he gave his famous "I Have a Dream" speech in Washington, D.C.:

> "Now is the time to make real the promises of democracy. Now is the time to rise from the dark and desolate valley of segregation to the sunlit path of racial justice. Now is the time to lift our nation from the quicksands of racial injustice to the solid rock of brotherhood. Now is the time to make justice a reality for all of God's children."[i]

As Martin Luther King Jr. and other activists like Malcolm X pushed for civil rights in the early 1960s, they found sympathetic allies in President Kennedy and President Johnson. American attitudes slowly began to shift. New laws were passed to protect African Americans' rights. For instance, the 1964 Civil Rights Act banned racial and gender discrimination against employees. That same year, King won the Nobel Peace Prize. The 1965 Voting Rights Act eliminated the poll taxes. Segregated schools, buses, and restrooms became a thing of the past. Sadly, King's untiring work generated enemies. In 1968, he was shot and killed in Tennessee. Days later, the Fair Housing Act was passed. It banned housing discrimination due to national origin, race, religion, or gender.

Martin Luther King Jr. giving his "I Have a Dream" speech [ss]

---

[i] Martin Luther King Jr., "'I Have a Dream' Speech." *History.* November 30, 2017. https://www.history.com/topics/black-history/i-have-a-dream-speech.

The "Post-racial" Era

America celebrated Barack Obama's election as president in 2009 as a monumental milestone for civil rights. Nevertheless, the struggle continues. African American men are three times more likely to be killed by police than White men. The poverty rate for Black people in 2023 was 17.9 percent compared to 7.7 percent for White people. Black babies are twice as likely to die as White babies. From a legal perspective, everyone has equal rights. Yet, in real life, America has a long journey.

Roundup Activity: Multiple Choice

Check your answers in the back of the book.

1. Which of the following did Abraham Lincoln believe about Black people?
    a. They could serve on juries.
    b. They could hold political office.
    c. They could marry White people.
    d. None of the above

2. Which of the following did Charles Darwin believe about White people?
    a. They were more evolved than people from Africa.
    b. Because White people evolved earlier, they should be in control.
    c. The civilized races would replace the savage races.
    d. All of the above

3. Dred Scott lost his court case for freedom because...
    a. The court ignored the "once free, always free" rule.
    b. The court said he was not a citizen.
    c. The court said he was an "inferior" slave with no rights.
    d. All of the above

4. Who got called "Scalawags"?
    a. Southern Democrats trying to keep Black people down.
    b. Formerly enslaved Black people.
    c. White people who advocated for formerly enslaved Blacks.
    d. All of the above

5. How did some White people retaliate against the bus boycott by Black people?
    a. The police arrested Martin Luther King Jr. and the carpool drivers.
    b. Racists bombed four Black churches.
    c. Racists bombed King's house.
    d. All of the above

Chapter 6: The War Against the World

The early twentieth century saw America dragged into two worldwide conflicts. World War I, which killed at least sixteen million people, was supposed to be the "war to end all wars." Yet, two decades later, World War II erupted as the bloodiest war in world history. America played a leading and decisive role in both. The collisions of nations placed America as the world's superpower—yet it came at a crushing cost.

World War I (1914-18)

World War I was horrific. The world had never seen a war involving so many countries. It raged between the Central Powers (Austria-Hungary, Germany, and the Ottoman Empire) and the Allied Powers (Britain, France, and Russia). Eventually, the United States got sucked in and fought for the Allied side. Before it ended, over thirty countries were fighting. Most battles were in Europe, where a regional conflict snowballed into a war encircling the globe.

What Triggered the War?

It all started in Sarajevo, the capital of Bosnia, a country in the Austro-Hungarian Empire. The Serbs were a Slavic ethnic group. Most lived in Serbia, next to Bosnia. Some lived in Bosnia and wanted independence from the Austro-Hungarian Empire. In June 1914, a teenage Serb shot and killed Archduke Franz Ferdinand and his wife Sophie. Ferdinand was the nephew of Austria-Hungary's emperor. He was supposed to be the next emperor.

"You plotted against my heir!" the emperor cried, declaring war on Serbia. Complicated alliances dragged most of Europe into the conflict. Russia and France supported Serbia, so Austria-Hungary invaded Russia. Germany supported Austria-Hungary, so it declared war on France. Luxembourg and Belgium were neutral, but they were in the way, so Germany invaded them to get to France. British troops arrived in France to defend their ally against Germany.

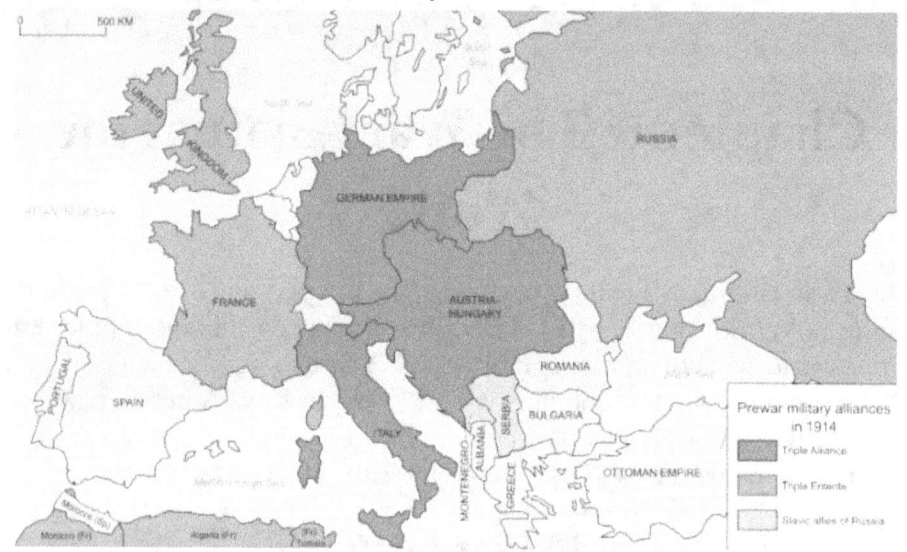

Map of Europe just before WWI began[27]

Within months, four hundred miles of trenches called the "Western Front" stretched through France near its borders with Belgium and Germany. Japan and Australia joined the Allies. Bulgaria and the Ottoman Empire, which controlled much of the Middle East, jumped in with Germany and Austria-Hungary (the Central Powers). In May 1915, Italy joined the Allies, although it had previously partnered with Germany and Austria-Hungary.

How Did the US Get Involved?

For three years, the United States remained neutral, even after the Germans torpedoed the *Lusitania* in 1915. It was the world's largest passenger ship, on its way from New York to England. By sinking it, the Germans killed 1,197 people, including 128 Americans. However, the

Lusitania was a British ship. President Wilson threatened Germany with war if they sank any American ships.

German submarines continued to prowl the seas, endangering shipping. On January 31, 1917, the Germans announced that they would attack every ship in the Mediterranean or near Britain and France. That's exactly what they did. In the next two months, they sank nine American ships flying under a neutral flag. America declared war on Germany on April 6, 1917, believing it was necessary for world peace and safe shipping.

Engraving of the Lusitania sinking by Norman Wilkinson, The Illustrated London News[28]

Once the US joined the Allies, Cuba, Greece, and China joined, followed by Nicaragua, Costa Rica, Haiti, and Honduras. The Allies breathed a sigh of relief. Many British soldiers were dead, wounded, or extremely exhausted. Half the surviving French soldiers were on strike, demoralized after losing the Second Battle of the Aisne. Meanwhile, Russia was in the middle of a violent revolution. The Marxist Bolsheviks, led by Vladimir Lenin, came to power and pulled out of the war.

What Was Different About This War?

Never before had so many nations been in the same war. Almost five million American soldiers fought. Meanwhile, women stepped into the men's places in factories and farms, doubling the female employment rate. Twenty-one thousand American women were nurses in the army, and thousands of "Hello Girls" worked as switchboard operators near the front lines. The navy recruited women as translators, radio operators, and truck drivers, freeing up men for combat.

A WWI recruitment poster for women[29]

World War I saw mind-blowing innovations in weapons, technology, manufacturing, and communications. Tanks were used for the first time, and WWI began the race for air supremacy. Machine guns were used for the first time on military airplanes in WWI and became a key weapon. Each US regiment had 336 machine guns by the war's end.

What Were Some Decisive Battles for the American Military?

America's first battle was at **Cantigny (May 1918)** in northern France. The French provided logistics, flamethrowers, and tanks. The US First Infantry Division's goal was to take the village of Cantigny. They did that in a half hour and captured 250 German soldiers. However, the Germans counterattacked the next day. They killed or wounded eight hundred American soldiers before abandoning the area.

In **June 1918**, the US 4th Marine Brigade joined French and British forces in the **Battle of Belleau Wood,** about one hundred miles east of Paris. This was the first large-scale battle for the US Marine Corps. The French ordered the US Marines to drop back and dig trenches as the Germans advanced through the woods. Instead, the Marine Corps commander ordered his men to hold their position and not open fire until the Germans were a hundred yards away. The hail of bullets killed many Germans, and they retreated. The next day, the Marines engaged in hand-to-hand combat in the thick woods. The Nazis killed or injured over one thousand Marines that day. But the tenacious Marines kept fighting for three weeks and finally chased the Germans away.

The **Hundred Days Offensive (August–November 1918)** was a series of battles along the Western Front in France. In one battle, a half million Americans and a hundred thousand French soldiers took back Saint-Mihiel. This was a stellar win because Germany had held the fortified town for four years.

At the Meuse-Argonne Offensive, one million American soldiers pushed the Germans forty miles back. Over 26,000 US troops died in America's most colossal battle in military history.

World War I trench warfare[80]

America's stunning victory at the Meuse-Argonne ended the war. Germany signed an armistice on November 11, 1918. The allies met in Paris in January 1919 to negotiate the *Treaty of Versailles*. They formed the *League of Nations,* a forum to resolve international disputes. Although America was in the war for less than six months, 53,402 US soldiers died in battle. Another 63,114 died from disease and accidents. The European Allies and Central Powers suffered far worse.

What happened to the Serbs in Bosnia—the ones who started the war? They won independence. The Austro-Hungarian Empire dissolved. Bosnia, Serbia, and other Slavic people formed the Kingdom of Serbs, Croats, and Slovenes (later Yugoslavia).

World War II (1939–45)

Nazi Germany's invasion of Poland triggered the Second World War, entangling nations around the globe in shocking violence. Once again, America tried to stay out of the war, but Japan's surprise attack changed everything. World War II killed over fifty million people and unleashed the atomic bomb. As the war ended, the horrified world learned of Hitler's Holocaust, which systematically murdered six million Jews.

Why Did America Get Involved This Time Around?

Most Americans preferred to sit this war out. It had only been two decades since the horrors of WWI. America was pulling out of the *Great Depression (1929-39),* a dreadful time when the economy collapsed and unemployment skyrocketed. Congress wanted to continue an *isolationist,* neutral position. They did not want to get involved in other people's fights.

However, in May and June 1940, Hitler's military swallowed up Belgium, the Netherlands, and part of France. What's worse, Hitler forged a fascist alliance with the Italian dictator Mussolini, planning to conquer Britain.

Fascism promotes a country's strength over its people's welfare. People living in fascist countries have few freedoms and face persecution if they criticize the government. Fascist leaders are usually violent dictators with unlimited power. They usually believe in a social hierarchy, the idea that some people are better than others. Hitler believed that the Germanic ethnicity was so superior that it had the right to rule the world and that Jews had no right to exist.

The Nazis were bombing London and torpedoing British ships. Would Hitler and Mussolini take over all of Europe? In addition, Japan wanted

Southeast Asia's Dutch, French, and British colonies. Germany, Japan, and Italy signed the *Tripartite Pact* in September 1940. The *Axis* powers pledged that if the United States attacked any of their three countries, the other two would defend them.

President Roosevelt still refused to join the war. However, he sent weapons to Britain. The US Navy escorted British merchant ships in convoys, protecting them from German attack. When Japan invaded Indochina, America cut off oil going to Japan.

Japan Attacks Pearl Harbor

Hitler wanted to avoid war with America, at least for the time being. He planned to conquer the Soviet Union first. However, Japan had other ideas. The Japanese wanted to control oil-rich Southeast Asia and did not want interference from the US military bases in Hawaii and the Philippines.

On December 7, 1941, the Japanese staged a surprise attack on Pearl Harbor, the American naval base in Hawaii. They sank four American battleships and damaged the other four in port. They took out eight other military ships and almost two hundred aircraft. The Japanese killed 2,393 Americans and wounded 1,178. It was the most lethal foreign attack on American soil up to that point.

The destroyer USS Shaw explodes from Japanese bombs at Pearl Harbor.[81]

Japan's reckless action enraged America. Now, everyone was up in arms and wanted revenge. President Roosevelt declared war against Japan the next day, December 8. Germany and Italy declared war against the United States three days later.

The Soviet Union knew it was in Hitler's crosshairs. Consequently, the Communists formed an unlikely union with Britain and America. The Chinese were already fighting Japan and decided that "the enemy of your enemy is your friend." China joined America, Britain, and the Soviet Union, forming the *Allied Big Four*. With twenty-two other countries, they signed a formal treaty called the *United Nations Declaration*.

Fighting on Two Fronts

America faced off against Japan, Germany, and Italy in its new global war. This forced it to fight in Asia and Europe at the same time. The United States sent food, weapons, tanks, and aircraft to the Soviet Union, which fought bravely against Germany and, later, Japan. It cost the Soviets twenty-seven million lives. Britain fought primarily in Europe, moving against Japan near the war's end.

China had been in the middle of a civil war between the Nationalist Party and the Communist Party. They stopped fighting each other and started fighting their mutual enemy when Japan invaded in 1937. The Chinese suffered horrible atrocities at the hands of the Japanese—war crimes they have not forgiven to this day. In the *Nanjing Massacre*, the Japanese killed 200,000 civilians and raped 20,000 women and children. At least fourteen million Chinese died in World War II.

America did not have a large standing army at this time. All men under age sixty-five had to register for the draft; however, most WWII soldiers were in their teens and twenties. Over sixteen million soldiers served in the US Army, Navy, and Marines during the war. More than 350,000 women joined America's armed forces, mostly in non-combat roles.

We Can Do It!

America had to quickly produce weapons, aircraft, tanks, ships, and uniforms. Three million women flocked to the factories and shipyards to do their part for the war effort. Recruitment posters featuring "Rosie the Riveter" became iconic. Teenagers and older men also rushed to work. America no longer had an unemployment problem. Factories ran around the clock with three shifts a day, seven days a week. In 1944, America produced over ninety thousand aircraft.

A recruitment poster by the War Production Board [32]

With many farmers at war and America helping feed the Soviet Union and Britain, civilians began growing their own vegetables and fruit in "Victory Gardens." People could only buy a small amount of coffee, sugar, and meat. With food rations, leftovers became a patriotic meal. The war effort demanded metal, so Americans scavenged their attics, basements, and yards for old mattress frames, pipes, pots, and junk cars. Carpools reduced the need for new tires so that rubber could go to military jeeps, tanks, and airplanes. Before the war, most Americans were exempt from income tax—only eight million paid taxes. Taxes increased to pay for the war. By 1945, most working adults paid income taxes.

Defeat the Nazis First!

President Franklin Roosevelt and his Joint Chiefs of Staff prioritized Europe. Their strategy was to defeat Hitler and then go after Japan. Nevertheless, they did not neglect Asia. Admiral Chester W. Nimitz was based in Hawaii and was Commander in Chief of the Pacific area. A submarine genius, he developed **underway replenishment (UNREP) techniques**, where weapons, food, and fuel are transferred from one ship to another at sea. Warships and submarines could stay out at sea, no longer needing to enter a port.

Battle of Midway (June 1942)

Six months after Japan bombed Pearl Harbor, the Japanese Navy attacked the US Navy fleet near the tiny island of Midway, about a thousand miles from Hawaii's main islands. Luckily, the US picked up the Japanese attack plans while monitoring signals, so the Americans plotted an ambush. The American forces were ready and waiting with 344 fighters, bombers, and patrol planes, three aircraft carriers, and the USS *Nautilus* submarine. The Japanese had 248 fighter planes and four aircraft carriers.

The Americans sunk all four Japanese aircraft carriers, along with 140 airplanes still on the carriers when they sank. They shot forty-eight more Japanese planes out of the sky. With no aircraft carriers to land on, some Japanese planes ditched at sea. Others flew to Midway, wishing they had not bombed the airfield earlier. One American aircraft carrier, the *Yorktown*, sank. The US lost 144 airplanes. Over 3,000 Japanese died, compared to 307 Americans. It was "the most stunning and decisive blow in the history of naval warfare," according to military historian John Keegan.[i]

D-Day, Battle of Normandy, France (June 1944)

The stakes for winning the Battle of Normandy were high. It was history's most extensive air, land, and sea invasion. The goal was to get a foothold in the European mainland so the Allies could retake it.

The English Channel lay between Britain and France. Hitler had built his "Atlantic Wall" along the channel's coast to prevent a British invasion on the beaches. However, now that America was in the war, the Allies had

---

[i] John Keegan, *The Second World War* (Penguin Press, 2005), 275.

more resources and manpower to cross the channel and retake Europe.

The Allies planned for five thousand landing boats to approach five beaches spread over fifty miles. Eleven thousand aircraft carried paratroopers and supported the land invasion. In the early morning of June 6, while it was still dark, twenty thousand American and British paratroopers floated down from the sky, landing behind enemy lines.

Wading to shore on D-Day [88]

At 5:30 a.m., waves of landing craft sailed up to the beach with 130,000 troops. They jumped into frigid, waist-high water. Struggling against a strong undertow, they waded to shore, holding their guns. Enemy fire peppered the beach and water. Once they reached the beach, they had to climb hundred-foot cliffs. By sunset, the Allies had breached Hitler's Atlantic Wall, although over ten thousand men were killed or wounded. This was a pivotal moment in the war in Europe.

Deaths of Mussolini and Hitler (April 1945)

After D-Day, the Allies took most of Europe in less than a year. In April 1945, the Soviets, led by Joseph Stalin, invaded the Nazi capital of Berlin, Germany. Hitler holed up in a bunker in the center of the city. As the Soviets closed in, Hitler received word that the Allies had killed Mussolini in Italy. Two days later, on April 30, Hitler committed suicide. The war in Europe was over.

Uncovering the Holocaust

As the Allies penetrated Germany, they found unimaginable horrors—the Nazi concentration camps. Reports had trickled out of the Nazi atrocities against Jews in Europe, but few realized how bad it was. Some American officials knew but did not care, as antisemitism was strong in America at the time. American officials in the Department of State blocked assistance for Jewish refugees and covered up intelligence reports of the Holocaust, saying "It's just a war rumor."[i]

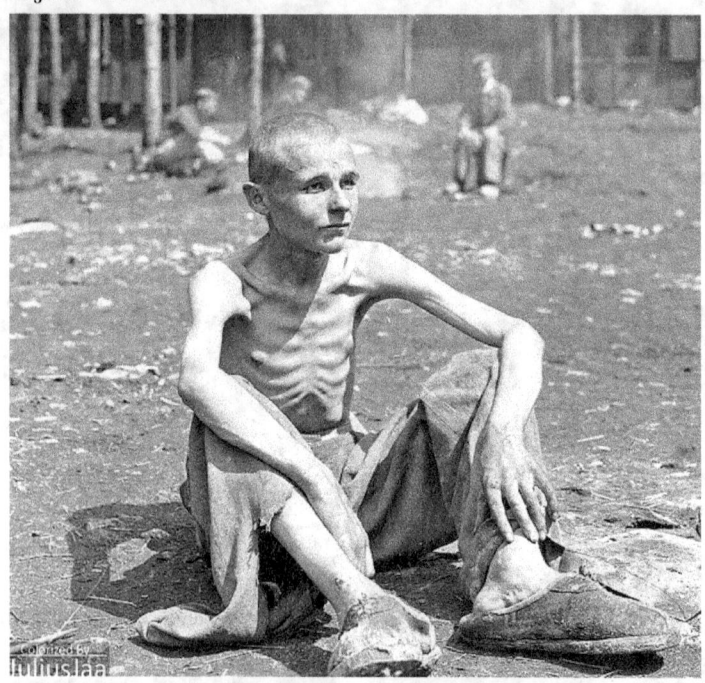

A teenager rescued from Ebensee Concentration Camp in Austria [ii]

In April 1945, American soldiers were eyewitnesses to the gruesome savagery of the Nazi concentration camps. "I saw walking dead people," one soldier reported. Men, women, and teens were nothing but skin and bone, their skin covered with sores. Six million Jews, including one million children, died in the Nazi Holocaust. Hitler's troops killed five million other people. His killing machine heartlessly murdered babies,

---

[i] "Americans and the Holocaust." United States Holocaust Memorial Museum, Accessed January 4, 2025, https://exhibitions.ushmm.org/americans-and-the-holocaust/main/state-department-obstruction-1#:~:text=In%20early%201943%2C%20US%20State,from%20reaching%20the%20United%20States.

children, and adults with Down syndrome and other disabilities. The mentally ill and political prisoners were also victims.

The Atomic Bomb Explodes (August 1945)

When the Italians and Germans surrendered, Japan lost its allies. On July 26, 1945, the Allies issued the ***Potsdam Declaration***, demanding Japan's immediate surrender. What if they refused? "Prompt and utter destruction," the Allies warned. Japan made the fatal mistake of ignoring the warning.

For months, American planes had dropped sixty-three million leaflets across Japan, warning the citizens to leave the cities. On August 6, 1945, an American B-29 bomber released "Little Boy," a nuclear bomb, on Hiroshima, Japan. It killed seventy thousand people instantly. Another thirty thousand died within months from radiation sickness. Inconceivably, the Japanese continued fighting. Three days later, another nuclear bomb called "Fat Boy" dropped on Nagasaki, killing at least forty thousand. The two bombs were the only atomic weapons ever deployed in war. On August 14, Emperor Hirohito announced his surrender. The war was over.

Fat Boy detonates at Nagasaki [85]

Roundup Activity: Crossword

Crossword Puzzle: World Wars I and II

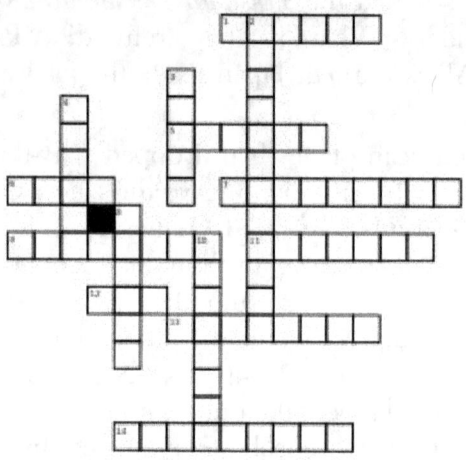

Down:
2. not getting involved in other nation's fights
3. staged a surprise attack on Pearl Harbor
4. the side America fought on in WWI
8. where America won a decisive sea battle against Japan
10. where WWI started

Across:
1. American admiral in Pacific during WWII
5. where Nazi Germany's invasion triggered WWII
6. union of Germany, Japan, and Italy against Allies
7. the city where America dropped the first atomic bomb
9. violent dictators with unlimited powers
11. where the Japanese killed 200,000 civilians
12. the war to end all wars
13. America's first WWI battle in France
14. the systematic murder of 6 million Jews

Image source[86]

Chapter 7: The Space Race and the Cuban Issue

The United States's relationship with its former allies, Cuba and the Soviet Union, grew icy during the Cold War. They were on opposite sides of the political ideology fence. Russia's revolution in 1917, led by Lenin's Bolshevik Party, overthrew the tsar and set up the world's first Communist government. In 1922, it formed the Union of Soviet Socialist Republics (USSR). Its empire grew to include fifteen states and achieved superpower status in World War II. At its peak, the Soviet Union was the largest nation on earth, covering one-sixth of the planet.

What Was the Cold War?

After World War II, America and its European allies grew increasingly nervous about the Soviet Union. Could the USSR take over all of Europe? Could it even control the entire earth? In 1949, America joined with Canada and twelve European allies to form *NATO*—the *North Atlantic Treaty Organization*. It was (and still is) a military alliance where the members pledged to defend each other from attack by a third party.

The most problematic third party was the Soviet Union. The USSR struck back in 1955 by forming the *Warsaw Pact* with *Eastern Bloc* countries. The Eastern Bloc nations embraced the Communist politics of the USSR. These two alliances—NATO and the Warsaw Pact—set off the *Cold War*. This power struggle persisted until the Soviet Union fell in 1991. The alliances avoided direct war—no one wanted World War III!

Yet, the rivalry and competition led to international incidents that almost plunged the world into nuclear war.

Churchill (UK), Truman (US), and Stalin (USSR) at the end of WWII [87]

The two sides were incredibly suspicious and resentful of each other, often with good reason. Both sides used sly tactics to convince other countries in Africa, Asia, Central America, and South America to align with them. They offered economic benefits and showered them with propaganda. *Propaganda* is information (often disinformation) used to convince people that one side is right and the other is wrong. *Disinformation* is false information intentionally spread to deceive people.

What Was the Arms Race?

America's policy during the Cold War was *containment*—preventing the Soviet Union from expanding any further. To this end, the United States built up its weapons like never before. America had already shown the world what it could do when it dropped two atomic bombs on Japan. It increased defense spending exponentially, developing and increasing nuclear weapons.

Of course, the Soviet Union had to keep up. It had already started developing an atomic bomb during World War II. The Soviets correctly suspected Britain, America, and Germany were doing the same. At the end of the war, the Soviets captured the German nuclear scientists and used them to surge ahead in making their own bomb.

The Soviets desperately needed uranium for their bomb project. The Americans had grabbed up most of Germany's uranium ore stash as

WWII ended. However, the Soviets found a hundred metric tons of uranium oxide (the refined product made from uranium ore) in Austria and another hundred tons in Germany. In 1949, the Soviet Union tested its atom bomb, "First Lightning," in Kazakhstan.

President Truman responded, "I have directed the Atomic Energy Commission to continue its work on all forms of atomic weapons, including the so-called hydrogen or superbomb."[i]

The race was on for the superbomb! What is the difference between an atom bomb and a ***hydrogen bomb***? Atomic bombs use split atoms (***nuclear fission***) to cause the explosion. Hydrogen (thermonuclear) bombs use both split atoms and fused atoms. A hydrogen bomb detonates when a small atom bomb triggers the reaction that fuses atoms (***nuclear fusion***). Hydrogen bombs are a thousand times more powerful than atom bombs.

In the 1950s and 1960s, Americans lived in terror of nuclear bombs. They dug bomb shelters in their backyards. The Federal Civil Defense Administration ordered schools to put children through "duck and cover" drills. Students watched training films featuring "Bert the Turtle." They practiced diving under their desks so they would know what to do if a bomb dropped.

A 1962 school "duck and cover" drill[ss]

---

[i] "Statement by the President on the Hydrogen Bomb," The American Presidency Project, Accessed January 4, 2025, https://www.presidency.ucsb.edu/documents/statement-the-president-the-hydrogen-bomb.

Would hiding under a desk have worked if an actual nuclear bomb hit? A bomb's shockwave and intense heat would immediately kill anything within about a mile. Flying debris would extend several miles, so the desks would have helped protect against shattering glass and falling objects. However, lethal radiation would travel up to a hundred miles, depending on the wind.

What Was the Cuban Missile Crisis? (1962)

The United States's relationship with Cuba, only ninety miles south of Key West, was complicated. Cuba had been independent since 1902, and the two countries initially enjoyed a close friendship. Americans, especially the rich and famous, flocked to Cuba to enjoy its beaches, palm trees, casinos, and vibrant nightlife. Then, Fidel Castro led a revolution against Cuba's brutal dictator Fulgencio Batista. In 1959, Batista fled Cuba, and Castro took power.

The United States recognized Castro's government immediately. However, the friendship fell apart when Castro formed a Communist government and established close ties with the Soviet Union. The CIA under President Kennedy launched the failed Bay of Pigs invasion in 1961. The CIA had trained 1,400 Cubans who had fled to America. In part one of the plan, the exiles were supposed to take out Cuba's air force. However, Castro discovered the plot and moved his aircraft in time.

The next part of the plan was to invade the Bay of Pigs on Cuba's southern shore. Despite the CIA's attempts to keep the raid a secret, word got out to the Cubans once again. What's worse, some of the exiles' ships hit reefs and sank, and their paratroopers landed in the wrong place. Castro's troops killed 114 exiles and captured most of the rest. Many people expected President Kennedy to send American troops in at this point. However, he refused. He did not want to spark the Soviets' wrath and start World War III.

The Cuban Missile Crisis erupted the following year. In this stressful, thirteen-day standoff between America and the Soviet Union, the Cold War suddenly got hot. The Soviets installed nuclear-armed SS-4 medium-range ballistic missiles in Cuba. The rockets were within easy striking range of Florida and other targets in the eastern United States. For the Soviets, it was payback for all the missiles America had aimed at them from Turkey and Western Europe.

In October 1962, an American pilot flying a spy plane high over Cuba spotted and photographed a missile. When President Kennedy got word, his executive committee wrestled with what to do. How could they get rid of the missiles without triggering nuclear war? They discussed invading Cuba or bombing the rockets. However, Kennedy's final decision was to place a blockade of Navy ships around Cuba to prevent the Soviets from sending more missiles. Next, he gave the Soviet Union an ultimatum: remove the missiles or face American military wrath.

Kennedy hashes out a plan with his generals.⁸⁹

Kennedy made a television broadcast on October 22, 1962, telling the American public about the missiles and what he was doing about it. Americans were on pins and needles. Some hoarded food and gasoline, certain they were on the brink of war. Two days later, Soviet ships approached the US Navy blockade around Cuba. Yet, they stopped. They did not try to get through.

Kennedy and his advisors breathed a sigh of relief. However, those missiles were still there in Cuba. Three days later, the Cubans shot down an American spy plane flying over Cuba. Tensions ran high. Kennedy's team had been exchanging communication with the Soviet leadership. Finally, Nikita Khrushchev, premier of the Soviet Union, blinked. On October 26, he messaged Kennedy. "I'll remove the missiles if you promise not to invade Cuba." The next day, he sent additional terms:

"Also, remove your missiles in Turkey."

Kennedy exhaled. He officially announced America would not invade Cuba. He pretended to ignore the part about the missiles in Turkey. Nevertheless, he quietly removed them. The Cuban Missile Crisis ended on October 28. The following year, the Americans and Soviets established a "hotline" between Washington D.C. and Moscow. They signed treaties regarding nuclear weapons. However, it was not the end of the Cold War. The Soviets shifted their focus to developing ballistic missiles that could reach the US from the Soviet Union.

Who Won the Space Race?

In the Cold War, the United States and the Soviet Union competed for a commanding influence on planet Earth, but they did not stop there. They also competed for space. America's history has always been one of exploration and expansion. Space became the final frontier—and yet the Soviets got into space first.

On October 4, 1957, the Soviet Union launched *Sputnik I* (Russian for "traveler"). It was the first manmade satellite to leave Earth's atmosphere. The Soviets used an R-7 intercontinental ballistic missile to thrust it 139 miles from Earth. It circled Earth 1,440 times for the next three months. Finally, aerodynamic drag pulled it out of orbit and back into Earth's atmosphere. The denser air levels caused friction and intense heat, and the satellite burst into flames and burned up. The Space Race involved not only getting an object into space but bringing it back safely.

One month later, the Soviet Union launched a second satellite, *Sputnik 2*. This satellite had a living passenger: a mixed-breed dog named Laika. She had been a stray on Moscow's streets. Laika died from overheating about five hours after the satellite launched. The insulation came loose, and the satellite's nose cone did not drop off as it should have. That caused the thermal system to malfunction, and the temperature rose to 104 Fahrenheit, too hot for a dog to survive for long. *Sputnik 2* orbited Earth for five months and then burned up when it reentered Earth's atmosphere as *Sputnik 1* had done.

Laika, the first animal in space[40]

The news about the two satellites stunned America. It was embarrassing that the Soviets got into space first. Yet, there were more insidious implications. The technology that got the satellites out there could easily deliver a nuclear warhead into the United States. America's rocket scientists were already making progress on their own space technology, and they ramped things up. It was time to show the Soviets what they could do.

President Eisenhower created NASA, the National Aeronautics and Space Administration, in 1958. On February 1, three months after *Sputnik 2* was launched, the Americans launched their first satellite, *Explorer 1*, from Cape Canaveral, Florida. *Explorer 1* circled Earth for twelve years and burned up when it reentered the atmosphere in 1970. In 1959, the Soviets sent the first (unmanned) spacecraft to the moon. It hit the moon at 7,400 miles per hour.

On April 12, 1961, the Soviets sent the first man, Yuri Alekseyevich Gagarin, into space. He orbited Earth one time. It took 108 minutes. Fortunately for Yuri, the Soviet rocket scientists had figured out how to get a rocket back into the atmosphere without bursting into flames. It did go into a spin as it entered, but Yuri managed to stay conscious. Four miles above Earth, the spacecraft ejected Yuri. His parachute opened at 8,200 feet, and he floated safely to the ground. Another parachute brought the spaceship to a gentle landing.

American Alan Shepard flew into space three weeks after Yuri Gagarin. Then, the Americans finally outdid the Soviets when they flew Neil Armstrong and Buzz Aldrin to the moon in July 1969. Armstrong was the first man to stand on the moon, saying, "One small step for man, one giant leap for mankind." Aldrin joined him on the moon's surface, and they spent over two hours exploring and collecting material to bring back to Earth.

Buzz Aldrin on the moon, 1969. Photo by Neil A. Armstrong. [41]

Who won the Space Race? Although the Soviets got a head start, America ultimately won. The Soviets never put a man on the moon. From 1968 to 1971, twelve American men walked on the moon.

Who won the Cold War? America did when the Soviet Union collapsed in 1991.

In recent years, a silly conspiracy theory has surfaced, arguing that walking on the moon was all a hoax. The theory is easily debunked. The astronauts videoed themselves on the moon. Millions of Americans were glued to their television sets, watching the men leap about on the moon, which has lower gravity than Earth. The astronauts took thousands of photos. They left footprints behind, which the Lunar Reconnaissance Orbiter (LRO) photographed in 2009. They also brought moon rocks and moon dust home to be tested.

Roundup Activity: Two Truths and a Lie

Spot which one of the three statements in each grouping is a lie. Check your answers in the back of the book.

- The USSR covered one-sixth of the planet at its peak.
- The USSR achieved superpower status before World War I.
- The USSR's political ideology was at odds with American democratic ideals.
- NATO was an alliance of the US, Canada, and European countries to defend themselves against a potential attack from a "third party" (primarily the Soviet Union).
- NATO and the Warsaw Pact alliances set off the Cold War.
- The Cold War ended in 1962 after the Cuban Missile Crisis was resolved.
- Atom bombs are much more powerful than hydrogen bombs.
- The Soviets used captured German nuclear scientists to develop an atom bomb.
- American schoolchildren had drills where they practiced hiding under the desk for protection from nuclear bombs.
- The USSR installed nuclear-armed ballistic missiles in Cuba, only ninety miles from Florida.
- President Kennedy put a navy blockade around Cuba.
- The Soviet missiles never got removed from Cuba.
- America sent the first man-made satellite into space.
- A dog named Laika was the first animal in space.
- America won the Space Race by putting men on the moon.

Chapter 8: The War on Terror

On September 11, 2001, the deadliest foreign attack on American soil ignited the War on Terror. That morning, nineteen Islamic al Qaeda (*el Kai duh*) terrorists hijacked four American passenger jets.

At 7:59 a.m., American Airlines Flight 11 left Logan International Airport in Boston, heading to Los Angeles. A few minutes into the flight, five terrorists attacked the crew and forced their way into the cockpit. They diverted the plane toward New York City in a suicide attack.

A flight attendant, Betty Ong, managed to call the reservations center in North Carolina. "The cockpit is not answering their phone. We can't get in. The door won't open. Our number one has been stabbed, our number five has been stabbed. And our purser had been stabbed." (Numbers one and five were flight attendants.)

Betty wasn't scheduled to be on the flight but had joined it to get to Los Angeles to meet her sister. They were planning a vacation in Hawaii. Unnoticed in the back of the plane, she stayed on the phone for twenty-six minutes. Her last words were, "Pray for us. Pray for us."

And then, eerie silence. "Betty? Betty? Are you still there?"

At 8:46 a.m., American Airlines Flight 11 flew into the North Tower of the World Trade Center, between floors 95 and 99. All ninety-two people on the airplane died. Seventeen minutes later, United Airlines Flight 175 crashed into the World Trade Center's South Tower, between floors 77 and 85. It killed the sixty-six people on board. The two crashes killed 2,606 people in the World Trade Center or on the ground, including 441 firefighters and other first responders trying to rescue the victims.

September 11, 2001, attack on the World Trade Center

As New York City erupted into confusion, more drama unfolded in the sky. Terrorists had already hijacked American Airlines Flight 77 on its way from Dulles International Airport in Virginia to Los Angeles. A passenger, Barbara Colson, and a flight attendant, Renee May, called their loved ones. Renee was pregnant with her first child. The hijackers turned Flight 77 around and headed east. At 9:37 a.m., the terrorists crashed into the Pentagon, killing everyone in the plane and 153 military and defense employees in the building.

United Airlines Flight 93 left Newark International Airport in New Jersey at 8:42 a.m., headed for San Francisco. It was behind schedule and only in the air for four minutes before the first plane flew into the World Trade Center. Air traffic control sent a warning to Flight 93 at 9:23 a.m. Confused, the pilot responded, "Confirm latest message, please." Two minutes later, the terrorists broke into the cockpit. The pilot screamed, "Mayday! Mayday!" as the plane dropped 685 feet.

By this point, the passengers were calling family members and officials on the ground. One passenger, Ted Burnett, called his wife several times. He told her the terrorists had stabbed a passenger and claimed to have a bomb. His wife told him about the attacks on the World Trade Center. Ted realized the terrorists were plotting the same thing with his plane. "Oh my God! It's a suicide mission!"

Ted and three other passengers—Mark Bingham, Todd Beamer, and Jeremy Glick—planned to retake the plane from the hijackers. The airplane was descending, and they knew it was targeting something.

"We're going to rush the hijackers," Glick told his wife. They planned to fly the airplane into the ground before it could hit the intended target. Beamer recited the Lord's Prayer and Psalm 23: "Yea, though I walk through the valley of the shadow of death, I will fear no evil, for thou art with me."

They stormed the cockpit. In the ensuing struggle, the airplane crashed into a field in Pennsylvania. The suspected target was the White House. President George W. Bush wasn't there. That morning, he was reading books to the children at Emma E. Booker Elementary School in Sarasota, Florida. The White House Chief of Staff whispered in his ear about the two attacks on the World Trade Center. Bush quietly got up to take a phone call from Condoleezza Rice, the national security director. After hanging up, Bush told his staff, "We're at war."

President Bush meets with his Security Council on September 12, 2001[a]

The war was not against a specific country. It was a war on terror. President Bush addressed the nation:

> "The attack took place on American soil, but it was an attack on the heart and soul of the civilized world. And the world has come together to fight a new and different war, the first, and we hope the only one, of the twenty-first century. A war against all those who seek to export terror, and a war against those governments that support or shelter them."[i]

---

[i] George W. Bush, "Global War on Terror," George W. Bush Presidential Library, Accessed January 4, 2025, https://www.georgewbushlibrary.gov/research/topic-guides/global-war-terror.

Who Was Osama bin Laden?

Osama bin Laden was the mastermind behind the September 11 hijackings. He was the son of a billionaire in Saudi Arabia's construction business, and his father was a close friend of the Saudi royal family. Interestingly, bin Laden had fifty-two brothers and sisters from his father's twenty-two wives. Muslims are only supposed to have four wives (at a time). His father stayed married to three of his wives but constantly changed out the fourth wife. Bin Laden's mother was from Syria and the last wife his father married.

Osama bin Laden attended King Abdul Aziz University, where he embraced an extreme, radical form of Islam. The Soviet Union invaded Afghanistan in 1979 when bin Laden was twenty-two. Since Afghanistan was primarily Muslim, bin Laden considered this an attack on Islam. He spearheaded a resistance movement using his family's money. In 1988, he created *al-Qaeda*, a network of militants recruited from around the Muslim world.

What Did the Taliban and Al-Qaeda Have in Common?

The Soviets withdrew from Afghanistan in 1989, and bin Laden made it his headquarters in 1996. By this point, the *Taliban* had taken over most of Afghanistan, and it welcomed bin Laden. The Taliban is a political and religious organization that follows strict Islamic law. Taliban rule was brutal and repressive, especially toward women. Even today, girls cannot attend school after sixth grade, and only a handful of jobs are available for women.

Al-Qaeda and the Taliban shared similar objectives and ideology. However, al-Qaeda's plans were global. The organization planned to create a *caliphate*, a political-religious state, led by a man following Islamic law. Al-Qaeda considered the United States its biggest enemy.

The Taliban's goals were modest and localized compared to Al-Qaeda. The Taliban wanted to subdue corrupt warlords in Afghanistan and establish a government with *Sharia law* based on the Quran (the Muslim holy book) and the opinions of Muslim teachers.

Bin Laden (l) and his advisor, Ayman al-Zawahiri in 2001[44]

Some examples of the Taliban's interpretation of Sharia law include banning women from many public areas. Women must have a male guardian with them and keep their hair and face covered whenever they step outside their homes. Sharia law says that if a Muslim leaves the Islamic faith, he must be killed. Al-Qaeda also followed Sharia law, but its members were slightly less strict with women and girls.

What Were Al-Qaeda's Goals in the September 11 Attacks?

Bin Laden believed the United States was already in a weakened state. For instance, America withdrew its troops from Lebanon after terrorists bombed the US Marine barracks in 1983. America withdrew from Somalia in 1993. Osama bin Laden wanted to further weaken the United States' standing in the world. More than anything, he wanted fear to reign—in America and worldwide. He hoped that the United States would stop supporting Middle Eastern governments that did not follow strict Sharia law.

President Bush's Response to the September 11 Attacks

On September 20, President Bush initiated the "GWOT" or "Global War on Terror" to find and stop terrorists worldwide. America partnered with other like-minded countries. Initially, the focus was on Afghanistan and then Iraq. However, it also used diplomatic and financial incentives to discourage other countries from harboring terrorists. "Our war on terror begins with al Qaeda, but it does not end there. It will not end until every terrorist group of global reach has been found, stopped, and defeated," Bush stated.

On October 7, 2001, Bush announced military strikes had begun against al-Qaeda and the Taliban in Afghanistan:

> "As we strike military targets, we'll also drop food, medicine, and supplies to the starving and suffering men and women and children of Afghanistan. The United States of America is a friend to the Afghan people, and we are the friends of almost a billion worldwide who practice the Islamic faith."

How Did Iraq Get Involved?

Iraq's president, Saddam Hussein, was a threat to peace in the Middle East. However, the CIA found no proof of a connection with bin Laden. Hussein hated the United States, which had led a coalition to fight against him successfully in the 1990-91 Gulf War. Hussein started the Gulf War by invading Kuwait and had started an earlier war by invading Iran in 1980. The Middle Eastern nations considered him a loose cannon, constantly stirring up trouble.

Fighter jets from the US, Canada, Qatar, and France fly over Saudi Arabia in the Gulf War. "

Hussein had committed horrible human rights violations, such as using mustard gas and Sarin nerve gas against Kurdish men, women, and children. He wiped out thousands of villages. President Bush reported Hussein was developing weapons of mass destruction, like anthrax and nuclear weapons. Hussein never developed an atomic bomb, but he did build a nuclear reactor. The only thing that stopped him from building a nuclear bomb was the lack of fissile material.

On March 19, 2003, the United States invaded Iraq to remove Hussein as Iraq's president. The country fell almost immediately, but Hussein disappeared. Finally, in December, American soldiers found him hiding in a hole in the ground. In June 2004, the US handed him over to the interim Iraqi government. It charged him with crimes against humanity, including torturing women and children and murdering 148 Shiite people. (The Shiites followed a different form of Islam.) The court found him guilty, and he died by hanging in December 2006.

The War on Terror Redefined

The War on Terror began as a coalition between the United States, the United Kingdom, and other allies. Their target was terrorists, specifically those in the Middle East. When Barack Obama became president in 2009, his goal in the Middle East was to get rid of al-Qaeda. Killing or capturing bin Laden was his top priority. When al-Qaeda was eliminated, the war would be over. It was no longer the "Global War on Terror." Now, it was part of "Overseas Contingency Operations." Journalists groaned. How could they sell headlines with a name like that?

Operation Neptune Spear: Navy Seals Take Out Osama bin Laden

When American troops moved into Afghanistan in 2001, bin Laden slipped into hiding. A decade passed, and US intelligence was unsure of his location. Intelligence officials did, however, gather several clues over the years. They knew he wasn't using phones anymore—they were too easy to track. They discovered he had been communicating with al-Qaeda through a trusted courier named al-Kuwaiti. Yet, where was al-Kuwaiti? Could he be on the run with bin Laden?

In 2007, US intelligence got more information on al-Kuwaiti. His real name was Ahmed, and he was from Pakistan. They heard a rumor that bin Laden was staying in Ahmed's family compound in Pakistan. They found Ahmed (al-Kuwaiti) in August 2010 and secretly followed him to his compound. Could bin Laden be in there?

The CIA studied surveillance photos of the compound. It appeared to be custom-built to hide someone. It was at the end of a dead-end road outside the city, surrounded by a twelve-foot concrete wall topped with barbed wire. The home had no internet or telephone service (making it hard to tap). While the neighbors set their trash out to be picked up by the garbage truck, the people in this home burned their trash. The CIA made the educated guess that bin Laden was there with his youngest wife and children.

On May 1, 2011, at 10:30 p.m., two helicopters carried twenty-three Navy SEALs from Team Six into Pakistan from Afghanistan. Typically, SEALs rappel down from a hovering helicopter; however, one of the helicopters destabilized and had to land inside the compound. As they approached a guesthouse wearing night vision goggles, someone shot at them through the door. They returned fire. Several minutes later, a woman opened the door with a baby on her hip and more children behind her. The SEALs went inside and found al-Kuwaiti (Ahmed) lying dead.

As they entered the main house, bin Laden's adult son, Khalid, shot at them from the second floor. They returned fire and killed him. The SEALs continued up to the third floor as bullets flew. They found Osama bin Laden in a bedroom with two of his wives. One wife rushed at the SEALs, blocking bin Laden and getting shot in the leg. A two-year-old boy wailed in the corner. Two SEALs threw themselves on the women to protect them. Bin Laden exchanged fire with the SEALs, and two bullets pierced his head. The mastermind of the September 11, 2001, attack that killed nearly three thousand people on American soil was dead.

A newspaper announcement of bin Laden's death [46]

Roundup Activity: Multiple Choice Quiz (first eight chapters)

1. How did the first Americans get to America?
    a. They crossed the Beringia land bridge.
    b. They crossed the Atlantic Ocean from Europe.
    c. They always lived there.
    d. They migrated from South America.

2. What did the Indigenous Americans teach the European colonists?
    a. How to farm with the Three Sisters planting system
    b. How to grow and use tobacco
    c. Both a and b
    d. None of the above

3. Who believed that all children—boys and girls—should be educated?
    a. The Catholics in Maryland
    b. The Puritans in New England
    c. The Spanish colonists in Florida
    d. The Virginia Colony

4. Who wrote the Declaration of Independence?
    a. Benjamin Franklin
    b. George Washington
    c. Paul Revere
    d. Thomas Jefferson

5. Which political party was pro-slavery when it first began?
    a. Democrat
    b. Libertarian
    c. Republican
    d. Socialist

6. Whose submarine sunk the USS *Housatonic*?
   a. The Confederates
   b. The Union
   c. The Canadians
   d. None of the above

7. Why did Mrs. Rosa Parks get arrested?
   a. She refused to move to the back of the bus.
   b. She helped organize a bus boycott.
   c. Both a and b
   d. None of the above

8. What was different about World War I?
   a. Tanks were used for the first time.
   b. Machine guns became a key weapon.
   c. The female employment rate doubled.
   d. All of the above

9. Who masterminded the September 11, 2001, attacks on the United States?
   a. King Abdul Aziz
   b. Osama bin Laden
   c. Saddam Hussein
   d. All of the above

10. How did the CIA figure out bin Laden was in the compound in Pakistan?
    a. They followed his associate Ahmed (al-Kuwaiti).
    b. The home had no internet or phone service.
    c. The people in the home burned their trash rather than using the garbage pickup.
    d. All of the above

Chapter 9: Presidential Progress

Who were the best presidents? Who were the worst? That, of course, is a matter of opinion. How do historians judge the best and worst? They consider their moral authority, international relations, vision, and how they handled crises. How well did they relate with Congress and handle the economy during their presidencies? Even the "best" presidents had severe flaws, yet they contributed positively to America's history.

This chapter reviews the seven best presidents, according to multiple historians, and what made them stand out. It also reviews the three worst presidents in American history. No one who has served in the past twenty-five years is on the list. Time needs to pass to assess a president's lasting impact. The presidents are listed in order of when they were president. However, most historians agree that George Washington, Abraham Lincoln, and Franklin Roosevelt were the top three.

Who Were the Seven Best Presidents?

George Washington (1789–97)

Washington was a war hero who led the colonists in winning independence. He also worked with other patriots to set up the United States government. He was the natural choice for America's first president and served for two four-year terms.

America was war-torn and almost bankrupt when Washington became president. He kept America from further wars by not getting involved in European conflicts. Washington paid each state's war debt from the federal treasury. He put a 5 percent tax on all imports so the treasury could pay the debt. The countries that imported goods were paying the debt, not the Americans.

George Washington in a 1796 painting by Gilbert Stuart [47]

Washington warned Americans not to have political parties but to work as a unit. "Parties will divide Americans!" Washington established the United States Mint, which made coins. He made the dollar America's official currency. Dollars were silver coins then; the US did not use paper money until 1861.

Thomas Jefferson (1801–09)

Jefferson was America's third president. In 1796, he lost to John Adams by three electoral votes. Jefferson became Adam's vice president due to a glitch in the Constitution. He barely won the next election. Jefferson cut military spending, reduced the budget, and decreased the national debt by one-third. In 1803, he bought the Louisiana Territory from France. It was a bit of a gamble because the Constitution did not permit the government to buy foreign territory. To his relief, the Senate voted 24-7 to approve the purchase.

Thomas Jefferson, 1805 portrait by Rembrandt Peale⁴⁸

Jefferson spent his second term trying to keep America out of Napoleon's wars in Europe. The British were boarding American ships and forcing thousands of American sailors into their navy to fight Napoleon. When three American sailors escaped the British Navy, Britain brazenly demanded them back. A British ship even fired on an American ship, killing three men. Jefferson passed the **Non-Intercourse Act of 1809** to end the nonsense. It stopped British imports and banned British ships from American waters.

Abraham Lincoln (1861–65)

Abraham Lincoln grew up in poverty on the Kentucky and Indiana frontier, coming of age during the Second Great Awakening. His mother died when he was nine, and he did not go to school much because he had to help his father on the farm. However, Lincoln learned to read, which became his favorite pastime. He borrowed books on history, law, and other themes and self-educated himself. His life exemplifies how anyone can succeed through dedication and determination.

Did you know that Lincoln only had a beard for the last four years of his life? When he was running for president, an eleven-year-old girl named Grace encouraged him to grow a beard to get more votes. He did, and he got elected!

Abraham Lincoln in 1860, just before growing a beard[49]

As we learned earlier, Lincoln was the president during the Civil War, which almost ripped the United States apart. He did everything within his power to preserve the Union. Lincoln had to make many difficult choices. It was impossible to please everyone. Nevertheless, he guided the nation through the crisis.

Lincoln was murdered just as the war ended, but he promoted reconciliation for the rebellious states rather than punishment. Just weeks before, at his Second Inaugural Address, he urged, "Let us strive to finish the work we are in; to bind up the nation's wounds ... to do all which may achieve and cherish a just, and a lasting peace."

Theodore Roosevelt (1901–09)

In 1901, an assassin shot President McKinley. Suddenly, Vice-President "Teddy" Roosevelt was America's new leader. He was the cowboy president. Before his political career took off, he went to North Dakota to hunt buffalo, fell in love with the plains, and bought a cattle ranch. Roosevelt was a "Rough Rider" (volunteer cavalry) during the Spanish-American War. President Roosevelt loved the great outdoors and gave federal protection to wildlife and land. He created 5 national parks, 51 bird reserves, and 150 national forests. He placed over 230 million acres under government protection.

Colonel Roosevelt, the Rough Rider, three years before becoming president[60]

Roosevelt had the Panama Canal built through a fifty-mile stretch of Panama so ships could pass from the Caribbean Sea to the Pacific Ocean (or vice versa). Before the canal, ships traveling between America's eastern shores and Asia had to sail around the bottom of South America, a long and dangerous voyage.

Roosevelt broke up giant business monopolies, like the ones controlling America's railroad lines. He used antitrust laws that promoted competition and fair trade to do this. In 1902, the coal miners in Pennsylvania went on strike. Winter was setting in, and people needed coal to heat their homes. Roosevelt called the mine owners and the miners to the White House, but the owners refused to negotiate. "Okay, then," Roosevelt replied with a glint in his eye. "I'll have my military seize the mines. I'll run them as a federal operation."

Suddenly, the mine owners were ready to negotiate. Roosevelt called it his "Square Deal" because everyone benefitted fairly. Roosevelt used a similar approach when dealing with other countries. He loved to say, "Speak softly and carry a big stick."

Franklin D. Roosevelt (1933–45)

Americans loved Franklin Roosevelt so much that they elected him to four terms. (In 1951, the US limited presidents to two terms.) Known as FDR, he was a distant cousin of Teddy Roosevelt. FDR became president in the fourth year of the Great Depression (1929-39). Twenty-five percent of America's workforce had lost their jobs. Could he pull the United States out of its economic slump?

Roosevelt's Emergency Banking Act let the Federal Reserve insure bank deposits. Even if a bank failed, people who had deposited money into the bank could get their money. His economic plans helped a little, but pulling out of the slump took years. FDR introduced Social Security for seniors and assistance for disabled people. He made "oppressive child labor" illegal and gave America the forty-hour work week and minimum wage.

FDR (center) with Churchill and Stalin at the Yalta Summit two months before he died[61]

As discussed earlier, Roosevelt successfully guided the United States through WWII. His health went downhill quickly in his fourth term, which his staff kept a secret. He died while in office on April 12, 1945. Mussolini's execution and Hitler's suicide were just days later. The war in Europe ended three weeks after Roosevelt's death.

John F. Kennedy (1961–63)

John F. Kennedy served less than three years before two assassin's bullets ended his life. Yet, he left a lasting legacy. In 1963, he signed the Limited Test Ban Treaty with the Soviet Union and the United Kingdom. It banned nuclear weapons testing above ground to prevent poisoning the air and water with radiation. Kennedy established the *Peace Corps*, a government program that sends trained volunteers to help developing countries. He picked up Dwight Eisenhower's *Apollo Program* and set the goal of putting a man on the moon.

John F. Kennedy and his nephew, Robert F. Kennedy Jr., with a pet salamander [52]

In his 1963 speech on civil rights, Kennedy asked, "If an American, because his skin is dark, cannot eat lunch in a restaurant open to the public, if he cannot send his children to the best public school available, if he cannot vote for the public officials who represent him, if, in short, he cannot enjoy the full and free life which all of us want, then who among us would be content to have the color of his skin changed and stand in his place?"

Kennedy made outstanding progress in integrating America's public schools and universities before his murder. Eight months after his death, the Civil Rights Act of 1964 passed. It banned discrimination based on race, religion, gender, or national origin and established equal employment.

Ronald Reagan (1981–89)

Ronald Reagan was the movie star who became president. After serving in WWII, he became a political activist, speaking out against racism and the Ku Klux Klan. Reagan became California's governor in 1966 and president in 1981, serving two terms. He was struck by a would-be assassin's bullet two months after becoming president. It punctured his lung and caused massive internal bleeding that put him in the hospital for six weeks.

Reagan meets with Prince Charles (now King Charles III of the United Kingdom).[68]

America enjoyed eight years of peace during Reagan's two terms. He appointed the first woman, Sandra Day O'Connor, to the Supreme Court. He also negotiated an arms reduction accord with the Soviet Union. Reagan worked closely with Soviet ruler Mikhail Gorbachev as he restructured the USSR from communism to a social democracy.

Reagan communicated his policies and goals in simple language that everyone could understand. He boosted the morale of the American people, who had become pessimistic and worried. He commented, "What I'd really like to do is go down in history as the President who made Americans believe in themselves again." Reagan achieved that goal.

His economic policy, nicknamed "Reaganomics," involved tax cuts that helped jumpstart the stagnating economy. He also tried to reduce government regulations over business. Unemployment dropped as twenty-one million new jobs opened. Inflation plunged, and production rose. However, critics pointed out that the rich got richer while more people became poor.

Who Were the Three Worst Presidents?

Interestingly, the three men most historians say were the worst presidents all served within twelve years of each other. This was in the era just before and immediately after the Civil War. It was an agonizing time for America.

Franklin Pierce (1853–57)

When the Democrats tried to nominate a presidential candidate in 1852, they sharply disagreed over the three top contenders. That's when Pierce came to mind. He was relatively unknown and did not have strong opinions on anything. People would not be able to find fault with him. He was the vanilla candidate. Pierce did not even campaign against his opponent, "Old Fuss and Feathers" Winfield Scott. People disliked Scott so much that Pierce won by a landslide.

Pierce became president a few years before the Civil War. Americans were hotly divided on the slavery issue.

Franklin Pierce, portrait by Mathew Brady"

Although Pierce was from New Hampshire, he opposed freeing enslaved people. He approved of returning escaped slaves to their owners in the South. In 1854, Pierce signed the Kansas-Nebraska Act that canceled a ban on slavery in the Northern territories. This act divided America even more intensely, leading to a political firestorm between the pro-slavers and the abolitionists. Pierce's attempts to stop the violent demonstrations were inept.

James Buchanan (1857–61)

Buchanan came after Pierce and inherited his mess. He felt the voters in the new territories should decide what to do about slavery. Of course, the voters were all White men. He also supported the Supreme Court decision that Dred Scott was not a citizen despite living his entire life in the United States.

James Buchanan by Matthew Brady [55]

In 1859, an anti-slavery activist named John Brown led an attack on a federal arsenal in Harper's Ferry near Washington, D.C. He wanted weapons for his struggle against slavery. Brown captured the armory and set the local enslaved people free. However, the following morning, the Marines stormed the arsenal and arrested Brown and several accomplices. Brown was hanged six weeks later with President Buchanan's approval. Tensions soared, and the divide between the North and South deepened, exploding into war two years later.

Andrew Johnson (1865–69)

Andrew Johnson became president when Abraham Lincoln was shot. Despite being Lincoln's vice president, Johnson had owned several enslaved people. He freed them in 1853 and kept them as paid servants. After unexpectedly becoming president, Johnson sparred with his advisors on what post-war America should look like. Would Black people have voting rights? What did the rebel states need to do to be readmitted into the Union?

President Johnson vetoed bills promoting equality and civil rights. He assured Missouri's governor, "This is a country for White men, and by God, as long as I am President, it shall be a government for White men." He was against the Fourteenth Amendment, which gave citizenship to formerly enslaved people. This led to a two-year battle between the president and the Republican Party, the bill's champions. In 1866, the Republicans took Congress by a landslide and pushed the bill through a year later.

Andrew Johnson, photographed by Mathew Benjamin Brady[48]

The Congress also tried to pass the *Civil Rights Act*, which gave formerly enslaved people full citizenship and said they had the same rights as Whites regarding property ownership and contracts. Similar wording was in the Fourteenth Amendment, but that had not passed yet. President

Johnson vetoed the Civil Rights Act. Congress passed the bill again, and Johnson vetoed it again. This time, however, the Republicans and other bill supporters had a two-thirds majority in the House and Senate and overrode Johnson's veto.

In 1868, Johnson fired his secretary of war, Edwin Stanton, without getting the Senate's go-ahead. Stanton was a Republican hired by Abraham Lincoln. The "Radical Republicans" impeached Johnson in February 1868 for breaking the Tenure of Office Act. However, seven senators voted against the impeachment, and Johnson survived as president. The seven senators were not fans of Johnson. The issue was that Johnson did not have a vice president. If they impeached him, the Senate president, Benjamin Wade, would become president. The senators thought he would be worse than Johnson.

Roundup Activity: Election Poster

Choose one of the above presidents and pretend you are part of his election campaign. Create an election poster with key facts you think would be essential to voters.

Chapter 10: Star-Spangled Heroes and Villains

The people in this chapter were not presidents or famous politicians. Most came from humble backgrounds. They rose to fame through other ways, like athletics, activism, and inventions. Some were heroes, and some were villains. Some were both. Yet, they all played a key role in shaping American history.

Benedict Arnold

Benedict Arnold was an American war hero who turned traitor. He was born in 1741 in Connecticut. His father was an alcoholic, and when he lost his business, Benedict had to leave school at age fourteen. His dreams of going to Yale crumbled. At sixteen, Benedict briefly served in the French and Indian War. He then opened a small store in New Haven, Connecticut, and soon became a wealthy businessman.

As a captain in the American Revolutionary War, Arnold successfully captured the British Fort Ticonderoga and Fort George in New York in 1775. However, he got passed over for promotion.

Arnold launched a successful defense when the British attacked a supply depot in Connecticut. A bullet shattered his left leg, and another bullet killed his horse, and it fell on his right leg. As blood gushed from Arnold's leg, his men finally got the dead horse off him. Due to the chaos of war, they could not get him to a hospital until four days later. Gangrene had set in, and antibiotics had not yet been discovered. The surgeon recommended amputating the leg. "I'd rather die," Arnold answered. All the doctors could do was clean and drain the wound. After months in the hospital in agonizing pain, he survived with a leg two inches shorter than the other. Despite all this, his political enemies gave a medal to another officer for the battle. However, George Washington intervened, and Congress promoted Arnold to major general.

Benedict Arnold in 1776, painted by Thomas Hart [57]

Arnold's enemies weren't done. Arnold was court-martialed and received a humiliating public reprimand in 1781 for a minor offense. Enough was enough! He began negotiating with the British about switching sides. Meanwhile, the unsuspecting American military put him in charge of West Point. Arnold secretly worked to weaken the fort's defenses.

The British rewarded him financially and made him brigadier general for coming over to their side. Arnold led two British attacks in 1781. In Virginia, he captured Richmond, and in Connecticut, he burned New London to the ground. He and his wife then sailed to Britain, where he died twenty years later.

Susan B. Anthony

Susan B. Anthony was an American hero who fought to end slavery and give women the right to vote. She was born in 1820 in Massachusetts to a Quaker family who taught the equality of all people before God. In 1845, Anthony's family moved to Rochester, New York, and their home became a central meeting place for the anti-slavery movement. She began traveling around, giving lectures against slavery. She even challenged Abraham Lincoln for being too moderate on the issue.

Anthony got a job as a teacher in 1848. She discovered male teachers made four times the salary of female teachers. She began fighting for women's equal rights, including **women's suffrage,** or the right to vote. Anthony met Elizabeth Cady Stanton, who organized the first women's rights convention. The ladies became lifelong friends as they pioneered women's rights and fought to end slavery.

Susan B. Anthony, engraved by G.E. Perine & Co.[58]

In 1863, Anthony formed the Women's Loyal National League with Stanton and Lucy Stone. They fought for an amendment to the Constitution to end slavery. Two years later, their dream came true when the Thirteenth Amendment abolished slavery. However, Anthony was disappointed when the Fifteenth Amendment passed. Black men could finally vote, but no women could vote.

In January 1869, Anthony held the first women's suffrage conference in Washington, D.C. She told women to go out and register to vote, even though it wasn't legal. In 1872, she and a group of ladies walked to a local barber shop, a place to register to vote in those days. The registrar was so surprised that he let them register. On Election Day, Anthony cast her vote in Rochester, New York. Two weeks later, she was arrested.

At her trial, which made headlines around the country, the judge told the twelve male jurors to find her guilty and did not allow Anthony to speak. He fined her $100.

In 1905, she met President Theodore Roosevelt at the White House to discuss women's right to vote. She was eighty-six years old and died the following year. The Nineteenth Amendment, nicknamed the "Susan B. Anthony Amendment," passed in 1920. Women finally had the right to vote!

Geronimo

Many Native Americans considered Geronimo a hero because he fiercely fought against people settling on their ancestral lands. Yet, his violent tactics made him a villain in the minds of most Americans and Mexicans of his day. Geronimo's real name was Goyahkla, and he was born in 1829 in Arizona or New Mexico. He belonged to the Bedonkohe people, part of the Chiricahua Apache tribe.

By the time he was seventeen, Geronimo had led four raids on the Navajo and Camanche tribes. Tragedy struck when Geronimo was twenty-two. He came home to find his wife, mother, and three small children murdered by Mexican soldiers. The Apache were not at war with the Mexicans at that time.

Finding their bodies changed Geronimo forever. Irrepressible rage boiled up. That devastating day began his lifelong vendetta against the Mexicans.

Geronimo [59]

The Mexicans were not his only problem. The United States had won the Mexican-American War in 1848, gaining most of the Southwest. Now, they wanted all the Indigenous Americans to move to reservations. Yet, the Apache could not bear to live in one place. They were nomads, following the herds of buffalo and other wildlife. Furthermore, the reservation was far from their ancestral lands.

In 1855, Geronimo led 135 Apache warriors, women, and children in an escape from the reservation. They roamed about, raiding American and Mexican settlements. Chased down by five thousand American troops, they eluded capture for five months. Finally, Geronimo surrendered. He spent the next fourteen years in custody at Fort Sill in Oklahoma, where he died.

Henry Ford

Henry Ford was both a hero of industry and a diabolical antisemite. Born in 1863, he only had an eighth-grade education. In 1892, he built a gasoline-powered "horseless carriage" in the shed behind his house. His "quadricycle" had four bicycle wheels and used a two-cylinder, four-horsepower gasoline engine. It wasn't the first car, yet it launched his epic automotive career.

In 1902, Ford opened the Ford Motor Company and began producing the Model A, a two-cylinder, eight-horsepower car. It had a top speed of around sixty-five miles per hour. He also made the "999" race car in 1902. It was the fastest car of its day with a top speed of ninety-one miles per hour.

Henry Ford (r) and his 999 race car with driver Barney Oldfield[60]

Ford's dream was mass-producing a car everyone could afford. In 1908, he introduced the Model T. He paid his workers almost twice what other factories paid. Within a decade, half of all cars in America were the Model T. He produced fifteen million Model T's in factories worldwide.

Ford owned the *Dearborn Independent* newspaper, where he discussed diverse topics. For instance, Ford approved of a minimum wage for workers but did not like labor unions. His most troubling view was blaming the Jews for war, crime, and immorality. Once a week, his paper's front page featured "The International Jew: The World's Problem." Ford felt that the Jews, who he thought controlled the world's banks, were profiting from World War I. He directly encouraged antisemitism in America.

The Wright Brothers

Wilbur (born 1867) and Orville Wright (born 1871) grew up in Ohio, fascinated by machines. Orville built a printing press when he was sixteen. Neither went to college nor finished high school. Instead, they worked together on business ventures like a bicycle shop. Their money from making and selling bicycles funded their dream to invent an airplane.

The winds and hills at Kitty Hawk on North Carolina's Outer Banks were ideal for their experiments. They built a glider in 1900 that could carry a man. Yet, how could they control it? Wilbur spent hours studying birds through binoculars, realizing they changed direction by modifying their wing shape. Using a pulley and cable system, the brothers learned to change their glider's wings like the birds.

However, they needed more lift. They built a wind tunnel in their bicycle shop and experimented. Finally, they hit upon a wing shape with better balance and lift. The next step was an engine. They made their own and also designed a propeller.

First flight at Kitty Hawk. Orville is flying, and Wilbur runs alongside.[61]

December 17, 1903, was the day! Orville went first. Lying on his belly, he flew their "Wright Flyer" about 120 feet in 12 seconds. Wilbur then flew for 59 seconds, covering 852 feet. A local man used their camera to get a shot of the flight. He had never used a camera before, and they weren't sure if he got the shot until they got home and developed the photo. In 1909, they began building and selling airplanes.

Jesse Owens

James Cleveland Owens was born in 1913, the youngest of ten children. When he was nine, his family moved from Alabama to Ohio in the Great Migration. His new teacher asked his name, and he said "J. C."–his family nickname. She wrote it down as Jesse, and it stuck. Jesse's astounding athletic abilities emerged in junior high. He scored a six-foot-high jump and a broad jump of almost twenty-three feet. In high school, he took all the track trophies, even the Ohio state championship, for three years straight.

As a high school senior, Jesse matched or broke three world records. He ran the 100-yard dash in 9.4 seconds, the 220-yard dash in 20.7 seconds, and pulled off a 24-foot,11.75-inch broad jump. College recruiters lined up with offers. However, he chose Ohio State despite it not having a track scholarship. Owens worked his way through college while setting intercollegiate records.

Jesse Owens at the 1935 Berlin Olympics [62]

In only forty-five minutes, Owens broke three world records and tied a fourth at the 1935 Big Ten Championships, despite recently falling down a flight of stairs. Buoyed by his victories, Owens competed in the 1936 Olympics in Germany. Hitler was sure the "superior" Aryan (White) race competitors would trump the other competitors. Owens proved him wrong. He was the first American to win four gold medals in track and field at the Olympics. In the words of President Jimmy Carter, "Perhaps no athlete better symbolized the human struggle against tyranny, poverty, and racial bigotry."

Maya Angelou

Born in 1928 in St. Louis, Missouri, Maya Angelou was an activist, author, dancer, poet, scholar, and singer. She wrote about events in her life, how they changed her, and what she learned from them. Her parents' marriage fell apart when she was three, and her father sent Maya to live with her grandmother. When she was seven, her father abruptly sent her back to her mother, where her mother's boyfriend raped her a year later. The man was murdered, probably by family members, and the trauma caused Maya to be mute for five years. In her silent world, she dove into books and developed a habit of listening, observing, and remembering things.

Maya was sent back to her grandmother, where a teacher, Mrs. Bertha Flowers, helped her to speak again by reciting poetry. Mrs. Flowers introduced her to classic literature and the writings of early Black female activists. At age fourteen, Maya went back to live with her mother. At sixteen, she got pregnant. She was terrified. Decades later, Maya shared about the experience on her Facebook page:

> "Back then, if you had money, there were some girls who got abortions, but I couldn't deal with that idea. Oh, no. No. I knew there was somebody inside me. So, I decided to keep the baby ... I'm telling you that the best decision I ever made was keeping that baby! ... Years later, when I was married, I wanted to have more children, but I couldn't conceive. Isn't it wonderful that I had a child at sixteen? Praise God!"[i]

---

[i] Bre Payton, "Maya Angelou Explains Why She Decided Against An Abortion," *The Federalist*, June 29, 2016, https://thefederalist.com/2016/06/29/maya-angelou-explains-why-she-decided-against-an-abortion/.

Maya Angelou with her first book in 1971[68]

Clyde Bailey (Guy) Johnson was her only child.

Angelou had talent as a calypso and cabaret singer and dancer. In the 1950s, she traveled as a performer around the United States, Europe, and North Africa. She published the story of her childhood and teen years in *I Know Why the Caged Bird Sings*, which became a bestseller. Many other books, plays, and poetry followed. She worked with Martin Luther King Jr. and Malcolm X in the civil rights movement. In Maya's own words, "You may not control all the events that happen to you, but you can decide not to be reduced by them."

Roundup Activity: Essay

Choose a person from this chapter that interests you the most. Write a two-to-three-paragraph essay explaining why this person intrigues you and what lessons can be learned from their life.

Answers to Roundup Questions

Chapter One Roundup Activity Answer Key

Tuscaloosa
Iroquois
Cahokia
Coosa
maize

colonizers
Anzick
Clovis
Columbus

Beringia
camelops
Hurons
Calusa

Image source[64]

Chapter Two Roundup Activity Answer Key

Most of the colonists in Virginia and New England came from **Protestant** groups. The Lost Colony disappeared from **Carolina's** Outer Banks. Among Jamestown's early leaders, **John Smith** was a former pirate and slave. After leaving England, the Puritans first went to **Holland** before sailing to America. **Squanto**, a Patuxet man, taught the Puritans to farm, hunt, and fish. The Puritans believed all children needed to be **literate**. The Spaniards in Florida offered freedom to slaves who escaped the British colonies and settled them at **Fort Mose**. **Jonathan Edwards** and **George Whitfield** were two ministers who helped spark the Great Awakening.

Chapter Three Roundup Activity Answer Key

(F) 1. The 1763 Treaty of Paris gave the French all the colonies east of the Mississippi River.

(T) 2. The Enlightenment thinkers preferred intellectual reason over faith and tradition.

(F) 3. The British trade policies with the American colonists were fair and profitable for all.

(T) 4. The Boston Tea Party led to the British closing Boston Harbor.

(T) 5. The Green Mountain Boys sent the canons from Fort Ticonderoga to Boston.

(F) 6. The Continental Congress wrote the Declaration of Independence at the war's end.

(T) 7. Thomas Paine's booklet *Common Sense* strengthened the resolve of the Americans.

(T) 8. Washington's troops won the Battle of Trenton on Christmas Day.

(T) 9. The Treaty of Paris recognized American independence and gave Florida back to Spain.

(T) 10. The Bill of Rights included freedom of speech and religion.

Chapter Five Roundup Activity Answer Key

1. Which of the following did Abraham Lincoln believe about Black people?

    d. <u>None of the above</u>

2. Which of the following did Charles Darwin believe about White people?

    d. <u>All of the above</u>

3. Dred Scott lost his court case for freedom because...

    d. <u>All of the above</u>

4. Who got called "Scalawags?"

    c. <u>White people who advocated for formerly enslaved Blacks</u>

5. How did some White people retaliate against the bus boycott by Black people?

    d. <u>All of the above</u>

Chapter Six Roundup Activity Answer Key

Crossword Puzzle: World Wars I and II

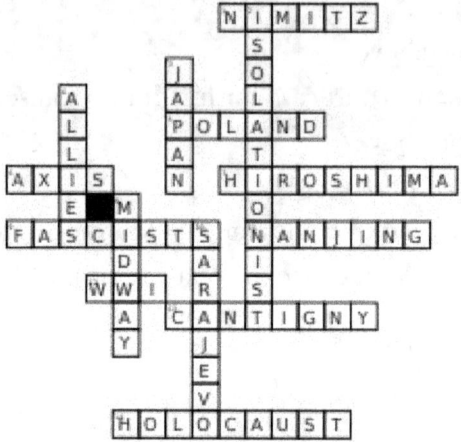

Down:
2. not getting involved in other nation's fights
3. staged a surprise attack on Pearl Harbor
4. the side America fought on in WWI
8. where America won a decisive sea battle against Japan
10. where WWI started

Across:
1. American admiral in Pacific during WWII
5. where Nazi Germany's invasion triggered WWII
6. union of Germany, Japan, and Italy against Allies
7. the city where America dropped the first atomic bomb
9. violent dictators with unlimited powers
11. where the Japanese killed 200,000 civilians
12. the war to end all wars
13. America's first WWI battle in France
14. the systematic murder of 6 million Jews

Image source[65]

Chapter Seven Roundup Activity Answer Key

The underlined statements are untrue.

- The USSR covered one-sixth of the planet at its peak.
- <u>The USSR achieved superpower status before World War I.</u>
- The USSR's political ideology was at odds with American democratic ideals.
- NATO was an alliance of the US, Canada, and European countries to defend themselves against a potential attack from a "third party" (primarily the Soviet Union).
- NATO and the Warsaw Pact alliances set off the Cold War.
- <u>The Cold War ended in 1962 after the Cuban Missile Crisis was resolved.</u>
- <u>Atom bombs are much more powerful than hydrogen bombs.</u>
- The Soviets used captured German nuclear scientists to develop an atom bomb.
- American schoolchildren had drills where they practiced hiding under the desk for protection from nuclear bombs.
- The USSR installed nuclear-armed ballistic missiles in Cuba, only ninety miles from Florida.
- President Kennedy put a navy blockade around Cuba.
- <u>The Soviet missiles never got removed from Cuba.</u>
- <u>America sent the first man-made satellite into space.</u>
- A dog named Laika was the first animal in space.
- America won the Space Race by putting men on the moon.

Chapter Eight Roundup Activity Answer Key

1. How did the first Americans get to America?
    a. They crossed the Beringia land bridge.
2. What did the Indigenous Americans teach the European colonists?
    c. Both a and b
3. Who believed that all children—boys and girls—should be educated?
    b. The Puritans in New England
4. Who wrote the Declaration of Independence?
    d. Thomas Jefferson
5. Which political party was pro-slavery when it first began?
    a. Democrat
6. Whose submarine sank the USS *Housatonic*?
    a. The Confederates
7. Why did Mrs. Rosa Parks get arrested?
    c. Both a and b
8. What was different about World War I?
    d. All of the above
9. Who masterminded the September 11, 2001, attacks on the United States?
    b. Osama bin Laden
10. How did the CIA figure out bin Laden was in the compound in Pakistan?
    d. All of the above

Part 2: The Civil War for Teens

An Enthralling Guide to a Major Event in American History

Introduction

Did you know that some soldiers in the American Civil War were as young as nine years old? Imagine being a kid and heading off to battle! Over 250,000 soldiers under the age of eighteen served in the Union and Confederate Army, making it a war fought by some very young heroes.

This book is specially designed for teen history buffs like yourself. You'll find everything you need to know about the Civil War. Learn how and when the Southern states withdrew from the Union, the war's daring battles and campaigns, America's transformation after the war, and how its brave participants are honored in the modern age.

History is so much more than just learning facts and dates. It's all about connecting the dots between past mistakes and triumphs so we can better understand the world we all live in today.

You won't find confusing, boring content here. Complex concepts are skillfully broken down and explained, and each chapter ends with a specially crafted activity that's guaranteed to boost your brain cells and keep you entertained as you learn. These pages are also full of maps and images that will stimulate your imagination and bring the content to life before your very eyes.

Get ready to go on an exciting adventure through time to learn more about the Civil War.

Chapter 1: The Lay of the Land

Imagine a cauldron or pot on the verge of boiling over. This gives you an idea of how chaotic the situation in America was before the Civil War broke out. The brutal conflict, lasting from 1861 to 1865, ravaged the nation with an unimaginable loss of life.

Scenes of the Civil War.[66]

A civil war is a violent conflict between people of the same country. It involves organized groups fighting to gain control over the nation. Sometimes, people seek independence for a specific region or want to change government policies.

The Buildup to the Revolutionary War

To form a crystal-clear picture, we will begin with the situation in North America during the late 1700s.

Britain reigned over the Thirteen Colonies. The colonists felt boxed in because they did not have enough say in Britain's *Parliament* (government), and Britain had imposed unfair taxes on them. Colonial trade had also been restricted, making it harder for the colonists to make money. As you may imagine, this made the colonists bitter and resentful.

The Revolutionary War Begins

Before the United States was a nation, most colonists wanted only some independence. They still wanted to stay under British rule. However, there continued to be tensions between the colonists and the British. Eventually, the Revolutionary War broke out. It started in Lexington and Concord, Massachusetts, on April 19th, 1775. The war was a grinding struggle for the colonies.

The Continental Congress, consisting of delegates from every colony, met to discuss important colonial matters, make decisions, and tackle issues affecting the colonies. On July 4th, 1776, the Second Continental Congress adopted the Declaration of Independence, which stated the colonists' right to independence.

The Declaration of Independence

Three brilliant brains were behind the Declaration of Independence: John Adams, Benjamin Franklin, and Thomas Jefferson. They were giants politically, intellectually, and ideologically—a powerful combination. The three men were key figures in the founding of the US. They are part of a group referred to as the Founding Fathers due to their significant contributions to the country.

The Declaration of Independence laid the foundation for a new nation founded on democratic ideals. The document stressed that every person is equal, no matter where they come from or who they are. The document states that everyone has the right to "life, liberty, and the pursuit of happiness."¹ However, this did not apply to slaves. They were excluded because they were regarded as property, not people.

It goes on to say that the government must protect the rights of all its citizens. Citizens had the right to push back if the government did not protect or violated people's rights. Citizens could even revolt and create a new government if necessary.

A painting of the signing of the US Declaration of Independence.⁶⁷

Back to the Revolutionary War for Independence

The colonists received a much-needed boost when France joined their cause in 1778. Spain also bolstered the colonies in 1779, and the Netherlands gave financial aid, boosting *morale* (confidence).

In October 1781, the war's course changed in favor of the *Continental* (American) forces. The colonists forced the British army to give up in Yorktown, Virginia.

After many battles, the war officially ended when the Treaty of Paris was signed on September 3rd, 1783. The US was now a self-ruling nation. In November of the same year, the remaining British soldiers returned home from New York.

The success of the American Revolution inspired anti-colonial movements globally. The US still had to form diplomatic relations and work hard for its place in the international community.

---

¹ United States. (1776). *Declaration of Independence*. Retrieved from National Archives.

Fresh Governance for the New US Nation

The end of British rule put America in high gear to get things moving. The first order of business was to draft and approve a constitution. This is like a rulebook that lays out the laws by which a country is governed. It defines citizens' rights and clarifies different governing bodies and their powers.

The Articles of Confederation were the country's first attempt at a national legal framework. However, the powers that be quickly realized that it was a flawed system. So, a group of delegates decided to create a brand-new constitution instead of just tweaking the old one.

The main goal was to give the *central* (national) government more power by redefining how the states worked together with it. New Hampshire sealed the deal as the ninth state to approve the Constitution. It came into effect on June 21st, 1788. The first federal government went to work on March 4th, 1789.

The modern US Constitution is based on the original one, but it has been changed, expanded, and modernized in many places since it was first made official. Let's examine what the Constitution was all about when it first came into effect in the late 1700s.

A Balancing Act Between National and Local Governance

There was a separation of powers between the federal level and individual state governments. This is known as a federalist system. This involves a power-sharing arrangement with all levels of government running simultaneously. America's federalist system put the national government squarely in the driver's seat, making decisions that affect the whole country. At the same time, each state had the power to make decisions about local matters but only if it acted within the boundaries of the Constitution.

The Northern and Southern Divide

Generally, the Northerners wanted the federal government to hold the most sway. From their standpoint, the governing framework was a pact between the nation's people, so it made sense to give greater power to the central government. The Southerners championed states' rights. They argued that this framework was a pact between the states that safeguarded each state's independence.

Clashes in the early 19th century over who should have more power were never-ending. A special rule known as the Supremacy Clause was applied to deal with this. In a nutshell, federal law wins when there's a disagreement between national and state laws. This is supposed to ensure uniformity across the country.

In practice, however, achieving national unity is much more difficult.

The US Constitution's Three Government Branches

Three separate bodies were defined in the country's governance system. The specific rules for how each had to be run were clearly laid out. What was the purpose of this? Well, it was important to safeguard against any one person or branch from having too much power. Let's learn more about each governing branch.

1. The US Congress

Congress consists of two parts: the House and the Senate. The House is made up of delegates chosen by each state's residents. The state's population size determines the number of delegates. More people means more delegates. The Senate has two senators per state.

- **The Powers of Congress**

Congress shapes policies by choosing laws the country should follow. Here's how it works. If Congress wants something done, they have to pass a bill to make it law. Congress makes rules about how companies and industries run, aiming to make sure things are fair and safe for everyone. Congress also manages the country's money. Congress can *impeach* (put on trial) federal officials, including the president, vice president, and judges.

2. The President

The president is the commander in chief of the US Armed Forces, leads the nation's foreign policy, and oversees the execution of laws. The president is a very powerful figure. As the country's leader, the president also has the authority to veto legislation passed by Congress. In these instances, Congress has the power to nullify the president's decision with a two-thirds vote in favor, causing a tug-of-war for power.

A strict election process is held to see who would hold this office. Each state chooses electors. The larger a state's population, the more electors it has. Together, these electors are known as the Electoral College. Every four years, they cast their votes for president, and the candidate who secures a majority of electoral votes secures the sought-after role. Citizens still vote for president, though. Typically, the electors vote for the candidate who won the majority of votes in their state.

The president holds this position for four years, provided they are not impeached or unable to complete their term. Interestingly, before the 20th century, there were no presidential term limits. Presidents could serve as many terms as they wanted, provided they won the election. This changed with the Twenty-second Amendment, passed in 1951, which capped a president to only two terms.

3. The Supreme Court

The Supreme Court is the land's highest court. It consists of justices who have to be appointed by the president after the Senate confirms their appointment. Justices serve for life unless they are impeached and removed. Many justices came from the world of politics rather than from lower courts. Although they are supposed to be *unbiased* (neutral), they tend to hold the same political views as the sitting president. Their political views are often well-known before their appointments.

- **The Supreme Court's Powers**

The Supreme Court is tasked with deciding whether laws passed by Congress or actions taken by the *executive branch* (the president and his Cabinet) align with the Constitution and past court cases. It also has to clarify the meaning and effects of constitutional *provisions* (conditions). The Supreme Court resolves clashes between federal and state laws, placing federal law at the highest level.

How the Constitution Helped Keep Slavery Alive

The US Constitution did not openly say that slaves were property and had no rights. However, slavery was flourishing at that time. Slavery was mentioned in a roundabout way in some of the Constitution's provisions. This inhumane institution was indirectly pardoned and even tolerated. Here's a breakdown of these slavery-related provisions:

1. The Three-Fifths Clause

The Three-Fifths Clause counted enslaved people as three-fifths of a person. This gave states with more slaves more power in the government. For example, even though Georgia's total population might have been smaller than the other states, its large slave population meant it got more representatives in Congress.

2. The Slave Trade Compromise

The Slave Trade Compromise prevented the federal government from banning the import of slaves from other countries until 1808. Northern states wanted to end the slave trade, but Southern states threatened to *secede* (withdraw) from the US if this happened. Neither side was ready for such a drastic situation to develop. So, the two sides agreed to delay the ban.

3. The Fugitive Slave Clause

Free states were forced to send back runaway slaves to their owners under the Fugitive Slave Clause. This denied enslaved people any chance of freedom. Over time, this clause was often ignored in the North.

The Evolving Right to Vote

At the start of the 1800s, only white male property owners could cast a ballot. Non-landholding white males could vote in the 1828 presidential election in most states. It would take decades before women, African Americans, and Native Americans could vote. By 1856, all states were on board with white males voting.

The Industrial Revolution and the Growing North-South Divide

Spanning from the late 1700s to 1861, the Industrial Revolution replaced America's agrarian economy with more lucrative manufacturing and industry. Hand tools and small-scale production were replaced by machinery and large-scale factories.

In the Northern states, manufacturing processes were improved and expanded by a growing population. The region became a hub for factories, which produced an array of goods. New inventions were created, including the cotton gin, a machine that separated cotton seeds from fiber. It sped up cotton processing and expanded the textile industry, greatly increasing the demand for raw cotton from Southern plantations.

A photograph of a cotton gin.[68]

The North used a mostly *free labor force* (not enslaved, paid workers). Northerners also made the most of new technology. The Southern states focused on their existing economic path, causing their dependence on *enslaved labor* (forced labor without pay) to skyrocket.

Industrialization continued in the North, and cities grew quickly. A new industrial middle class appeared. The region invested greatly in infrastructure, making transportation of people, goods, and ideas easier. A growing segment of Northern society viewed slavery as an outdated and immoral institution. Many believed it was out of step with the principles of their modern, industrialized nation.

The Southern economy heavily depended on their vast landholdings and the cultivation of cash crops (primarily cotton). The South's hierarchical social structure created a huge gap between wealthy farm-owning, smaller farmers, and slaves. Southerners resisted industrialization, fearing it would chip away at the institution of slavery. They believed it would ruin their existing way of life.

As you can see, the Northern and Southern states were like two different worlds.

The Westward Expansion: Pioneers of the American Dream

In 1803, America bought a large chunk of North American land from France. The Louisiana Purchase doubled the size of the US. All this new territory made Americans eager to move and settle in new regions.

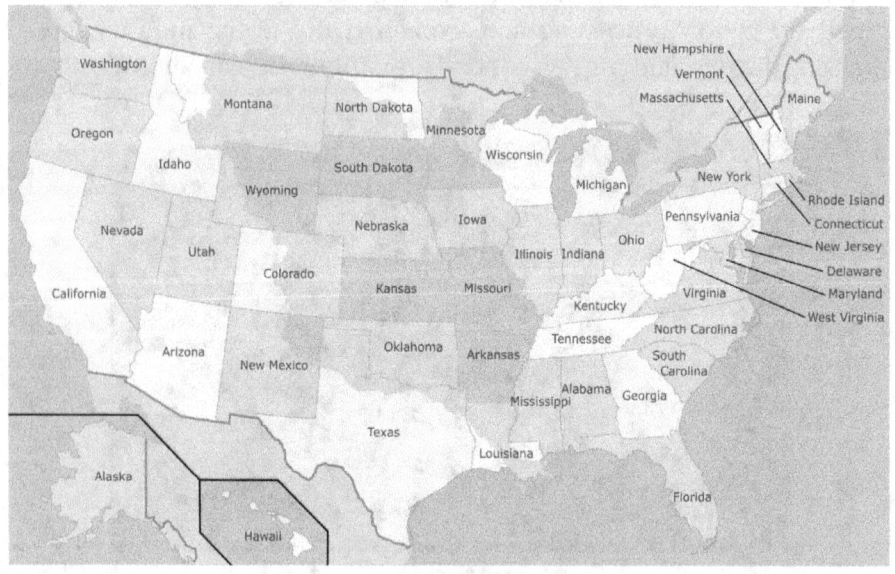

A map of the areas included in the Louisiana Purchase.[60]

The Erie Canal, completed in 1825, spanned 363 miles across New York State. The canal opened a passageway to the Northwest Territories (now Michigan, Ohio, Indiana, and Illinois). It provided a waterway for trade and migration.

Interestingly, this caused freight trade costs to drop by 90 percent! It spurred the first great wave of settlers to move westward. New York became a thriving business hub, and trade between different regions increased greatly.

By 1840, nearly seven million Americans, around 40 percent of the nation's population, lived in the trans-Appalachian West. The Oregon Trail, a two-thousand-mile route, was used by American pioneers in the 1840s to travel westward from Missouri to Oregon. Thousands of people used the trail. However, railroads became the most used method of transportation in the late 1860s.

The 1840s also saw the growth of Manifest Destiny, a belief that Americans were divinely *ordained* (meant) to migrate westward and settle throughout the continent. This *philosophy* (way of thinking) drove 19th-century US territorial growth, promising to spread democracy and *capitalism* (business opportunities) throughout North America. The *Mormon* (a religious group) mass migration to Utah in the 1840s set up a larger settlement in the West.[i]

A painting depicting Manifest Destiny. This was widely distributed in the 1800s as an engraving called "Spirit of the Frontier."[70]

---

[i] O'Sullivan, J. L. (1845). Annexation. *The United States Magazine and Democratic Review*, 17, 5-10.

Westward Expansion Fueled Tensions

As Americans moved westward, the slavery issue came to the forefront. Would freedom or shackles be the order of the day in the new states? Two key developments muddied the waters even more:

- **The Missouri Compromise of 1820:** This set of laws allowed Missouri to enter as a slave state and Maine as a free state. It balanced the number of free and slave states, but it also highlighted regional opinions.
- **Political Power Struggles:** As new states were formed, the balance of power in Congress naturally shifted. This snowballed into increased struggles between pro-slavery and anti-slavery groups.

The North's Growing Anti-Slavery Attitude

The anti-slavery movement in the US was complex and driven by moral beliefs. However, there was more to it. Unpaid slave workers created competition for paid free workers. An anti-slavery attitude became more popular, as people wanted to protect their chance of earning a living.

During that time, many white people felt they were entitled to more than African Americans and Native Americans. By abolishing slavery, white workers hoped to gain more control over the labor market, ensuring fairer competition and protecting their jobs and wages from being undercut by unpaid labor.

If slavery stopped spreading, African Americans could gain rights in the long run. Many white people believed that when this happened, they could maintain social dominance through *segregation* (exclusion, separation) laws and *discriminatory* (unfair) practices. (Segregation is when people are kept apart based on their race, religion, or other characteristics. It usually leads to unfair treatment and fewer opportunities for the separated group.)

Many white people in the North believed that if slavery continued to spread, the Southern states would gain more political influence. This would shrink the Northern states' political voice. By stopping the spread of slavery, they aimed to weaken the South's political power and strengthen the Northern states' control over national policies. This would, in turn, protect the jobs, wages, and overall power of white people in the North.

Many people also hated slavery because it was morally wrong. However, what can't be ignored is the fact that many wanted slavery banned because they were looking out for their own best interests. They were not necessarily fighting for the rights of slaves.

The Mexican-American War and Expansion

The Texas Revolution kicked off in October 1835. In this conflict, colonists in what is now Texas fought to gain independence from Mexico, which had banned slavery in 1829. The Texas colonists gained independence in April 1836. After this, they created a pro-slavery constitution.

When Texas became the twenty-eighth US state in 1845, a dispute erupted between Mexico and the US about where the Texas border was. Resolving this seemed impossible without a war. Not too long afterward, the Mexican-American War started in April 1846. The war ended after several battles in favor of the US. The Treaty of Guadalupe (*gwa-duh-loo-pe*) Hidalgo (*he-dal-go*) was signed in February 1848.

This US victory added a whopping 500,000 square miles of Mexican territory to its land. Mexico *ceded* (gave up) present-day California, Texas, New Mexico, Utah, Nevada, and Arizona to the US for fifteen million dollars. Expansion continued, widening the existing divide over slavery.

The war's land gains also paved the way for the California Gold Rush and further settlement. Gold was found at Sutter's Mill in Coloma, California, in early 1848. Fortune seekers from all over the world set off to California. Around 300,000 people from various countries and parts of the US flocked there and settled along the Pacific Coast.

The Compromise That Shaped a Nation

The Compromise of 1850 was a package of five Congress bills passed in September 1850. It was mostly the result of debates over slavery in the new territories created after the Mexican-American War. The Compromise of 1850 was designed to briefly create a better situation between slave and free states because they were becoming angrier with each other. Many think this compromise delayed the nation's war by around a decade.

California became part of the Union as a free state. New Mexico and Utah were given the choice to allow slavery through "popular sovereignty." This means that the government gets its power from the people, and the people decide who will be in charge and what laws will be made. To put it simply, the people of each state could vote on whether to allow slavery or not without government involvement.[i]

The Compromise of 1850 included strengthening the Fugitive Slave Act of 1793. Stricter measures allowed slave owners and their agents to search for escaped slaves in free states. Upon showing proof of ownership, the escapees had to be returned. Harsh punishments could be imposed on anyone aiding escaped slaves. This put anti-slavery supporters helping slaves to escape at risk and increased tensions between the North and South.

From the Compromise of 1850 to the Kansas-Nebraska Act

To organize the new western territories, the Kansas-Nebraska Act was passed in 1854. Its goal was to make westward expansion easier and build a railroad from coast to coast. The focus was on the vast Nebraska Territory, which included future states like Kansas, Nebraska, Montana, and the Dakotas.

The act also canceled the Missouri Compromise of 1820. The Kansas-Nebraska Act stated that new territories could decide on slavery through popular sovereignty. This had a dangerous snowball effect, as it was up to the states to choose to become a free or slave state.

A stage of violent clashes broke out when separate factions flooded into Kansas to sway the vote. This period was so concerning that it even gave rise to the nickname "Bleeding Kansas" (1854-1859). *Electoral fraud* (vote rigging) was also widespread, and people with different opinions were prepared to do just about anything to get their way.[ii]

Our next chapter will examine slavery in America through a microscope. For now, though, it's time to test your knowledge with this chapter's activity!

---

[i] McPherson, J. M. (2003). *Battle Cry of Freedom: The Civil War Era*. Oxford University Press.

[ii] Etcheson, N. (2004). *Bleeding Kansas: Contested Liberty in the Civil War Era*. Lawrence: University Press of Kansas.

Chapter 1 Activity

Answer whether the statements listed below are true or false.

1. North America was divided into thirteen colonies under British rule in the 1700s.
2. The Declaration of Independence is an important document that was drafted by the president of the US after the colonists had won the Revolutionary War.
3. The US Constitution defines five separate governing branches: Congress, the House, the Senate, the President, and the Supreme Court.
4. The Louisiana Purchase added several Canadian provinces and the Caribbean islands to the US territory.
5. Manifest Destiny refers to the belief that Americans were divinely ordained to spread out across the entire continent, spreading democracy and capitalism.
6. The Mexican-American War happened mainly because the Mexicans wanted to ally with the Southern states.
7. Popular sovereignty means that the people of each state could vote on whether to allow slavery or not without government involvement.
8. The Missouri Compromise of 1820 allowed Missouri to enter as a free state and Maine as a slave state.
9. In the 18th century, presidents could only serve two terms in office.
10. When the president vetoed a decision by Congress, the Supreme Court could overrule it if the justices felt it was an unfair decision.

Chapter 1 Activity Answers

Answer whether the statements listed below are true or false.

1. North America was divided into thirteen colonies under British rule in the 1700s. **True.**
2. The Declaration of Independence is an important document that was drafted by the president of the US after the colonists had won the Revolutionary War. **False.**
3. The US Constitution defines five separate governing branches: Congress, the House, the Senate, the president, and the Supreme Court. **False.**
4. The Louisiana Purchase added several Canadian provinces and the Caribbean islands to the US territory. **False.**
5. Manifest Destiny refers to the belief that Americans were divinely ordained to spread out across the entire continent, spreading democracy and capitalism. **True.**
6. The Mexican-American War happened mainly because the Mexicans wanted to ally with the Southern states. **False.**
7. Popular sovereignty means that the people of each state could vote on whether to allow slavery or not without government involvement. **True.**
8. The Missouri Compromise of 1820 allowed Missouri to enter as a free state and Maine as a slave state. **False.**
9. In the 18th century, presidents could only serve two terms in office. **False.**
10. When the president vetoed a decision by Congress, the Supreme Court could overrule it if the justices felt it was unfair. **False.**

Chapter 2: A History of Slavery in America

Slavery was a major part of the Civil War. Now is a good time for us to track the evolution of this institution in America.

A picture depicting the main deck of a slave ship.[71]

The Story of Slavery

Slavery is an unfair institution where people are treated like things or property, not like humans. They're not viewed as citizens, so they do not have rights. Slaves are owned by other people who are free and have rights. Slaves are forced to work without payment and must do whatever their owners expect of them.

Slavery was used by ancient societies, going back as far as hunter-gatherer groups. In those days, hereditary slavery was common. (Hereditary slavery means slavery is passed down from one generation to the next. The children born to slaves are automatically regarded as slaves.) Then, civilizations like the advanced Sumerians (*soo-mehr-ee-anz*), around five and a half millennia ago, created more organized slavery systems. From there, it spread globally, reaching Africa, Asia, and Europe.

The Atlantic Slave Trade

European nations set about exploring the world from the 15th to the 17th centuries. They conquered and laid claim to various parts of the globe. This period is known as the Age of Exploration.

The Portuguese began the process of kidnapping Africans and forcing them into bondage. They traded native Africans with other nations and colonies for money and other goods. As early as the 1480s, African slaves were already being transported to Cape Verde and the Madeira Islands in the eastern Atlantic.

As time passed, other nations did the same thing. They were often aided by local African leaders and traders. Africa lost many of its young adults to this trade, marking the onset of one of history's most dreadful periods.

Slaves were moved over the Atlantic Ocean by boat through the Middle Passage. The Middle Passage was the middle leg of the Africans' forced journey to the Americas. The slaves were kept in shocking conditions and handled like cargo. During these voyages, many slaves died of abuse, malnutrition, and sickness. However, many survived.

Slavery's Arrival in America

In 1619, the *White Lion* docked at the British colony of Jamestown in Virginia. It was reportedly carrying twenty Africans to be sold as slaves. They were the first slaves to arrive in what would become the United States.

Throughout the 1600s, more colonies were formed on the continent, increasing the need for slaves. In the 1700s, it was estimated that several million Africans were forcibly shipped to North America.

The Anti-Slavery Movement

Anti-slavery attitudes in America popped up gradually, beginning in the 17th century. In 1688, one of the first concrete steps toward abolition happened when German Quakers in Pennsylvania created the Germantown Quaker Petition Against Slavery. The Quakers are still a religious group today. The *Mennonites* (another religious group) joined them in speaking out against slavery.

Organized anti-slavery efforts were few and far between. There was too much pressure on people to accept the *status quo* (the present situation). Speaking out was frowned upon.

The abolitionist movement was a dedicated effort to stop the practice of slavery. Anti-slavery activists, better known as *abolitionists*, included people from all walks of life and all races. Driven by moral views and their passion to achieve equal human rights, they worked tirelessly to expose the unfairness of slavery and stop its use. Just about all means were used, including public speeches, petitions, political activism, and underground networks.

The slave trade reached its height in the US at the end of the 1700s and the early part of the next century. The anti-slavery movement also began to make advances.

Slavery during the American Revolution

During the Revolutionary War, colonists battled it out for their own freedom. However, they continued to deny freedom to enslaved people. Some enslaved people believed they would be freed in exchange for their service and fought for the British. An estimated one thousand to two thousand Virginian enslaved African Americans fled to the British side.

The Continental Army initially stopped African American soldiers from joining, but this policy eventually changed due to manpower shortages. Approximately five thousand African American soldiers and sailors, free and enslaved, took part in the war. Some enslaved people escaped to freedom, mostly in areas occupied by British forces. It's estimated that thousands of slaves escaped and gained freedom during this war.

During the war, Vermont made slavery against the law in its 1777 constitution. However, enslaved boys and girls at the time the law was passed would remain slaves. They were only able to be freed at the ages of twenty-one and eighteen, respectively. Pennsylvania passed a law in 1780 to slowly phase out slavery. As you can see, progress was slow.

Slavery after the Revolutionary War

After the American Revolution, the Massachusetts Supreme Judicial Court ruled that enslavement was unconstitutional in 1783. In 1784, Connecticut introduced a law to end slavery through a slow process. Rhode Island followed suit in the same year with their law to slowly phase out slavery. It was a start; however, these state laws did not put an immediate end to slavery.

The Religious Society of Friends (the Quakers) played a big part in helping abolitionist groups after the revolution. Benjamin Franklin played a big role by helping with anti-slavery efforts. In 1787, he became the president of a group in Pennsylvania that worked to end slavery slowly over time. They also helped free slaves, providing them with aid to get on their feet.

In 1788, anti-slavery campaigners breathed a light sigh of relief when kidnapping and slave trading was outlawed in Massachusetts. Slave traders faced serious punishment and fines after this law took effect. Other states also banned slavery over the next few decades.

However, these laws were painfully slow to make change and take effect, leaving slavery to thrive for decades after America gained its independence.

Prince Hall: The Famous Abolitionist

Prince Hall was an African American man born around 1735. The exact date and place remain uncertain. He was a slave in Boston when the city's massacre took place on March 5th, 1770.

A crowd of colonists harassed a lone British soldier on King Street. British Captain Thomas Preston dispatched troops to calm the disturbance. When the crowd started throwing snowballs and becoming more hostile toward the growing number of British soldiers, the situation got out of hand. Soldiers eventually fired into the crowd, resulting in the deaths of five colonists and wounding several others.

This event helped bring about the Revolutionary War, introducing new ideas about freedom and equality. These ideas promoted change for slaves in Massachusetts and other colonies. People began to see the contradiction in fighting for liberty while keeping slaves.

In 1775, Hall's owner willingly freed him through the legal process of manumission. After being set free, Hall aided the colonists in the war for independence.

In the 18th century, Masonic lodges were *fraternal* (brotherly) organizations. They were places of fellowship and support and had secret rituals and moral teachings. They were closed to people of color.

In 1775, Hall and a group of free African American men formed the first Masonic lodge for people of color in the world. It was called the African Lodge. These men delivered powerful speeches and wrote petitions calling for the abolition of slavery. Hall and the African Lodge faced constant unfairness, but they continued to fight for equality.

In 1777, Hall drafted a petition calling for a gradual process of freeing those enslaved in Massachusetts. Hall opened a school for African American children in his home and secured funding for African American schools in Boston in 1796. His input was invaluable in passing legislation outlawing the slave trade in Massachusetts. He died on December 7th, 1807.

A portrait of Prince Hall.[78]

The Growing Abolitionist Movement

During the first half of the 19th century, abolitionists made a name for themselves. Let's take a closer look at some of the most famous anti-slavery activists.

- **David Walker**

Born around 1785, David Walker became an important African American abolitionist from North Carolina. His early life is shrouded in mystery, though it's clear he was a self-educated man.

In 1829, he published his influential work, *An Appeal to Colored Citizens of the World*, urging African Americans to resist slavery by any means necessary, including through the use of violence. Read by white people and African Americans, Walker's writings inspired many to join the abolitionist movement.

Walker's whereabouts after this book was published are unknown, but he was a target for pro-slavery activists. Some historians believe he might have died in 1830, either from natural causes or because of foul play.

- **William Lloyd Garrison**

An important white abolitionist, William Lloyd Garrison was born in 1805. He founded *The Liberator*, an anti-slavery weekly newspaper, in 1831. Published in Massachusetts and distributed throughout the Northern free states, it gained a dedicated following in the US and abroad.

Garrison often wrote opinion pieces and articles. The newspaper also published firsthand accounts of enslaved people's lives and descriptions of slave auctions. The goal was to urge readers to reconsider their views on slavery and take action.

A portrait of William Lloyd Garrison.[78]

Garrison played a key role in the formation of the American Anti-Slavery Society in 1833. During his lifetime, slavery was abolished. The Thirteenth Amendment was approved in 1865. In 1879, he died of heart disease in New York City and was buried in Boston at Forest Hills Cemetery.

- **Harriet Beecher Stowe**

Another important white anti-slavery activist was Harriet Beecher Stowe. She was born in Connecticut in 1811. After marrying a professor and moving to Cincinnati, Ohio, she was exposed to the growing abolitionist movement. There, she witnessed the brutality of slavery.

A picture of Harriet Beecher Stowe. [74]

Horrified by what was happening and by the introduction of the Fugitive Slave Act of 1850, she put pen to paper and started writing a novel. In 1851, her son tragically passed away, likely from a disease, inspiring her to finish her book.

Uncle Tom's Cabin, published in 1852, became an instant bestseller. The book depicted the inhumane treatment of slaves and brought about widespread sympathy for slaves' suffering. Harriet Beecher Stowe wrote many more novels and rallied support for the abolitionist movement by giving speeches, writing articles, and spreading its message.

After her death in 1896, she was buried in the family plot at the Old North Cemetery in Hartford.

- **Frederick Douglass**

Born into slavery in 1818, Frederick Douglass grew up in Talbot County, Maryland. Douglass's mother was an enslaved African American, and his father was a white man, likely their enslaver. Through self-education and the help of kind white women, Douglass learned to read and write, which became invaluable tools in his later years.

In 1838, Douglass disguised himself as a free African American sailor and fled to New York. He gained his freedom and eventually made his way to Massachusetts. *Narrative of the Life of Frederick Douglass*, released in 1845, was written by Douglass. The book became a bestseller and opened the eyes of people to the realities of life as a slave.

The book was republished many times, with added chapters that detailed Douglass's abolitionist efforts as a free man.

A portrait of Frederick Douglass.[75]

He died on February 20th, 1895, in Washington, DC, and was buried at Mount Hope Cemetery in Rochester, New York.

- **Harriet Tubman**

Harriet Tubman, born Araminta Ross, was born a slave around 1822 in Maryland. A serious head injury during her childhood left her with ongoing medical problems, including seizures. Later in her life, she accepted her seizures as signs from the heavenly realm.

A photograph of Harriet Tubman.[76]

She took on the last name of her free African American husband, John Tubman, and later changed her first name to Harriet. As you may imagine, Harriet's status as a slave strained their relationship. Terrified she could be sold, Tubman escaped slavery and made her way alone to Philadelphia in 1849.

Determined to free others, Tubman became a conductor on the Underground Railroad. She made many trips to Maryland to lead enslaved people to freedom in the North. The Underground Railroad was a *clandestine* (secret) network of people who helped enslaved people escape the South.

Secret routes and safehouses were used by escaping slaves along their journey to the Northern states and Canada, where they would gain their freedom. Avoiding being caught was an essential part of this network's undertakings. Communication was done through a system of codes, signals, and hidden messages.

The Underground Railroad operated from the late 18th century until 1865, when the Civil War also ended. It's believed thousands escaped to freedom thanks to this interconnected outfit. Nicknamed the "Moses of her people," Tubman helped hundreds to freedom. She's believed to have never lost one of her passengers. Her fame spread, resulting in a bounty on her head.

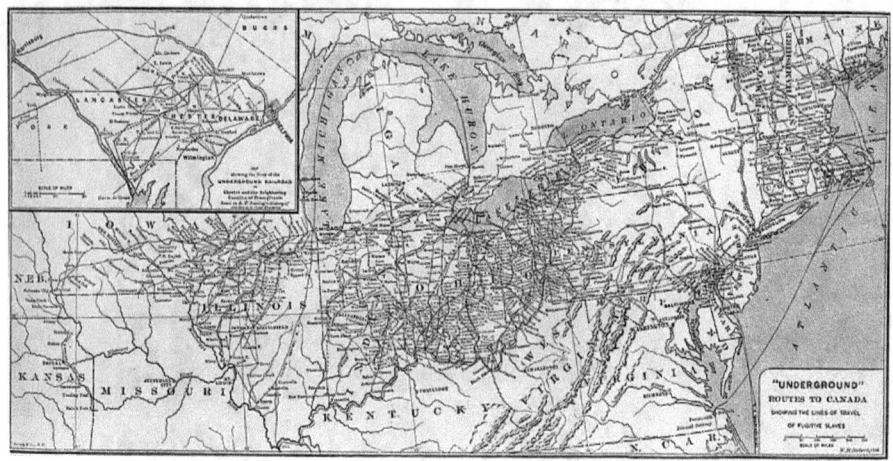

A map of the routes of the Underground Railroad.[77]

During the Civil War, Tubman was a scout, spy, and nurse for the Union Army. She was involved in the Combahee Ferry Raid. The Northern forces conducted this military operation on June 2nd, 1863. During the operation, Tubman led a group of soldiers and escaped enslaved people in capturing the ferry. Seven hundred and fifty slaves were freed, and they went on to aid the Union Army by joining the fight.

After the war and the abolition of slavery, Tubman devoted much of her time to fighting for the rights of people who had once been enslaved. Even though Tubman received a pension from the US government for her service, she faced monetary hardship in her later years. She died in New York in 1913 and was buried with full military honors.

Nat Turner's Brutal Slave Rebellion

The abolitionist movement was not the only form of resistance to slavery. Enslaved people took drastic and violent actions themselves. Let's look at one example.

Born in 1800, Nat Turner was an enslaved African American preacher from Virginia. He was not an abolitionist, but he was a complex figure in the early 19th century. He led one of the most violent slave revolts in American history.

In 1831, Turner and a group of his followers, mostly slaves, rebelled against white slaveholders in Southampton County. On the night of August 21st, the group took weapons and horses after killing the Travis family on their farm.

Over the following day, the rebels moved through the county, attacking white settlements and recruiting other enslaved people to their cause. Their main targets were white families, and their revolt caused the deaths of around sixty white people, including women and children.

The group avoided capture for several weeks, hiding in swamps and forests. They relied on African American communities for support. In response to the rebellion, an intense manhunt was launched by white *militias* (private armies) and bounty hunters. They eventually trapped the rebels.

Turner was captured in a cave near Dismal Swamp, North Carolina, on October 30th of the same year. After this, he was quickly tried, found guilty, and executed on November 11th, 1831. Others involved were also captured and severely punished. They were sold away from the region or executed.

Today, Turner is still a topic of heated debate. Some view him as a courageous individual who fought against the injustices of slavery. Others see him as a violent criminal who caused great harm.

In an effort to prevent more uprisings, white slaveholders increased *stakeouts* (spying and monitoring) of enslaved people, and stricter slave codes were enforced. (Slave codes were laws in the South that restricted enslaved people's rights and movements. They were designed to keep control and stop slave rebellions from happening.)

Slave codes included measures that prevented slaves from being outside their designated areas during certain times. They also restricted slaves from traveling to nearby towns and plantations without permission. Slaveholders could also prevent slaves from gathering in large groups.

Slavery Just Before the Civil War

By 1860, slavery was not only fixed in the American way of life, but it had also formed part of American history for around 250 years. Even with progress in some places and states, slavery stayed unshakeable in many others.

Slavery had become a cycle. Enslaved people were considered property, and their offspring were automatically inherited as such. This created a continuous cycle of slave labor, doing away with the need to import more slaves through the slave trade.

And so, with this solid understanding of slavery's progression in America, it's time to complete this chapter's roundup activity!

Chapter 2 Activity

Find the following words in the word search below.

- Abolish
- Underground
- Liberator
- Rebels
- Slavery
- Bondage
- Exploration
- Property
- Activists
- Fraternal

F	R	A	T	E	R	N	A	L	H	D	F	D	V	P
Y	R	D	X	C	J	F	N	B	G	E	D	S	X	E
A	O	O	O	P	L	M	D	D	V	C	H	G	H	V
S	R	F	D	C	X	A	C	T	I	V	I	S	T	S
P	O	N	G	R	E	S	S	G	C	A	F	T	N	Z
R	E	B	E	L	S	Z	T	U	I	R	E	R	T	U
O	S	M	L	P	W	S	R	Q	S	A	C	G	R	Q
P	P	S	U	P	R	E	M	E	Q	T	Q	S	D	I
E	U	Y	U	N	D	E	R	G	R	O	U	N	D	O
R	S	Z	X	C	V	B	L	M	R	O	D	F	S	E
T	N	S	U	S	T	R	I	A	L	N	T	F	C	X
Y	H	L	H	J	N	G	B	M	T	Y	R	E	W	P
O	I	A	Y	A	B	O	L	I	S	H	M	C	X	L
W	E	V	T	W	A	R	D	F	J	K	O	P	L	O
H	F	E	H	J	K	L	I	B	E	R	A	T	O	R
P	D	R	S	C	S	D	R	D	F	T	Y	H	G	A
V	A	Y	D	F	G	H	J	U	Y	T	V	C	X	T
E	F	R	A	N	K	L	I	N	G	F	L	N	M	I
A	T	U	B	O	N	D	A	G	E	Z	N	D	S	O
E	V	O	T	O	P	Y	O	F	E	D	P	W	A	N

Chapter 2 Activity Answers

Find the following words in the puzzle of scrambled letters below:

F	R	A	T	E	R	N	A	L				
					A	C	T	I	V	I	S	T	S
P												
R	E	B	E	L	S							
O												
P												
E			U	N	D	E	R	G	R	O	U	N	D
R													E
T		S											X
Y		L											P
		A		A	B	O	L	I	S	H			L
		V											O
		E			L	I	B	E	R	A	T	O	R
		R											A
		Y											T
		R											I
			B	O	N	D	A	G	E				O
													N

Chapter 3: A Government in Turmoil

Decades of ever-changing, complex politics paved the way for the nation's historic conflict. Understanding the political parties of the time is key to unraveling their role in sparking the war.

Andrew Jackson and the Democratic Party

Andrew Jackson was born on March 15th, 1767. He qualified to practice in the legal profession and chose Tennessee to settle and work as an attorney. He became wealthy and an important political figure. He had a post in the House of Representatives and was in the Senate for a short period. He also did military service.

The Democratic-Republican Party splintered in 1828. Jackson organized a revamped party that focused on limiting the federal government's power and strengthening the power of

A portrait of Andrew Jackson.[78]

state governments. The Democratic Party was born! The party was also against monopolies and a strong central bank. It favored individuals' opportunities over big business interests. This Democratic Party was different from today's Democratic Party. In the modern day, Democrats want a stronger central government.

Jacksonian Democrats believed in equal rights for white men. They were firmly behind westward expansion. Many Democrats were farmers, *frontiersmen* (roaming settlers), and Southern planters.

With all white men being allowed to vote, voter turnout increased. Powerful local party organizations were formed to deal with this. Jackson was elected in 1828, and his presidency lasted from 1829 until 1837. Jacksonian democracy saw the government's authority change. Regular folks (meaning average white males) had more of a say in how the country was run.

This is a good time for us to look at some of the major actions taken during Jackson's presidency.

Jacksonian Democracy in Action

Jackson put the spoils system into action. This was a process in which loyal supporters were rewarded with government jobs. The Indian Removal Act of 1830 was another action taken by Jackson. This law allowed the government to force Native American tribes to leave their homes and move to selected areas.

Jackson's time in office included major political battles, including the Nullification Crisis. The crisis started with the Tariff of 1828, which imposed high taxes on imported goods. This helped Northern manufacturers, but it hurt the South's economy. Outraged, South Carolina passed the Ordinance of Nullification in 1832. This *ordinance* canceled the tariffs of 1828 and 1832 within the state. (An ordinance is a type of law or rule made by a lawmaking branch.)

Jackson was furious. He called this an act of treason. The Force Bill was passed in 1833. It authorized the president to use military force to collect tariffs from South Carolina. A *concession* (allowance) was also made in the form of the Compromise Tariff of 1833, which guaranteed a reduction in the tariff over a period of years. South Carolina accepted this, and the crisis was sorted out without the state leaving the country.

The Bank War took place during Jackson's term. Jackson believed the Second Bank of the US was too powerful. It was controlled by wealthy elites and unstable. By rejecting the proposal to continue the financial institution's existence, he caused it to be shut down. Jackson's image as a champion of the common man was boosted by this result.

Stopping people from buying large amounts of land quickly just to sell it for a profit later was another move made by Jackson. He did this by making a rule that people had to pay for government land with real gold or silver coins, not paper money.

Jackson died at his home in Tennessee on June 8th, 1845.

The Whig Party

Politicians who were against Jackson's autocratic leadership style planned and started a new party in 1834. It was called the Whig Party. The party aimed to limit presidential power. The Whigs were firmly in favor of a strong federal government. They supported tariffs, infrastructure improvements, and a national bank to grow the nation's economy.

The party started to run into problems in the 1850s. Members were unable to agree on what should be done about slavery. By 1856, most Northern Whigs had joined the newly formed Republican Party. Not long after this, the Whig Party disbanded.

The Free-Soil Party

The Free-Soil Party was formed in 1848. It called for free land for settlers. Free-Soilers pushed to stop slavery because it was unwanted competition for paid white workers.

This party merged into the Republican Party in 1854.

The Republican Party

The Republican Party was formed directly after the Kansas-Nebraska Act came into law. The party was a *coalition* (alliance) of various groups that opposed the expansion of slavery. The party was firmly against the concept of popular sovereignty, believing it would only cause slavery to spread. Party members included former Whigs, Free-Soilers, and anti-slavery ex-Democrats.

Free Soil, Free Labor, Free Men

The Republican Party's core *ideology* (viewpoint) is fully covered by the phrase "free soil, free labor, free men."[ii] This ideology would ultimately define the party and its role in the nation for decades to come. Let's explore what each of the points means:

---

[i] Foner, E. (1995). *Free Soil, Free Labor, Free Men: The Ideology of the Republican Party before the Civil War.* Oxford University Press. Pg. 23.

- **Free Soil:** The Republicans believed the western territories should be reserved for white farmers and laborers without slave labor competition. This was a practical economic concern, as well as a moral stance.
- **Free Labor:** This term pushed the idea that white workers should be free to choose their own jobs and employers. This, in turn, would ensure no meddling from the slaveholding aristocracy.
- **Free Men:** This was a broader statement. It was about the Republican Party's commitment to individual liberty and equality. While it primarily referred to white men, it laid the groundwork for future arguments in favor of civil rights for everyone.

The party grew rapidly. People joined the party in droves, particularly in the Northern states. The party appealed to a broad base, including urban workers, middle-class voters, and businessmen. Surprisingly, even some farmers backed this party.

Protecting the Union was of the utmost importance to this party. This meant keeping the US as a single united nation. Several fed-up Southern states wanted to form their own country. through a process called *secession* (withdrawal).

A few other issues were front and center. The Republican Party was geared at modernizing the economy with projects such as railroad development. Republicans were also committed to expanding public education. Many Republicans were active in the temperance movement, believing that alcohol consumption was a primary cause of poverty, crime, and domestic violence. The movement aimed to reduce the consumption and sale of alcoholic beverages.

Abraham Lincoln as the Standard-Bearer

Running for president as the Republican nominee, Lincoln was a strong candidate in the 1860 election campaign. Why was he the party's first choice? Let's find out by learning more about his journey from humble beginnings to his rise as an influential and powerful man.

In 1809, Lincoln was born in Hardin County, Kentucky. Thomas Lincoln, his father, was a frontiersman. He constantly moved his family in search of a better life. Several of Lincoln's siblings died due to illness, and the family farm couldn't provide for the family. Lincoln had to work long hours on the farm and later as a storekeeper and boatman to help support his family. He was a mostly self-educated man. He had little formal education and mainly taught himself by reading books.

After working many jobs, he became a lawyer in Illinois. Lincoln then started his life as a politician in the Whig Party, holding a position in the Illinois General Assembly. From 1847 to 1849, Lincoln served as a congressman from Illinois. He opposed the Mexican-American War during his time in this post. After his term, he returned to Illinois to continue his law practice. He became popular for his honesty and skill in the courtroom.

A portrait of Abraham Lincoln.[79]

During his debates with Stephen A. Douglas, Lincoln gained fame due to his exceptional ability as a public speaker. Douglas was the Illinois Democratic senator. The debates happened during the Illinois Senate race in 1858.

Lincoln ran for president in the 1860 election. He kept a middle-of-the-road viewpoint on slavery. This helped him to achieve popularity among a broader voter base. Having strong support from abolitionists, Free Soilers, and other anti-slavery groups certainly gave him an edge.

The plan to present Lincoln's public image was brilliant. He was shown as a self-made man, striking a chord with many voters. Lincoln had exceptional political skills, and he ran a great campaign.

Hannibal Hamlin

Hamlin was born in Maine in 1809. He had success as a lawyer and later worked in the US House of Representatives from 1843 to 1847. He served multiple terms in the US Senate, being elected for the first time in 1848. Hamlin strongly opposed slavery. He left the Democratic Party to join the Republicans for this very reason.

A portrait of Hannibal Hamlin.[80]

In 1857, Hamlin had a short stint as governor of Maine, but he returned to the Senate. To balance the ticket for the 1860 election, Lincoln chose Hamlin to run alongside him. Here are some of the reasons why combining these men as partners was a great move:

1. They covered a broader section of the country. Lincoln was a favorite in Illinois, and Hamlin was popular in the northeast, with a proven following in Maine.
2. Lincoln was a former Whig, and Hamlin was a former Democrat. This made them appealing to a broad range of people.

3. Hamlin had extensive political experience, which helped to balance Lincoln's shorter political career.

Hamlin served as vice president from 1861 to 1865 during Lincoln's first term. After his vice presidency, Hamlin continued to be active in politics. He even served another term in the Senate. Hamlin died on July 4th, 1891, in Bangor, Maine. He passed away from a heart attack while playing cards at the Tarratine Club (a social club).

The Democratic Party's Fracture

There was an unusual fracture in the Democratic Party. It was possibly the reason this party was weakened by the time the 1860 presidential election rolled around. But before we get into the election, let's grasp the divisions among the Democratic leadership.

Things came to a head at the 1860 Democratic Convention in Charleston, South Carolina. Unable to agree over slavery, the Democratic Party separated into two. The party held two separate conventions, which nominated different candidates. How did the Democratic Party deal with this?

The party decided the votes would be divided among the two candidates, particularly in key swing states. What are swing states? They are states where the outcome is uncertain and can be won by any major candidate. Key swing states where the competition was intense in this election included Illinois, Indiana, and Pennsylvania.

The party's Northern supporters were led by Stephen A. Douglas. They backed giving regions the freedom to choose for themselves on the issue of slavery. The Southern Democrats were led by John C. Breckinridge. They demanded that slavery be protected by the federal government.

The Constitutional Union Party

In the mid-19th century, former Whigs and Know-Nothings formed the Constitutional Union Party. They aimed to prevent the country from splitting over slavery. The Know-Nothings were active in the 1840s and 1850s. They were anti-immigrant and secretive. When asked about their activities, they often claimed to "know nothing."

John Bell was the Constitutional Union Party's nominee for president, and he firmly backed the Union and the protection of the Constitution. This party had no interest in having any say over slavery. The party called out to moderate voters who were unhappy with the extreme positions of either major party. Bell's campaign emphasized national unity and the rule of law.

Bell won three states in the South, showing some support for a middle-ground approach. However, the party's success was short-lived. It quickly dissolved after the election as the nation moved toward war.

The Election of 1860 and Its Controversies

The presidential election of 1860 saw candidates focus on different issues, making their campaigns controversial. The intense interest and the high stakes involved created a much higher voter turnout.

Lincoln won 180 electoral votes, although he was just under 40 percent of the popular vote. Lincoln's victory on November 6th, 1860, was largely due to his success in the Northern states. Remember, they had more electoral votes. He became the country's 16th president. However, trouble was on the horizon.

A picture depicting Lincoln returning home after winning the 1860 presidential election.[81]

Do you think this election result caused the nation's war? It was certainly a trigger. However, there were many long-standing tensions. Many historians agree that the Civil War was inevitable. Overcoming the deep-rooted and *irreconcilable* (opposing) differences between the North and South seemed too hard to do peacefully.

At this stage, it's important to reinforce that Lincoln's election came with a high price. After he was elected, seven Southern states seceded from the Union. This happened before Lincoln's inauguration on March 4th, 1861. And secession was only the beginning of what was about to unfold.

We'll cover everything you need to know about secession in our next chapter. But before we get into all that, it's time to complete this chapter's activity!

Chapter 3 Activity

Complete the sentences below by inserting the correct words in the blank spaces provided.

1. In 1834, the _____ Party started in opposition to _____ bossy leadership style.

2. The Republican Party included former members of the _____ Party, the Free-Soilers, and Democrats who were _____.

3. The _____ movement aimed to reduce the sale and consumption of _____ beverages.

4. From _____ to _____, Lincoln served as a US congressman from Illinois.

5. During the Illinois _____ race in _____, Lincoln debated against Stephen A. Douglas.

6. _____ served as the vice president during Lincoln's first term from _____ to _____.

7. The Democratic Party split caused _____ to lead the Northern Democrats and _____ to lead the Southern Democrats in the 1860 presidential election.

8. Lincoln became the _____ US president after he won the election in 1860.

Chapter 3 Activity Answers

Complete the sentences below by inserting the correct words in the blank spaces provided:

1. In 1834, the **Whig** Party started in opposition to **President Andrew Jackson's** bossy leadership style.

2. The Republican Party included former members of the **Whig** Party, the Free-Soilers, and Democrats who were **anti-slavery**.

3. The **temperance** movement aimed to reduce the sale and consumption of **alcoholic** beverages.

4. From **1847** to **1849**, Lincoln served as a US congressman from Illinois.

5. During the Illinois **Senate** race in the year **1858**, Lincoln debated against Stephen A. Douglas.

6. Hannibal Hamlin served as the vice president during Lincoln's first term from **1861** to **1865**.

7. The Democratic Party split caused **Stephen A. Douglas** to lead the Northern Democrats and **John C. Breckinridge** to lead the Southern Democrats in the 1860 presidential election.

8. Lincoln became the **sixteenth** US president after he won the election in 1860.

Chapter 4: Secession Sparks the War

The election's result made secession a full-blown reality. Determined to keep their way of life intact and uphold their right to slavery, Southern states wasted no time in forming a new nation. Like dominoes, these states left the Union one after the other.

The factors affecting the timing of each state's decision played an important role. Let's look at this in more detail.

Secession of the Southern States in the Buildup to the Civil War

In December 1860, South Carolina held a state convention. Delegates had serious discussions over whether to go ahead and withdraw from the Union. On December 20th, 1860, the convention unanimously adopted the Ordinance of Secession, forming a short-term government shortly afterward.

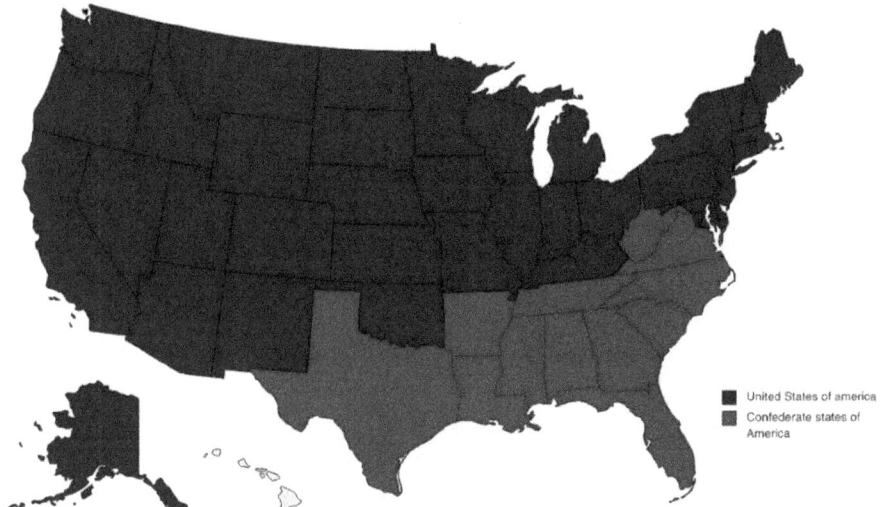

A map of the United States of America and the Confederate States of America in 1861. The two northernmost red states on the map are West Virginia and Virginia. In 1861, Virginia and West Virginia were one state. Virginia became part of the Confederacy in 1861. However, in 1863, part of the state split over the issue of slavery. It formed a separate state, West Virginia. West Virginia became a border state. It was not part of the Confederacy after its formation. [82]

This ordinance declared South Carolina an independent state. The federal government viewed this move as illegal and unconstitutional. The ordinance stated several reasons for secession. These included the violation of states' rights, the federal government's interference with the institution of slavery, and the election of Lincoln.

These reasons were used by all states that seceded. Here's the order in which the other states seceded:

1. Mississippi was quick on South Carolina's heels, voting to secede on January 9th, 1861.
2. Florida seceded on January 10th, 1861.
3. Alabama joined the secession movement on January 11th, 1861.
4. Georgia declared secession on January 19th, 1861.
5. Louisiana seceded on January 26th, 1861.
6. Texas voted to secede on February 1st, 1861.

Seven states had seceded by early February. On February 4th, 1861, several delegates from these states met in Montgomery, Alabama. They formed the Confederate States of America.

At this convention, Jefferson Davis, a former US senator from Mississippi, was elected as the Confederacy's provisional president. Lincoln refused to recognize the Confederacy and vowed to preserve the Union. You will learn more about Jefferson Davis in Chapter 9, so keep reading!

The flag of the Confederate States from 1861 to 1863.[83]

The Attack on Fort Sumter

Fort Sumter was located in Charleston, South Carolina. It was a federal garrison that had been blockaded by Confederate forces since the state seceded. In April 1861, Confederate General P. G. T. Beauregard demanded the surrender of Fort Sumter. Federal Major Robert Anderson, the fort's commander, refused.

On April 12th, 1861, Confederate artillery opened fire on the fort, starting a bombardment that lasted for thirty-four hours. Fort Sumter's federal leadership was outnumbered and outgunned. After major damage had been done, Major Anderson surrendered the fort on April 13th, 1861. No one died in the attack.

A painting depicting the attack on Fort Sumter.[84]

The attack forced Lincoln to take decisive action. He called for seventy-five thousand volunteers to join the cause and stop the rebellion. Many in the South saw this as an attack, and more states withdrew from the Union.

- **Virginia** left on April 17th, 1861.
- **North Carolina** seceded on May 20th.
- **Arkansas** voted to secede on May 6th.
- **Tennessee** left the Union on June 8th.

The Union vs. the Confederacy

The war pitting North and South against each other was underway. What were the strategies of each side?

- **The Union Strategy**

The Union's strategy was aggressive. The Union had a much larger and more powerful navy, so blockading Confederate ports would not be difficult to do. If the Union could do this, it would give it control of the seas. The Union's Anaconda Plan involved blocking Southern ports to cut off trade and stop the Confederates from exporting cotton and importing essential goods, crippling the South's economy.

Another part of the plan was getting control of the Mississippi River to divide the Confederacy. The plan was named after a snake that squeezes its prey to death, which is what the Union sought to do to the Confederates.

The Union had a much larger population, which made mobilizing a larger army possible. Because the Union controlled most of the nation's industries, it had an advantage over the South when it came to manufacturing weapons, ammunition, and supplies.

The broader plan included a total war approach. This involves putting the enemy out of action by targeting their armies and the infrastructure supporting their economy and civilians.

The rapid movement of troops and supplies was far easier for the North due to their more extensive railroad network.

- **The Confederate Strategy**

The Confederates planned to avoid large-scale battles that could lead to heavy losses. Instead, they wanted to focus on smaller engagements to gradually weaken the enemy. They hoped that by prolonging the war, they would wear the enemy down.

The Confederacy was fighting on its own territory. This was a major benefit, as it kept their supply lines intact. The Confederates also had a far better understanding of their territory than the Union did. Confederate soldiers were highly driven by the belief that they were fighting for their way of life and the defense of their homeland.

Skilled cavalry units were valued for raids and scouting. The Confederacy was well known for its ability to produce excellent units when needed. The South's defensive strategy relied on fortifications and natural barriers to slow the Union advance.

A picture of the Confederates' uniform.[85]

Something that perhaps made the Civil War trickier was that many of the Union and Confederate military leaders had fought alongside one another in the Mexican-American War. They formed solid relationships, but now, they were fighting against each other. This war also gave the Union and Confederate leaders a good knowledge of large-scale warfare tactics and operations.

The Border States

There was a group of states found on the border between the two warring regions. These were known as the border states. They included Delaware, Maryland, Kentucky, Missouri, and West Virginia. These states controlled key transportation routes and resources, such as coal and iron, which were essential for the war effort.

Internally, they were deeply divided over the issue of slavery. Some of the counties supported the North, while others supported the Confederacy. Although slavery was legal in these states, they did not join the Confederacy, mostly because the Union sought to keep them happy. The Union sent troops to protect key cities and infrastructure in border states and offered these states economic benefits to encourage their loyalty.

In the end, the pressures of war, including economic hardship, loss of life, and the destruction of property, made it difficult for the border states to stay neutral. Many chose to remain with the Union despite their internal divisions.

The Role of Foreign Powers

Even though both sides tried to gain aid from the international community, foreign help was limited.

Great Britain remained neutral throughout the war, even though many Brits sympathized with the Confederacy. This neutrality was influenced by Britain's economic interests and the potential risks of war.

France also remained neutral. However, it did form diplomatic relations with the Confederacy. It was driven by its economic interests in cotton and its desire to expand its territory in Mexico.

Russia provided diplomatic and material support to the Union, bolstering the US' standing on the international front. This support was motivated by Russia's competition with Great Britain.

The Confederacy and the Union employed blockade runners to sidestep naval blockades and supply their forces. The Confederate blockade runners are widely known for their role in smuggling goods through Union blockades. However, the Union had its own fleet of blockade runners that helped supply its troops. These vessels often sought refuge in foreign ports. They engaged in trade with foreign powers, highlighting the global reach of the Civil War.

The European powers were worried, perhaps even threatened, that a Union victory could strengthen the US as a global power. This concern was driven by a variety of factors, including the potential for increased economic competition, a more powerful military, and the spread of democratic ideals.

Our next chapter delves into the major battles and campaigns of the Civil War. So, it's time to test your knowledge as you complete this chapter's activity!

Chapter 4 Activity

Answer whether the statements listed below are true or false.

1. Alabama joined the secession movement on January 21st, 1861, making it the second state to secede.

2. South Carolina formed a provisional government after adopting the Ordinance of Secession.

3. The federal government viewed the Ordinance of Secession as unconstitutional and illegal.

4. Fort Sumter was a federal garrison that had been blockaded by Confederate forces since the state's secession.

5. The border states included Delaware, Maryland, Kentucky, Missouri, and West Virginia.

6. Great Britain provided military support to the Union during the Civil War.

7. Spain aided the Confederacy by providing soldiers and artillery.

8. Tennessee was a border state and did not join the Confederacy.

9. Jefferson Davis was chosen as the president of the Confederacy at the convention in Alabama.

10. Louisiana seceded on January 26th, 1861.

Chapter 4 Activity Answers

Answer whether the statements listed below are true or false.

1. Alabama joined the secession movement on January 21ˢᵗ, 1861, making it the second state to secede. **False.**

2. South Carolina formed a provisional government after adopting the Ordinance of Secession. **True.**

3. The federal government viewed the Ordinance of Secession as unconstitutional and illegal. **True.**

4. Fort Sumter was a federal garrison that had been blockaded by Confederate forces since the state's secession. **True.**

5. The border states included Delaware, Maryland, Kentucky, Missouri, and West Virginia. **True.**

6. Great Britain provided military support to the Union during the Civil War. **False.**

7. Spain aided the Confederacy by providing soldiers and artillery. **False.**

8. Tennessee was a border state and did not join the Confederacy. **False.**

9. Jefferson Davis was chosen as the president of the Confederacy at the convention in Alabama. **True.**

10. Louisiana seceded on January 26ᵗʰ, 1861. **True.**

Chapter 5: The Eastern Theater

The word "theater" in the phrase "Eastern theater" refers to a broad geographic area where military operations happened during the Civil War.

The Eastern theater stretched across Virginia, Maryland, Pennsylvania, and portions of North Carolina and Tennessee. What made this area so important? It was close to the nation's capital, Washington, DC, and its control of vital transportation channels.

The Army of the Potomac

The Army of the Potomac mostly consisted of troops from the northeastern states. It was formed in 1861. It was the Union's principal army. General Winfield Scott, a Mexican-American War veteran, was in command at first. However, it became necessary to replace him because of his older age. At seventy-five years old, he was still a brilliant leader, but he was physically unable to lead troops in combat.

A painting depicting the Army of the Potomac.[46]

The First Battle of Bull Run

General Irvin McDowell took the helm next, leading the Union forces in the First Battle of Bull Run. It's also referred to as the Battle of First Manassas since it took place just north of this town. It happened on July 21st, 1861, in hilly terrain in brush and open spaces. General Beauregard charged his Confederate forces against the Union in Prince William County, Virginia.

The railroad junction at Manassas was important because it allowed for the rapid movement of troops and supplies. This helped the Confederates, led by General Joseph E. Johnston, when supplies arrived by train. The Union Army advanced. However, with General Thomas "Stonewall" Jackson in charge, the Confederates counterattacked.

A picture depicting the brutal First Battle of Bull Run.[87]

Interestingly, it was during this battle that Jackson earned his nickname "Stonewall." Confederate General Barnard E. Bee Jr. noticed Jackson's brigade standing firm against a strong Union assault. Bee Jr. shouted, "There stands Jackson like a stone wall!" This sturdy defense stopped the Union forces in their tracks. They had to pull back and return to Washington, DC.

A portrait of Confederate General "Stonewall" Jackson.⁸⁸

Many civilians, including senators and congressmen, had accompanied the Union Army to witness the battle. It was almost like going to watch a show. They ended up fleeing in panic.

It was an embarrassing defeat for the Union. McDowell was dismissed soon after. Estimates suggest the Union *casualties* were around 2,800, while the Confederacy's were around 1,800. (Casualties refer to civilians or army members who are killed, wounded, or caught.)

Lincoln stepped into action, calling for fifty thousand extra volunteer soldiers. He appointed General George B. McClellan as the army's new leader. McClellan completely overhauled the army, making important reforms and reorganizations. Considerable time and energy were put into improving training, discipline, and confidence.

The Civil War's First Naval Clash

This war also included naval attacks. The Civil War was the first time ironclads were used. Unlike the warships in use up to that time, ironclad warships could block most enemy cannon fire due to their design, which featured heavy armored iron plating.

Ironclads were equipped with heavy cannons to fire on enemy ships, and their heavy construction made them stable in rough seas. However, they were slower than other types of warships. It was very expensive to construct them, and their great weight slowed them down.

The Battle of Hampton Roads started on March 8th, 1862. The first day involved the Confederate ironclad CSS *Virginia* sinking the Union's wooden vessel USS *Cumberland*. The USS *Congress* was also damaged and ran aground, ending up in flames. This was not a good result for the Union.

However, the Union forces stepped up to the plate, sending their revolutionary designed ironclad USS *Monitor* the next day on March 9th. Thankfully for them, they managed to stop further damage. The battle ended on the same day with no clear winner.

A picture depicting the raging Battle of Hampton Roads.[89]

The Peninsula Campaign

Back on land in March of 1862, McClellan launched the Peninsula Campaign by moving troops up the York River Peninsula. It was part of a daring plan to capture Richmond, the Confederate headquarters. The Union's powerful naval force controlled the waterways leading into the region.

Advancing toward Richmond was not easy. From June 25th to July 1st, 1862, fierce battles, known as the Seven Days' Battles, happened. These battles earned their name because they lasted for seven straight days. During this period, Confederate General Robert E. Lee, who commanded the Army of Northern Virginia, launched a series of aggressive attacks, starting with the Battle of Oak Grove and continuing with engagements at Beaver Dam Creek, Gaines' Mill, and Savage's Station. Each clash pushed the Union forces farther back. By the time they reached Malvern Hill, the Union troops were forced into a defensive position. They suffered heavy casualties.

Turning back was the only choice for McClellan's troops. Lee protected Richmond.

McClellan's leadership style was questioned for being cautious and indecisive during the Peninsula Campaign. His decisions left Lincoln and other Union officials frustrated. McClellan was temporarily removed from command and replaced by General John Pope.

The Second Battle of Bull Run

The next major battle took place at Manassas and lasted from August 28th to August 30th, 1862. It's known as the Second Battle of Bull Run. General Lee commanded the Confederate forces, and the Union troops were led by General Pope. A clash at Brawner's Farm on August 28th, 1862, set off this battle. The Union Army outnumbered the Confederate Army by an estimated ten thousand men.

Confederate General Stonewall Jackson positioned his troops in a defensive stance. On August 29th, Pope bombarded Jackson's position with several attacks. On August 30th, Confederate General James Longstreet and his men joined the battle. Homes and farms were damaged, leaving locals badly affected. Again, the Union Army had no choice but to turn around and go back to the nation's capital.

The Union suffered about fourteen thousand casualties, while the Confederates had around eight thousand. Pope's lack of success led Lincoln to put McClellan back in charge of the army. The Union regrouped and strengthened positions closer to Washington.

The Maryland Campaign

General Lee's reputation was greatly boosted by this latest victory, pushing him to go ahead with the Maryland Campaign. The aim was to invade the North to gain supplies and sway Northern public opinion.

Lee moved his army, crossing the Potomac River into Maryland on September 4th, 1862. Then, he divided his army into four parts to complete the mission.

A fascinating development happened when Union soldiers discovered Lee's Special Order 191. This revealed his battle plans to McClellan. This was a disaster for Lee. The discovery aided the Union in winning on September 14th when they attacked the Confederates at South Mountain. This area is part of the Blue Ridge Mountains, stretching across Maryland and Pennsylvania. This natural barrier separates the Hagerstown and Cumberland Valleys from the eastern part of Maryland.

On September 15th, 1862, Jackson's troops captured the Union garrison at Harpers Ferry near Sharpsburg. Harpers Ferry, a small town in West Virginia, sits where the Shenandoah and Potomac Rivers join together. Lee ordered General Jackson to rejoin the main army positioned near Antietam Creek. He did this in preparation for the next attack. The two combined their forces after Jackson arrived.

Union General George B. McClellan learned of Lee's plans through Special Order 191. He moved his units to cut the Confederates off. On September 16th, skirmishes began near Antietam Creek, just outside Sharpsburg.

The Battle of Antietam

The campaign culminated in the Battle of Antietam on September 17th, 1862. It's viewed by many historians as America's worst one-day battle. The estimates of casualties go as high as twenty-three thousand.

On that morning, the Union struck their rival's left flank, with major fighting even happening in the cornfields near Dunker Church. For nearly four hours, the two sides attacked each other on a heavily used, worn-out path that has since been referred to as "Bloody Lane."

The bridge over Antietam Creek was solidly guarded, making it difficult for Union General Ambrose Burnside's soldiers to cross. Confederate General A. P. Hill's division had traveled from Harpers Ferry and met the group that afternoon. The battle ended without a real winner, but it stopped Lee from breaking into Northern territory. He had no choice but to go back to Virginia. The Union felt they had won by forcing the Confederates to turn back.

A picture depicting the intense Battle of Antietam.⁹⁰

Off-the-Battlefield Consequences

1. **Emancipation Proclamation:** The Union's performance at Antietam was the good news Lincoln was waiting for, so he released the preliminary Emancipation Proclamation on September 22nd, 1862. This stated that all those enslaved in the Confederacy would be free as of January 1st, 1863. It shifted the war's focus to include banning slavery as a main goal for the Union.

2. **Diplomatic Impact:** The Union's strategic success at Antietam made European powers, particularly Britain and France, less willing to accept the Confederacy. The battle proved that the Union could stand against Confederate advances, reducing the likelihood of the South getting foreign aid.

3. **Political Developments:** The battle influenced the 1862 midterm elections in the North. It helped to lessen the growing weariness of the war and criticism of the Lincoln administration.

4. **Public Perception:** Photographs taken during this battle by Alexander Gardner and others were widely circulated. This visual evidence of the war's human cost influenced public opinion.

5. **Union Morale:** The Union's ability to drive back Lee's troops renewed the North's determination to continue with the war. It boosted the morale of those in the military and those who were not. People believed the Union could stand strong in the long run.

McClellan was dismissed in November 1862, mostly because he couldn't make up his mind and often avoided sending his troops into combat situations. General Ambrose Burnside became the new head of the Army of the Potomac.

The Battle of Fredericksburg

The Battle of Fredericksburg took place in Virginia. The Union Army was trying to use float bridges to move over the Rappahannock River in the eastern part of the state. The battle started on December 11th, 1862, and featured the first combat in a town's streets. Most of the battle involved repeated Union assaults on the heavily fortified Confederate position at Marye's Heights. This is a strategic ridge west of Fredericksburg.

Lee's forces, particularly those under General James Longstreet, effectively fought off Union attacks from strong defensive positions. The battle was fought under cold and harsh winter conditions, adding to the soldiers' hardships. The two sides were badly affected. They lost many men during this conflict.

After several days, Burnside ordered his men to withdraw by moving back over the Rappahannock River. The battle ended in a definite win for the Confederacy on December 15th. Burnside's leadership was criticized, and General Joseph Hooker replaced him.

The Chancellorsville Campaign

Hooker commanded the Chancellorsville Campaign. On April 30th, 1863, his soldiers made it over the Rappahannock River and attacked the Confederates from the west. In a bold move, Lee chose to divide his men and attack even though they were outnumbered.

On May 2nd, General Stonewall Jackson executed a surprise flank attack on the Union's right. On that same night, Jackson was accidentally shot by his own men. He later died from his wounds. Hooker was forced to retreat. The assault ended in a win for the Confederates on May 6th.

Hooker's failure was frowned upon by other leaders. Major General Meade replaced him. The Chancellorsville Campaign is viewed as Lee's greatest victory.

The Gettysburg Campaign

Lee's second attack on the North is known as the Gettysburg Campaign. Setting off on June 3rd, 1863, Lee's forces moved north out of Fredericksburg.

The campaign kicked off when the two sides came to blows at Brandy Station. On June 9th, 1863, the Union cavalry, led by General Alfred Pleasonton, unexpectedly struck the Confederate cavalry under General J. E. B. "Jeb" Stuart. The battle featured attacks at Fleetwood Hill and St. James Church. Even though the Union made some headway, the Confederate forces did not back down.

The Union had no choice but to pull out of the area. Lee's army moved over the Potomac River, arriving in Maryland in mid-June. At Winchester, Virginia, the Union garrison was attacked by the Confederates from June 13th to June 15th. The Confederates seized it. Lee's men made it to Pennsylvania. They moved to the Susquehanna River. The Confederates were determined to destroy Union supply chains and stock up on provisions from Northern farms and villages.

Three army corps were formed by Lee. The leaders chosen for each corps were Generals James Longstreet, Richard S. Ewell, and A. P. Hill. Harrisburg, Pennsylvania's state capital, was in danger.

Hooker was removed from leadership on June 28th, and General Meade took control of the Union troops again. They traveled up through Maryland, getting closer to Lee's troops. Lee's soldiers were scattered, and he commanded them to rally near Gettysburg, Pennsylvania. The Union cavalry under General John Buford arrived in Gettysburg on June 30th, 1863.

The Battle of Gettysburg

The battle started on the morning of July 1st when the Confederates collided with the Union's mounted soldiers west of the town. It was a chance encounter. The rival armies just happened to be there at the same time. Confederate divisions under Generals Henry Heth and Jubal Early stayed on course toward Gettysburg.

As the first clashes grew more intense, both armies sent reinforcements to the region. The Union formed a defensive line south of Gettysburg on the elevated terrain of Cemetery Hill.

The army's formation looked like a fishhook on Cemetery Hill, Cemetery Ridge (a long high hill), and Culp's Hill (a high hill to the east). This gave them a far better view of the battlefield. General John Buford managed to withstand the enemy's combat until the Union infantry arrived.

On July 2nd, Lee attacked the Union flanks, targeting Little Round Top, a small, rounded hill. There was also conflict at Devil's Den, a rocky, rugged area. Union soldiers in the Wheatfield and the Peach Orchard were also bombarded, including the 20th Maine under Colonel Joshua Chamberlain.

Chamberlain's troops successfully defended Little Round Top. Both armies lost several troops when they clashed at Devil's Den. The Union blocked the Confederate strikes on Culp's Hill.

A picture depicting the Battle of Gettysburg.[91]

On July 3rd, Lee ordered his soldiers to overrun the enemy on Cemetery Hill. This strike is known as Pickett's Charge. During this assault, approximately 12,500 Confederate soldiers made their way across grasslands through heavy shooting from enemy soldiers. However, the Union soldiers did not back down.

Entire regiments were wiped out during the fighting. Makeshift hospitals and surgeries were set up in the grasslands. It was another bloody battle, resulting in approximately 51,000 casualties.

A painting depicting Pickett's Charge.⁹²

On July 4th, 1863, Lee's men retreated to Virginia. Rain-swollen rivers and the Union cavalry's chase complicated the Confederate withdrawal on July 5th and 6th. Even though Meade's army was chasing them, there wasn't serious fighting during this stage.

Finally, the Union had gained the upper hand in the war. Lee's second Northern invasion ended in failure. Lee's army successfully made it back over the Potomac River on July 14th. Between July 13th and July 31st, the two armies maneuvered in Virginia. There were skirmishes but no major assaults.

During August, the Union Army began a series of operations in northern Virginia, including the Bristoe Campaign, to pressure Lee's forces. In September, Lee sent reinforcements to the Western theater, weakening his army in Virginia.

In October 1863, Meade and Lee had their troops take part in clever schemes and battles, including the Battle of Bristoe Station on October 14th. The Mine Run Campaign took place in November, with Union forces trying to strike Lee's army. The Union withdrew after undecisive clashes.

Lincoln delivered his famous yet remarkably short speech on November 19th, 1863. It's known as the Gettysburg Address and was given at the dedication of the Soldiers' National Cemetery. It only lasted about two minutes.

A poster displaying Lincoln's famous Gettysburg Address.[98]

Lincoln's Proclamation of Amnesty and Reconstruction

Lincoln unveiled his Reconstruction plan on December 8th, 1863. It was presented alongside his third annual message to Congress in the capital of Washington, DC.

Known as the Proclamation of Amnesty and Reconstruction, its goal was to make sure that the seceded states came back into the Union, making the US whole again. A full pardon and restoration of property, not including slaves, was available to all who had partaken in the rebellion. However, the highest Confederate officials and military leaders were excluded from this.

The terms included individuals taking an oath of loyalty to the US. Agreeing to abide by all federal laws and proclamations regarding slavery was needed for amnesty. The "10 Percent Plan" was also included. Under this plan, a new state government could be formed once 10 percent of a Southern state's voters took the oath.

The proclamation mentioned existing laws, such as the Confiscation Acts, which allowed for the seizure of property from rebels. The Confiscation Acts were laws passed by Congress during the Civil War. They were designed to weaken the Confederate war effort by freeing enslaved people and seizing property used to support the rebellion. Here is a breakdown of these acts:

- **The Confiscation Act of August 6th, 1861**: This act authorized the Union to confiscate property, including slaves. This early lawmaking step allowed for the freedom of slaves being used by the Confederacy.
- **The Confiscation Act of July 17th, 1862**: This more aggressive act, enforced only in Union-controlled territories, expanded the scope of confiscation to allow property to be seized from any Confederate supporter or official within sixty days.

In Congress, some Radical Republicans thought this went too easy on the Southern states. (Radical Republicans wanted Southern states to be harshly punished for their participation in the Civil War. They wanted slavery abolished instantly, and they wanted equal rights for African Americans.) However, others in Congress went along with this because they preferred President Johnson's less strict policies. Our next chapter covers this in detail, so don't go anywhere!

The War Rages On

In the winter from 1863 to 1864, both armies hunkered down in their winter quarters. A positive change for the Union Army happened in the spring of 1864. General Ulysses S. Grant became its commander.

The Overland Campaign was a series of battles by Grant's army against Lee's troops in Virginia. It began on May 4th, 1864. Its main goal was to capture the Confederate capital of Richmond. How did this play out? The Army of the Potomac crossed the Rapidan River in north-central Virginia, moving into the Wilderness of Spotsylvania, a densely forested region. From May 5th to May 7th, intense clashes took place in the thick forests.

From May 8th to May 21st, Grant's forces repeatedly attacked the Confederates. There were heavy losses on both sides. From May 23rd to May 26th, Lee's forces took strong defensive positions along the North Anna River. This prevented Grant from breaking through.

From May 31st to June 12th, Grant launched a massive assault on well-entrenched Confederate positions, which resulted in heavy Union casualties.

Grant carried out a strategic maneuver by crossing the James River. On June 15th, 1864, Grant's army attacked the Confederate earthworks east of Petersburg. At this stage, the campaign changed into the siege of Petersburg. The aim was to cut off Confederate supply lines to Richmond.

The siege had the two sides digging complex networks of trenches to be used for trench warfare. This type of warfare was a type of fighting where soldiers dug holes in the ground to hide from bullets and then attacked from these safe places.

On July 30th, 1864, Union forces blew up a mine beneath the Confederate lines, creating a massive crater. However, the Union's next assault failed. On August 21st, 1864, the important Confederate supply channel, Weldon Railroad, was captured by the Union.

The Valley Campaigns

Virginia's Shenandoah Valley was an important target for the Union to destroy. It was a major supply point for the Confederates. The Union kicked off the Valley campaigns in May 1864. They lasted until October 1864. Initially, the Union soldiers were led by Major General Franz Sigel. The Confederacy was under the leadership of Lieutenant General Jubal Early.

The Lynchburg Campaign was the first phase of the Valley campaigns. It started on May 15th with the Battle of New Market, where Sigel was wiped out by General Breckenridge's troops. Sigel was replaced by General David Hunter, who won the Battle of Piedmont, which lasted from June 5th to June 6th. His men captured Staunton, Virginia.

Hunter went on to raid Lexington and destroy the Virginia Military Institute. However, General Early managed to fend off Hunter's attack at the Battle of Lynchburg, which lasted from June 17th to June 18th. Hunter and his troops withdrew.

Lieutenant General Early's Valley Campaign

On June 19th, General Early steered his troops into the Shenandoah Valley toward Maryland. On July 9th, near Frederick, Maryland, Union General Lew Wallace's army was crushed in the Battle of Monocacy. However, they managed to delay the Confederacy's advance toward Washington, DC.

On the outskirts of the capital, Early's forces fought the Battle of Fort Stevens. However, they were repelled by Union reinforcements. Interestingly, this battle was the only one fought within the boundaries of Washington, DC. Lincoln's presence on the battlefield makes this battle stand out. He even came under fire from Confederate sharpshooters.

The Second Battle of Kernstown took place on July 24th. Early secured the Shenandoah Valley after winning against Union General George Crook's soldiers.

On August 7th, General Philip Sheridan was appointed the Union leader in the Shenandoah Valley.

Sheridan's Valley Campaign

Sheridan's tactics included destroying resources to prevent their use by Confederates. This is known as *scorched earth tactics*. Sheridan started with an undecided battle at Summit Point on August 21st, 1864. However, the Union's luck changed with a win on September 19th at the Third Battle of Winchester. This successfully drove the Confederates out of the lower Shenandoah Valley.

Fueled by this success, the Union won again on September 22nd at Fisher's Hill. On October 9th, at the Battle of Tom's Brook, the Union gained more control of the valley. On October 19th, Early attacked the Union without warning at Cedar Creek, but Sheridan's counterattack was too strong.

From December 1864 to February 1865, the armies suffered a harsh winter in their trenches. The Union continued to receive reinforcements and supplies.

Looming Doom for the South

Lee's army was undergoing serious shortages of men and supplies by March 1865. Something needed to be done. Fort Stedman was lightly guarded by the Union and close to Confederate lines. Capturing this stronghold could help the Confederates resupply. Major General John B. Gordon led the pre-dawn Confederate assault on March 25th.

The Confederates overpowered the Union at Fort Stedman. They also captured Batteries 10, 11, and 12. The Union forces quickly responded. Major General John G. Parke commanded the Union IX Corps in successful counterattacks. Over 1,900 Confederate soldiers were captured during the battle. It was another blow to the South.

Five Forks was a crossroads south of Petersburg. Five key roads and supply lines met at this point, and it was vital for the Confederacy's operations. The Union wanted to capture it to cut off Lee's supplies and force him to retreat.

On April 1st, the Confederate right flank collapsed during the Battle of Five Forks, and the Union captured the area. After this, Sheridan cut off Lee's army's primary supply line from the city. Lee and his men left the defensive lines, leaving them vulnerable to attack.

On April 2nd, 1865, the Union forces broke through the Confederate lines, causing the collapse of Petersburg. The siege of Petersburg was officially over after 292 days of combat. Richmond had also fallen.

A picture depicting the dramatic fall of Petersburg.[94]

The following day, the Confederates left the city willingly after dark on April 2nd, and the Union troops took over. Lee's army began retreating westward. They wanted to regroup and resupply at Amelia Court House. However, there were delays and supply shortages.

Meanwhile, Grant's forces were in hot pursuit of Lee's army. They wanted to prevent him from joining forces with General Johnston in North Carolina. At Sailor's Creek, many Confederate soldiers were captured or killed on April 6th, 1865.

Hoping to reach Lynchburg for desperately needed supplies, Lee continued to move west. Grant sent Lee a letter on April 7th, urging him to avoid more bloodshed and surrender.

Lee's forces were tired and hungry. Sheridan's Union cavalry continuously harassed them. On April 8th, Union forces captured Confederate supply trains at Appomattox Station. At this point, there was very little hope for Lee's army to resupply.

On the morning of April 9th, Lee tried a final breakout at Appomattox Court House. Strong infantry reinforced the Union cavalry. They surrounded Lee and his troops. Lee met with his generals and assessed their position. They ultimately decided to give up. Lee sent a message to Grant requesting a meeting to talk about the conditions of surrender. That afternoon, Lee and Grant met in Wilmer McLean's home in Appomattox Court House.

There's a remarkable coincidence here! Let's rewind to the First Battle of Bull Run. A Union artillery shell landed in McLean's kitchen, disrupting a family meal. Seeking to escape the war, McLean moved his family in 1863. In a twist of fate, the war found McLean again. McLean is often quoted as saying, "The war began in my front yard and ended in my front parlor." Legend has it that Union soldiers took many of McLean's household items as souvenirs, leaving him with little more than the house itself.

Grant offered the Confederates generous terms. Their soldiers could return home with their personal possessions, sidearms, and horses. Lee agreed. The Confederate soldiers were paroled and given rations by Union forces. The official ceremony took place on April 12th, 1865. Even after this surrender, the war continued for several months.

A sketch depicting General Lee's surrender.[95]

You will read a whole lot more about the war's eventual end in Chapter 7. Right now, though, it's time for this chapter's activity!

Chapter 5 Activity

In the table below, a date is listed in the left column. Your task is to fill in the corresponding historical battle that occurred on each date in the blank column on the right.

July 21, 1861	
March 8, 1862	
August 28 to August 30, 1862	
September 17, 1862	
December 11, 1862	
April 30 to May 6, 1863	
July 1, 1863	
June 5 to 6, 1864	
June 17 to 18, 1864	
September 19, 1864	

Chapter 5 Activity Answers

July 21, 1861	The First Battle of Bull Run
March 8, 1862	The Battle of Hampton Roads
August 28 to August 30, 1862	The Second Battle of Bull Run
September 17, 1862	The Battle of Antietam
December 11, 1862	The Battle of Fredericksburg
April 30 to May 6, 1863	The Battle of Chancellorsville.
July 1, 1863	The Battle of Gettysburg
June 5 to 6, 1864	The Battle of Piedmont
June 17 to 18, 1864	The Battle of Lynchburg
September 19, 1864	The Third Battle of Winchester

Chapter 6: The Western Theater

During the Civil War, the Western theater was mostly dominated by the Union. Vital rivers, including the Mississippi, the Tennessee, and the Cumberland, were in this region. This sector included border and Confederate-loyal states.

Various railroads connected key cities and military installations, and it was an agricultural hub. Naturally, the North and South fought hard for control of this territory.

Early Western Theater Campaigns and Battles

In November 1861, Union operations kicked off in the Western theater with their victory at the Battle of Belmont. In February 1862, the Union won the Battle of Fort Henry, which gave the North control of the Tennessee River. They took control of the Cumberland River after defeating the Confederates at Fort Donelson on February 16th. These wins meant the Union could move troops and supplies deep into Confederate territory, disrupt the Confederacy's supply lines, and isolate the South.

A painting depicting the Battle of Fort Donelson.[96]

These battles involved naval and land forces. The Union was far better equipped in these naval battles. They mostly used *gunboats* (small, shallow-draft vessels armed with heavy cannons and rifled guns). Confederate forces used civilian vessels that had been adapted for military use. These were known as river steamers. They had a limited number of lower-powered cannons and no extra firepower. They were larger and slower than Union gunboats. However, they could still transport supplies and provide support to forces on land.

The Union's Mississippi Valley Campaign

The Battle of Shiloh took place near Shiloh Church in Tennessee along the Tennessee River. Here's what happened during the two-day battle. On April 6th, Confederate forces, commanded by General Albert Sidney Johnston, launched a surprise attack on the Union encampment under Grant's command. General Johnston was mortally wounded during the battle. Union reinforcements arrived later that afternoon.

On April 7th, the Union forces took back the lost ground. The Confederates retreated southward, abandoning their plans to invade Kentucky. This turned out to be a brutal conflict. There were over twenty-three thousand casualties in total.

The campaign forged ahead, moving on to Corinth, Mississippi, which was firmly under Confederate control. This area's railroad junction connected the Mobile and Ohio Railroad with the Memphis and Charleston Railroad. The Union needed to besiege it in order to take it over. This battle took place from April 29th to May 30th, 1862.

Major General Henry Halleck commanded around 120,000 Union troops. Beauregard's army had only around half that number. The Union forces slowly gained ground in the city over the next month.

Throughout this siege, there were continuous exchanges of fire. The Union's approach worked for them. By May 29th, the Confederates had withdrawn. On May 30th, the Union took over the city with little resistance.

An Important Naval Battle in the Western Theater

The Battle of Memphis took place on June 6th, 1862, on the Mississippi River just north of Tennessee. Many of the city's residents witnessed the battle. The Union forces, consisting of the Western Gunboat Flotilla and the United States Ram Fleet, clashed with the Confederate River Defense Fleet. The Union fleet included four rams and five ironclads. The Confederate fleet was made up of eight vessels.

A painting depicting the Battle of Memphis.[97]

The battle, which lasted less than two hours, resulted in a decisive Union victory. All but one of the Confederate vessels were either sunk or captured. Approximately a hundred Confederate soldiers were killed or wounded. Another 150 were taken prisoner.

The capture of Memphis, a key Confederate city on the Mississippi River, significantly affected the Confederacy's ability to defend its territory.

Leading the Union forces were Flag Officer Charles H. Davis and Colonel Charles Ellet. The Confederate forces were commanded by James E. Montgomery and M. Jeff Thompson. The Union fleet included ironclads such as the USS *Louisville, Carondelet, St. Louis*, and *Cairo*. On the opposite side, the Confederate fleet included vessels like the CSS *General Beauregard*, CSS *General Bragg*, and CSS *General Sterling Price*.

By noon of the same day, the city of Memphis surrendered to federal authority after this purely naval battle that did not involve land forces. The engagement featured a stark contrast between the Union ironclads, which were equipped with the most modern technology of the time, and the Confederate vessels, which relied on older weaponry.

On August 30th, 1862, Union forces under Brigadier General William H. Lytle advanced south into Kentucky. Confederate forces led by Major General Kirby Smith counterattacked, driving the Union forces back across the Kentucky River. This happened in the Battle of Richmond.

On October 8th, 1862, another bloody but indecisive conflict occurred when Confederate forces, under the leadership of General Braxton Bragg, advanced toward Louisville, Kentucky. At the Battle of Perryville, Union General Don Carlos Buell managed to hold off the invasion but not without paying a high price. He suffered around four thousand casualties. Bragg left Kentucky due to logistical issues and the possibility that reinforcements might arrive to aid the Union.

The year rounded off with a Union defensive battle in central Tennessee. Bragg made a sneak attack on Union General William S. Rosecrans's army on December 31st in the Battle of Stones River. On January 1st, 1863, the Union forces recovered enough to push the Confederates out. There were many casualties on both sides. The battle was over on January 2nd. The Confederates did not take control of the area.

The Vicksburg Campaign

General Grant was tasked with capturing Vicksburg, a Confederate stronghold in Mississippi. General John C. Pemberton led the Confederate garrison at Vicksburg. On May 18th, 1863, the campaign reached its peak when Grant and his men encircled the city. The Union

Navy set up a blockade of the Mississippi River, preventing supplies and reinforcements from reaching the Confederate garrison. Continuous Union heavy artillery strikes damaged the Confederate defenses.

On July 2nd, 1863, the Union forces launched a final assault on Vicksburg, but they were pushed back by the Confederate defenders. By this stage, the siege had caused severe hardship and damage to the morale of the city's civilians. They had experienced ongoing food and supply shortages. With all this in mind and facing the inevitability of defeat, the Confederates surrendered on July 4th, 1863.

This win gave the Union complete control of the Mississippi River. It was a crushing blow to the Confederacy. Its western part had been cut off from its eastern part.

The Battle of Chickamauga

From September 18th to September 20th, 1863, another important battle took place near Chickamauga (*chi-kuh-maw-guh*) Creek in southeastern Tennessee and northwestern Georgia. The Confederates, led by Bragg, wanted to capture a key Union stronghold in Tennessee called Chattanooga (*cha-tuh-noo-guh*). They successfully attacked the Union soldiers in fields and forests. After this defeat, Rosecrans's troops retreated to Chattanooga.

A painting depicting the fierce Battle of Chickamauga.[96]

The Confederates followed close behind them, but they did not keep up the same pace due to exhaustion and the lack of supplies. They decided to camp on the city's outskirts and began laying siege shortly afterward.

Chattanooga Campaign

The Chattanooga Campaign aimed to break the Confederate siege of the city, which lasted from September to November 1863. Things happened quickly during this campaign because time was of the essence. Let's run through the key events as they unfolded.

Grant was ordered to leave Vicksburg on September 29th. He was to take twenty thousand soldiers with him and head to Chattanooga to lift the siege. On October 16th, the War Department issued General Order No. 337, creating the Military Division of the Mississippi and placing Grant in charge of all Union forces in the Western theater.

On October 18th, Rosecrans was replaced by Major General George Henry Thomas. Grant arrived in Chattanooga on October 23rd and took command of operations. Then, from October 28th to 29th, Union forces, under Major General Joseph Hooker, fought off a Confederate counterattack at the Battle of Wauhatchie (*waw-hat-chee*). This secured the "Cracker Line," which enabled supplies to reach the besieged Union troops.

On November 23rd, near Chattanooga, the Union Army of the Cumberland advanced from Chattanooga's fortifications, seizing the strategic high ground at Orchard Knob. On the following day, Union Major General Sherman's army crossed the Tennessee River and occupied the northern end of Missionary Ridge. Sherman's troops did not confront the Confederates on this day. That same day, November 24th, Hooker's men drove the enemy away at the Battle of Lookout Mountain.

Missionary Ridge offered a bird's eye view and unbeatable defense. Bragg led his troops there to scout for the oncoming enemy. The Union only held part of the ridge.

A well-planned Union attack took place on November 25th at Missionary Ridge. Sherman attacked the right Confederate flank but made little progress. However, Major General George Henry Thomas's forces surged to the top of Missionary Ridge, routing the Confederate Army.

The Confederates were left with no choice but to back away and leave, with the Union soldiers hot on their heels. On November 27th, it all came to a head in the Battle of Ringgold Gap. The Confederates escaped, but the siege of Chattanooga was officially over. Chattanooga became a vital supply and logistics base for the Union.

This Union victory also opened the Deep South to a Union invasion.

The Atlanta Campaign

Capturing Atlanta, Georgia, was always a primary mission for the Union. Atlanta was a major transportation and industrial center for the Confederacy. To that end, General Sherman commanded three armies: the Army of the Tennessee, the Army of the Cumberland, and the Army of the Ohio.

Confederate General Joseph E. Johnston used a defensive strategy to slow the enemy's advance. On June 27th, 1864, the Union started a full-frontal bombardment on the Confederate strongholds on and around Kennesaw Mountain in Cobb County, northwest of Atlanta. The Union was almost crushed.

After this defeat, Sherman realized that a direct assault was simply not going to do the trick. He moved more cautiously, employing flanking maneuvers to outflank the Confederate defenses at Kennesaw Mountain. This worked! As Sherman's forces threatened to cut off their supply lines, the Confederate forces were forced to retreat from Kennesaw Mountain. This allowed the Union Army to continue advancing toward Atlanta.

The Battle of Atlanta

The Confederates set up several defense blockades around the city. Johnston commanded his troops and resisted repeated attacks by the Union, which started on July 22nd.

Nevertheless, on September 1st, Union forces managed to break through and enter Atlanta. It did not take long at all. On September 2nd, Confederate forces were forced to retreat from the city, leaving it in the Union's hands. There were around 1,500 Union casualties, while the Confederacy had around 1,200.

A painting depicting the Battle of Atlanta.[99]

Sherman's March to the Sea

Sherman's March to the Sea was a military campaign conducted by the Union. The fall of Atlanta was enough of a boost for Sherman to start his preparations, dividing his army into two columns, the Right Wing and the Left Wing. The troops' orders were crystal clear: destroy everything in their path.

On November 15th, 1864, Sherman's army of approximately sixty thousand troops left Atlanta, heading southeast toward the coast. Sherman's army carried its own supplies, including food, ammunition, and medical supplies.

As they went along, soldiers destroyed railroads, bridges, factories, and plantations. They also burned towns and cities, leaving a trail of devastation in their wake. The Confederate soldiers were simply not in a position to fight back. Many people lost their jobs and homes. On December 10th, Sherman's army laid siege to Savannah, a main Confederate port city. By December 21st, the Confederates had given up.

A cover of sheet music for "Sherman's March to the Sea."[100]

The Carolinas Campaign

In early 1865, Charleston, South Carolina, was operated by the Confederates. The Union wanted to defeat the remaining Confederate forces in the Carolinas, destroy Confederate infrastructure, and link up with their own forces in Virginia. The plan to achieve this was known as the Carolinas Campaign. Sherman was to head the Northern soldiers in this quest since they had already taken over Savannah. The army was split into two sections to cover more ground and apply pressure on multiple fronts.

Union Major General Henry W. Slocum commanded the left wing, which consisted mostly of the XIV and XX Corps. Its goal was to advance toward Raleigh, North Carolina. Major General Oliver O. Howard led the right division, which included the XV and XVII Corps. Its goal was to move toward Goldsboro, North Carolina, where railroads connected to the coast.

Howard's army approached South Carolina's capital of Columbia in February. Confederate General Wade Hampton III tried to avoid confrontation and evacuated the city on the 16th. Confederate forces tried to burn cotton supplies to stop the Union from getting hold of them.

The evacuation and later occupation led to panic and disorder among the city's residents. Martial law was declared in Columbia on February 16th to keep order. On the morning of the 17th, Union forces occupied the city without a struggle.

Much of Columbia was burned, although it's still unclear whether the fires were started by the retreating Confederates, Union forces, or both. Union forces set up a *provost guard* to garrison the city and control the fires. (A provost guard is a detachment of soldiers under the authority of a provost marshal. Provost guards had to ensure that soldiers followed military regulations and that order was kept in the army and occupied territories.)

Another valuable supply point was Cheraw, South Carolina, because it was on the Pee Dee River. On March 1st, Howard's army battled with Lieutenant General William J. Hardee's ten thousand-man-strong army. The Confederates were defeated in the Battle of Cheraw.

On March 16th, Hardee's army fought again in the Battle of Averasborough (*aver-az-bur-uh*), this time with Slocum's army. This was one battle that took place in two counties that are right next to each other, Harnett and Cumberland counties, North Carolina. It ended without a clear winner.

The Battle of Bentonville

On March 19th, Johnston's army surprised Slocum's army with an attack in Johnston County near the village of Bentonville. The Battle of Bentonville lasted three days. The Union Army had around sixty thousand soldiers, and the Confederates numbered around twenty-two thousand men.

On the first day, the Confederates attacked the XIV Corps and routed two divisions. The next day, Howard's army joined Slocum's men in the battle. There were only minor skirmishes on this day. However, Sherman sent reinforcements because the Confederate attack had routed two divisions.

On the third day, Major General Joseph A. Mower's division attacked the Confederate rear. The Confederates managed to repulse Mower's attack. However, casualties were high, reaching around 2,600 for the Confederates and the Union with around 1,500. Johnston decided to withdraw from the battlefield on the night of March 21st.

Johnston's army moved toward Smithfield, North Carolina, to regroup. The Union continued its advance, making it to Goldsboro on March 25th and linking up with Northern soldiers under Major Generals John M. Schofield and Alfred H. Terry.

On April 10th, Johnston's forces were still retreating westward when news of Lee's surrender reached the Confederates and the Union armies. The collapse of the main Confederate force was devastating news for Johnston. On April 12th, Sherman received official confirmation of Lee's surrender, and the following day, the Union took charge of Raleigh. Meanwhile, Johnston's soldiers continued moving toward Greensboro.

By this stage, Johnston's hope had diminished. He estimated that his soldiers were outnumbered by around eighteen to one. His army was running low on supplies, and his troops were hungry, with many soldiers abandoning the cause and returning home. On April 14th, under a flag of truce, he sent a letter to Sherman, who halted the fighting and agreed to meet and negotiate a surrender on April 17th at the Bennett Farmhouse in North Carolina.

The Mobile Campaign

Mobile, Alabama, was a key Confederate port and a hub for the cotton trade. It was also the Confederacy's fourth-largest city. On March 26th, 1865, Union Major General Edward Canby led a campaign to capture the city. General Dabney H. Maury led the Confederates in this area.

The Battle of Spanish Fort took place in Baldwin County, Alabama. Canby's troops, which numbered around 30,000 soldiers, crossed the Fish River at Marlow Ferry. They moved along the eastern shore of Mobile Bay.

On March 27th, they began the siege of Spanish Fort. Confederate Brigadier General Randall L. Gibson was in charge of the Southern troops, which numbered only around two thousand. By April 1st, the Union had enveloped the garrison and began a massive bombardment. Outnumbered, the Confederates returned fire.

On April 8th, the 8th Iowa Infantry crushed the defensive barriers of the Confederates. Most of the Confederate forces managed to escape and flee to Mobile, leaving the Union to capture the fort the same day.

The Battle of Fort Blakely

On April 2nd, the siege of Fort Blakeley began. It was located around six miles north of Spanish Fort. Liddell's Confederates were outnumbered. They had around 3,500 soldiers, while the Union had 16,000. Union forces built three rings of earthworks and began a massive bombardment. The Confederates held out until they heard that Spanish Fort had fallen.

An illustration depicting the storming of Fort Blakely.[101]

On April 9th, Brigadier General John P. Hawkins led the Union troops in a final assault. Liddell and his soldiers surrendered within half an hour. Many Confederates were captured.

The End of the Mobile Campaign

From April 2nd to April 9th, around forty-five thousand Union soldiers fought around six thousand Confederate soldiers. The Union Navy blockaded Mobile Bay successfully in the Battle of Fort Blakeley. It concluded with Confederate forces evacuating Mobile and the Union occupying the fort without resistance.

And on that note, it's time for the next brain-boosting chapter activity!

Chapter 6 Activity

Find the following words in the word search below:
- Cumberland
- Railroads
- Rivers
- Shiloh
- Beauregard
- Vicksburg
- Rosecrans
- Sherman
- Bentonville
- Mobile

A	M	S	D	A	W	E	N	M	H	G	F	D	V	B
Y	O	D	X	S	H	I	L	O	H	F	D	S	X	E
A	B	O	O	P	L	M	N	D	V	C	H	G	H	N
S	I	F	C	U	M	B	E	R	L	A	N	D	E	T
G	L	S	X	C	A	H	N	G	C	V	F	T	N	O
O	E	F	R	A	I	L	R	O	A	D	S	R	T	N
G	S	M	L	P	W	S	Q	Q	S	X	C	G	R	V
V	P	J	G	F	T	Y	B	V	Q	W	Q	S	D	I
O	U	Y	N	B	V	G	F	V	C	H	R	N	B	L
M	S	Z	X	C	V	B	N	M	R	E	I	F	S	L
X	J	W	S	A	X	Z	Z	S	E	R	V	F	C	E
E	H	J	H	J	N	G	B	M	T	Y	E	E	W	Q
O	I	U	Y	H	B	F	D	G	B	N	R	C	X	D
M	X	D	R	O	S	E	C	R	A	N	S	P	L	M
H	F	G	H	J	K	V	B	N	E	W	Q	R	T	D
B	E	A	U	R	E	G	A	R	D	T	Y	H	G	B
V	A	S	D	F	G	H	J	U	Y	T	V	C	X	Z
E	W	V	I	C	K	S	B	U	R	G	L	N	M	V
A	T	U	I	E	R	F	V	D	Y	Z	N	D	S	O
M	Z	C	Z	B	I	M	F	S	H	E	R	M	A	N

Chapter 6 Activity Answers

Find the following words in the puzzle of scrambled letters below:

	M										B
	O		S	H	I	L	O				E
	B										N
	I		C	U	M	B	E	R	L	A	N	D	T
	L										O
	E		R	A	I	L	R	O	A	D	S		N
											V
											I
									R		L
									I		L
									V		E
									E		
									R		
			R	O	S	E	C	R	A	N	S	
B	E	A	U	R	E	G	A	R	D		
		V	I	C	K	S	B	U	R	G		
							S	H	E	R	M	A	N

209

Chapter 7: The War's Last Gasp

With the Eastern theater in the Union's hands and the Western theater on the verge of following suit, the war's end was on the horizon. However, another tragedy was about to occur before this would happen.

The Death of a Legend

Lincoln was at Ford's Theatre in Washington, DC, watching a presentation of the play *Our American Cousin*. It's a comedic play written by Tom Taylor in 1858. The story revolves around a somewhat *uncouth* (ill-mannered) American who travels to England to claim an inheritance.

On April 14th, 1865, at around 10:15 p.m., Lincoln was shot in the back of the head. The shooter was John Wilkes Booth. He was a staunch supporter of the Confederacy's policies and a well-known actor. After shooting the president, Booth wasted no time escaping. He leaped onto the stage, breaking his leg in the process. He still managed to get away successfully.

The president was carried across the street after the incident to Petersen House. After receiving medical attention, he died the following morning at 7:22 a.m.

A slide depicting John Wilkes Booth taking aim to shoot President Lincoln.[109]

It was discovered later that Booth was angered after hearing Lincoln's speech backing voting rights for African Americans on April 11th, 1865. He was part of a larger conspiracy involving several others, including Lewis Powell, David Herold, and George Atzerodt. They were all loyal to the Confederacy. Lewis Powell attacked Secretary of State William H. Seward at his home. He severely injured Seward and several others. George Atzerodt was supposed to kill Vice President Andrew Johnson, but he lost his nerve and did not follow through.

A massive manhunt ensued for Booth and his accomplices. Booth fled to Virginia, where he was found hiding in a barn on April 26th, 1865. During his capture, he was shot and killed by Union soldiers. Following this, eight conspirators were tried by a military commission. Four of them, including a woman named Mary Surratt, were executed by hanging on July 7th, 1865.

The Country's New President

Andrew Johnson was born in 1808. His childhood was filled with trials. He lost his father at the tender age of three, and his life was filled with financial hardship. Johnson was raised in Raleigh, North Carolina. He became a tailor's apprentice at the age of fourteen, but he ran away a couple of years later.

At nineteen, Johnson started his own shop, producing tailored items in Greenville, Tennessee. He made a good name for himself. He was elected as the town's mayor and served in the Tennessee House of Representatives from 1843 to 1853. In 1853, he became Tennessee's governor, a position he held until he became a US senator in 1857.

Johnson was a Southern senator who stayed loyal to the Union during the nation's war. This did not go unnoticed and led to his appointment as the military governor of Tennessee from 1862 to 1865.

Andrew Johnson was chosen to run with Lincoln in the 1864 election because he was a Southern Democrat who was loyal to the Union. It was believed this would help Lincoln by appealing to Democrats. Being from Tennessee, Johnson helped Lincoln appeal to voters in border states and the South. Johnson's support for the working class broadened the appeal of Lincoln's campaign as well. Johnson became the vice president on March 4th, 1865.

Johnson was sworn in as the seventeenth president just hours after Lincoln's death. He hit the ground running with efforts to manage the war's end.

A portrait of President Andrew Johnson.[108]

The Reconstruction Plan

Johnson's plan for the *post-war* (after the war) efforts is known as "Presidential Reconstruction." Johnson wanted to quickly reintegrate the Southern states into the Union. He wanted to make minimal changes to how they existed before the war. High-ranking Confederates and wealthy Confederate landowners had to apply individually for a pardon. Most who applied were successful.

Some of the key issues addressed in the plan included the following:

- Southern states had to hold conventions to rewrite their constitutions, abolish slavery, and reject secession. These conventions began in the summer of 1865.
- Provisional governors in Southern states were appointed by the president. They had to oversee the transition and ensure that loyal Unionists were elected to office. This process started in May 1865.

Johnson had an extremely tolerant approach. His policies allowed many former Confederate leaders to regain power. In late 1865 and early 1866, many Southern states were even allowed to enact Black Codes, restricting the rights of newly freed African Americans.

Johnson's policies faced strong opposition from Radical Republicans. They wanted stricter measures against the South to protect the rights of freedmen. Ensuring a more thorough transformation of Southern society was at the top of their priority list.

If you're curious to know more about the Reconstruction process, our next chapter covers it in far more detail. So, keep reading!

Johnston's Surrender in the Western Theater

Let's step back to the Western theater to see what was happening after Lincoln's assassination. Remember, Sherman had planned a meeting with Johnston?

On April 17th, 1865, Sherman rode out to meet Johnston and his generals at the Bennett Farmhouse near Durham Station. Sherman had received news of the president's assassination. However, he chose to keep it a secret to avoid affecting the morale of his men.

This was the first time Sherman and Johnston had met in person. Their discussion happened inside the farmhouse, although there were no witnesses. Sherman handed Johnston the telegraph announcing Lincoln's assassination. They began negotiating the terms of surrender, focusing on ending hostilities and dismissing the Confederate soldiers. No final agreement was reached on April 17th. They planned to get together the next day.

On April 18th, the men had another face-to-face at the Bennett Farmhouse. Sherman was told by Johnston that it was within his power to surrender all the Confederate soldiers still on the ground. They drafted and signed an agreement that included political terms that were more generous than those given to Lee. The two men planned to meet again to revise the terms so they were in line with the Union government's guidelines.

A picture depicting General Johnston's surrender.[104]

Sherman sent the draft agreement to Washington, DC, for approval. However, on April 24th, the terms were rejected by the Union government because they included political conditions beyond military surrender. Sherman was instructed to offer terms like those given to Lee.

On April 26th, Sherman and Johnston met again at the Bennett Farmhouse. They agreed solely on terms of a military surrender. Johnston formally surrendered his army, which included about ninety thousand troops. In essence, the war was over in the Carolinas, Georgia, and Florida. However, there was still more to do.

The Surrender in Alabama

Confederate General Richard Taylor commanded forces in the Trans-Mississippi Theater. General Taylor reached out to Canby to discuss surrender terms. On May 4th, they met at Citronelle and agreed on terms like those given to Lee. The surrender of naval forces under Commodore Ebenezer Farrand was included in the agreement. Operations east of the Mississippi River were over at this point. During a formal surrender ceremony, Confederate soldiers laid down their arms.

The Capture of Jefferson Davis

Jefferson Davis, his wife Varina, and a small group of Confederate officials and soldiers had been fleeing from Union troops since they evacuated Richmond. Union General James H. Wilson was tasked with raiding Alabama and Georgia. They wanted to disrupt Confederate infrastructure and capture key figures.

On the night of May 9th, Davis's group camped near Irwinville, Georgia. Two of Wilson's cavalry groups, the 4th Michigan and 1st Wisconsin, converged on Davis's camp. There was a brief clash, and two Union soldiers died. At dawn on May 10th, Davis was captured. Davis was reportedly wearing his wife's black shawl, leading to rumors he was disguised as a woman. The Northern press ridiculed Davis as a coward trying to escape in disguise.

Davis was taken to Savannah before being transported to Fort Monroe, Virginia. Once there, he was imprisoned in a damp holding cell and put in leg irons. After a few months, Davis was moved to better quarters.

Texas during the Final Stage of the War

Most Union troops had been taken out of the Rio Grande Valley after July 27th, 1864. By early 1865, an informal ceasefire had been called between the Union and Confederacy in southern Texas. The Mexicans across the border tended to side with the Confederates because of the lucrative cotton export trade.

In the spring of 1865, the war was drawing to a close. Union forces, led by Colonel Theodore Barrett, had recently been assigned command of a unit composed entirely of African American soldiers. On May 11th, 1865, Barrett took charge of these troops at Brazos Santiago, Texas.

That evening, Barrett decided to strike Confederate camps located near Brownsville. By doing this, he went against the unofficial ceasefire. He dispatched three hundred men, including African American infantry and white cavalry, under the leadership of Lieutenant Colonel David Branson.

The Union troops marched through the night, hoping to surprise the Confederates at their camps. However, they were spotted by Confederate soldiers stationed on the Mexican side of the Rio Grande. They reached the outskirts of White Ranch on May 12th, where a brief skirmish took place.

The Union cavalry, led by Captain W. N. Robinson, retreated toward the ranch, and Branson's men withdrew to a nearby hill. As the day wore on, Branson requested reinforcements. Colonel Barrett arrived with additional troops, bringing the total number of Union soldiers to five hundred. The Confederates also received more soldiers.

The War's Final Conflict

On May 13th, 1865, Colonel Theodore Barrett's Union forces launched an attack on the Confederate camp at Palmito Ranch. The Confederates, led by Colonel John Salmon Ford, also known as "Rip" Ford, counterattacked with artillery support.

The Confederate forces received artillery support from French troops stationed across the Rio Grande in Matamoros, Mexico. The Union troops were outgunned and outmaneuvered. They were forced to retreat back to Brazos Santiago. The battle was a decisive victory for the Confederates, who inflicted heavy casualties on the Union forces.

While the war had officially ended weeks earlier, the Battle of Palmito Ranch is considered to be the final battle of the Civil War. Union Private John J. Williams was killed during this battle. He is believed to be the last soldier to die in the war.

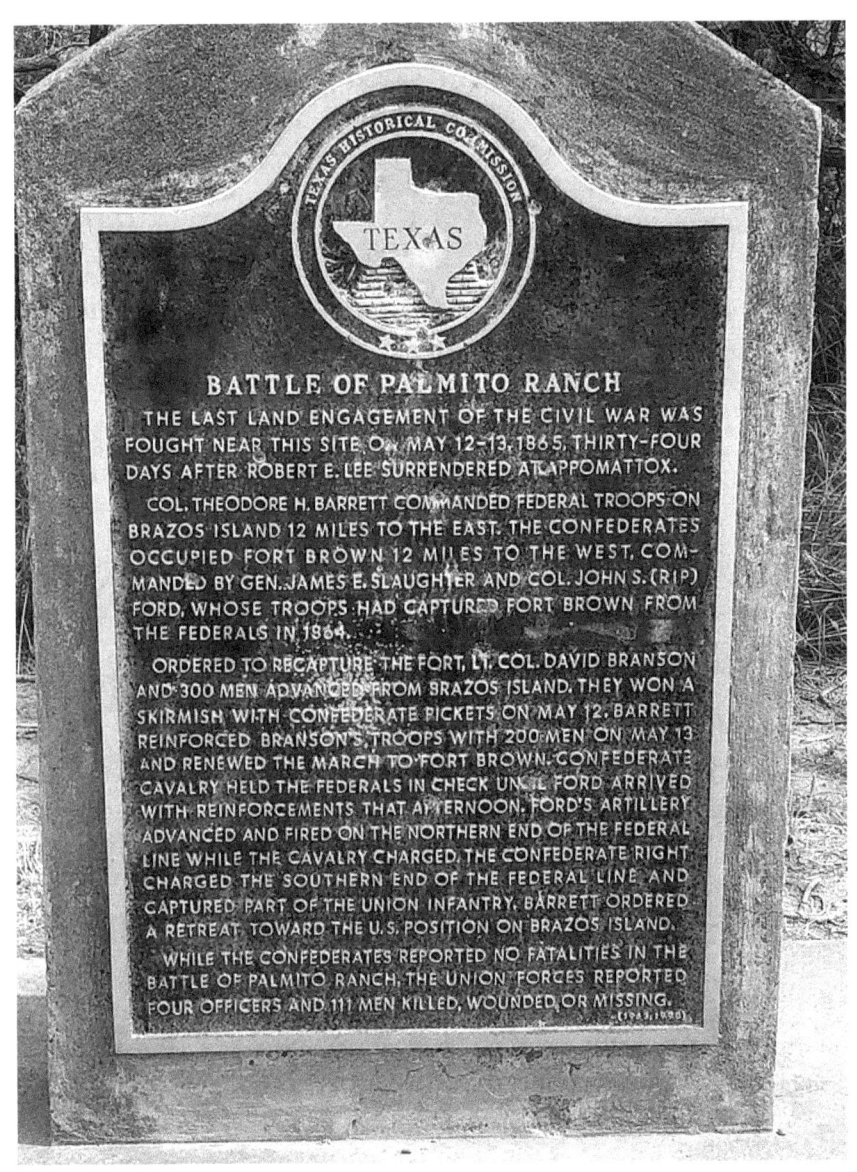

A photograph of a Battle of Palmito Ranch marker in Texas.[105]

Interestingly, Colonel Ford had served as a Texas Ranger, a Confederate officer, a doctor, a lawyer, and a journalist. The nickname "Rip" originated from his time as an *adjutant* (administrative staff officer) during the Mexican-American War. His duties included writing death notices. Ford frequently used the phrase "Rest in Peace" on these notices, which was shortened to "Rip" by his fellow soldiers. This nickname stuck with him for the rest of his life.

The Trans-Mississippi Department Surrender

On May 26th, 1862, the Trans-Mississippi Department was formed to oversee Confederate military operations west of the Mississippi River. It had several commanders, including Major Generals Thomas C. Hindman and Theophilus H. Holmes, as well as Lieutenant General Edmund Kirby Smith.

This department was vital for protecting the border with Mexico and ensuring a steady cotton supply for the Confederacy. In 1865, the department's forces were greatly reduced due to heavy casualties and desertions. By that stage, the Union had also made significant gains in the region.

On May 25th, Confederate leaders Buckner and Price met with Union General Canby in New Orleans to discuss terms of surrender. General Smith, who had the power to decide on this surrender, was not present at the meeting; he was in Galveston, Texas. After he received word of the meeting, Smith officially surrendered the Trans-Mississippi Department on May 26th under similar terms as Lee. This was the true end of the Confederacy's military.

The Proclamation of Amnesty and Reconstruction

On May 29th, 1865, President Johnson issued a proclamation offering forgiveness and a pardon to most people who had fought for or supported the Confederacy during the war. However, it was conditional. To receive it, these individuals had to take an oath of loyalty to the US, promising to support and defend the Constitution and the Union. Certain individuals still had to apply for special pardons.

The Last Confederate Soldier's Surrender

Stand Watie was born in 1806. He was one of the few Native American generals in the Confederate Army. He led the 1st Cherokee Mounted Rifles and later the Indian Brigade, which included soldiers from various Native American tribes, such as the Cherokee, Creek, Seminole, and Osage.

Throughout the war, he fought in several important battles and was promoted to brigadier general in May 1864. By February 1865, Watie oversaw the Indian Division in Indian Territory (now Oklahoma). Despite the Confederacy's weakening position, Watie continued targeting Union supply lines and communications.

On June 23rd, he surrendered his command at Doaksville near Fort Towson in Indian Territory. After the war, Watie returned to his home in Indian Territory and focused on rebuilding his plantation and community. In 1871, he died of natural causes at his home.

The Last Shot Fired

In October 1864, the Confederacy bought a British merchant ship named *Sea King* and converted it into a warship called the *Shenandoah*. It was under the command of Captain James Waddell, and it was to be used to capture and destroy Union merchant vessels. The Confederates particularly wanted to target the whaling fleet in the Bering Sea between Russia and Alaska.

On June 22nd, 1865, the *Shenandoah* fired what would be the last shot of the war. However, the crew was unaware that the war had already ended. It wasn't until August 2nd that year, when they encountered the British ship *Barracouta* (*bar-uh-koo-tuh*), that they learned of the Confederacy's defeat.

Waddell decided to sail to Liverpool, England, where he hoped to surrender the ship to the British authorities. To avoid detection, Waddell ordered the ship's weapons to be dismantled and stowed below deck during the journey. The hull was painted to resemble a merchant vessel.

On November 6th, the ship reached Liverpool and anchored next to the British warship HMS *Donegal*. Waddell then lowered the Confederate flag for the last time and surrendered the ship to the British Marines. The British Admiralty Court investigated whether the ship's actions during the war were legal. Eventually, the crew was released.

And with that, we've reached the end of another chapter. It's time to boost those brain cells with the next chapter activity!

Chapter 7 Activity

For each topic below, list five important facts. Try remembering as many facts as you can. Refer back to the content of Chapter 7 to refresh your memory. When you are done, verify that the information you have provided is accurate.

1. President Lincoln's assassination

_____
_____
_____
_____
_____

2. Andrew Johnson

_____
_____
_____
_____
_____

3. The Capture of Jefferson Davis

_____
_____
_____
_____
_____

Chapter 8: Beyond the Battlefield

Off the battlefield, the Union was making important changes to the Constitution. Congress was hard at work, approving several new laws.

The Reconstruction era aimed to reunite the nation after the Civil War. It focused on bringing the Southern states back under federal control, ensuring their loyalty to the Union government. The government also had to figure out how to rebuild the war-torn South. Another major goal was abolishing slavery and protecting the legal and civil rights of African Americans.

Three key amendments were passed during this time. They are known as the Reconstruction Amendments. Let's take a closer look at them.

The Thirteenth Amendment's Approval

The Thirteenth Amendment made slavery illegal in all US territories. Do you remember that the Emancipation Proclamation aimed to abolish slavery? The Thirteenth Amendment set that in stone.

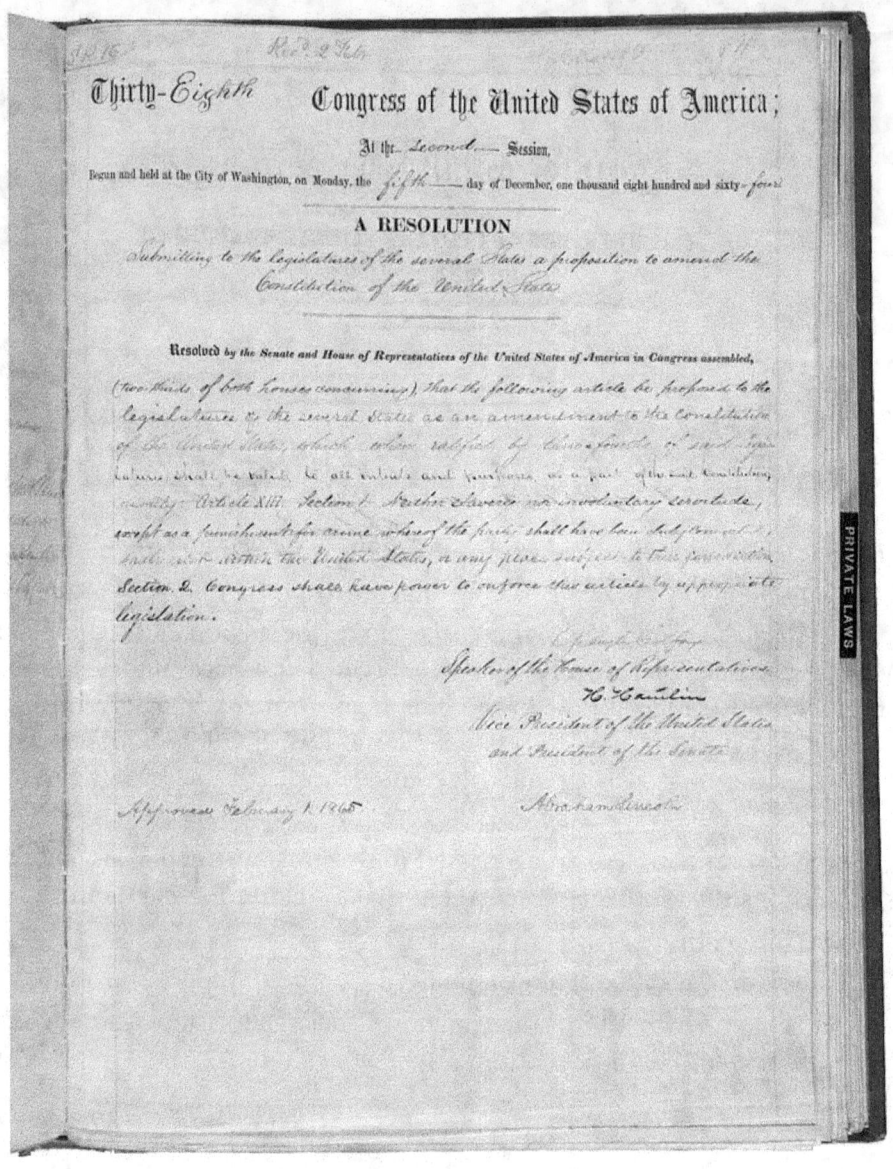

A photograph of the Thirteenth Amendment.[106]

Senator John B. Henderson from Missouri introduced this bill. The bill declares, "Neither slavery nor involuntary servitude, except as a punishment for crime whereof the party shall have been duly convicted, shall exist within the United States, or any place subject to their jurisdiction." This means that slavery is illegal in the US, and no one can be forced to work without pay, except as a punishment for a crime they have been found guilty of.

The Senate passed the amendment on April 8, 1864. The House of Representatives approved the amendment on January 31, 1865, and Lincoln signed the joint resolution to send the amendment to the states for ratification on February 1, 1865. The amendment was ratified with the necessary number of states on December 6, 1865. It was officially proclaimed on December 18, 1865.

The Black Codes

After the Thirteenth Amendment abolished slavery, the Black Codes (a set of several laws) were proposed and enacted by the former Confederate states in 1865 and 1866. The laws aimed to control and exploit newly freed African Americans. In practice, they trapped African Americans in low-paying positions on plantations, which kept them in poverty. The working conditions were poor.

In late 1865, Mississippi and South Carolina became the first states to set the Black Codes in motion. By June 1866, Louisiana, Alabama, Georgia, Tennessee, Florida, and North Carolina had also adopted these laws. Local and state governments enforced the Black Codes. They were assisted by white supremacist groups.

Some Northern states had Black Codes. However, the enforcement of these codes in the North was mostly prevented by the Freedmen's Bureau. Radical Republican state governments canceled these laws during the Reconstruction era.

What did the Black Codes mean for African Americans who had to navigate these laws daily? These laws ensured that African Americans had to provide cheap labor. Vagrancy laws meant they had to find and keep jobs to avoid arrest. They had to agree to yearly work contracts, with penalties if they left early. They had to adhere to strict *curfews* (time limits), limiting their movement at night. Moving around freely was difficult because travel required special permits.

African Americans grappled with strict limitations on owning property, especially in certain areas. African Americans couldn't testify against white people in court, and interracial marriages were banned. For large gatherings, a white person had to be present, and owning firearms was forbidden. African American children could be forced into apprenticeships; in many cases, this happened with their former enslavers.

Breaking these laws could result in fines, jail time, or forced labor.

Let's look at the measures Congress took to protect the rights of African Americans in early 1866, and then we'll return to the Black Codes.

The Civil Rights Act

On January 5th, 1866, Illinois Senator Lyman Trumbull introduced the Civil Rights Act. The act proposed to declare all US-born persons to be citizens, excluding untaxed Native Americans. This granted all citizens the same rights to make and enforce contracts, sue, give evidence, and inherit, purchase, lease, sell, hold, and convey real and personal property.

The act faced significant opposition. The Senate passed the bill on February 2nd, 1866, with a vote of thirty-three to twelve. On March 13th, 1866, the House ratified the bill with a vote of 111 to 38.

However, on March 27th, President Johnson vetoed the bill, arguing that it infringed on states' rights and exceeded federal authority. On April 6th, the Senate overrode Johnson's veto. The House did the same on April 9th.

The Fourteenth Amendment

Drafted in April 1866, the Fourteenth Amendment was inspired by Senator Jacob Howard and House member Thaddeus Stevens. This aimed to guarantee all citizens "equal protection of the laws." This means that everyone in the US has the same rights under the law, and no one can be treated differently because of their race, religion, or other reasons.

Representatives had to be divided up among the states according to their populations, excluding untaxed Native Americans. Federal and state governments were released from paying Confederate-incurred debts. Confederates who held a government office before the war were barred from holding a federal or state office unless they secured a two-thirds vote in Congress.

On June 8th, 1866, the amendment was passed by the Senate. The House followed suit on June 13th. President Johnson vetoed this bill. He was against constitutional changes being made without adequate Southern state representation in Congress. However, the amendment came into full force on July 9th, 1868.

The Formal End of the War

On August 20th, 1866, the president issued a proclamation saying that peace and order had been restored throughout the US. He officially declared the war's end. It was the official end of the state of *insurrection* (rebellion). However, some Southern states stayed under military occupation to enforce Reconstruction policies. Southern states continued to hold conventions. They rewrote their constitutions so they'd be allowed to rejoin the Union.

Radical Republicans and Their Proposed Act

The Radical Republicans demanded protection for freedmen and a guarantee of emancipation. Led by figures like Thaddeus Stevens and Charles Sumner, they played a significant role in shaping the Reconstruction era and the rights of African Americans. Their policies aimed to ensure that the South was punished for its role in the war and its support for slavery. They firmly backed protecting newly freed African Americans' rights.

In early 1867, Radical Republicans drafted their proposed way forward for Reconstruction. The act divided the former Confederate states (except Tennessee) into five military districts, which would be overseen by Union generals.

Johnson vetoed the bill. On March 2nd, 1867, Congress overrode the veto. The Southern states had to ratify the Fourteenth Amendment and meet the conditions set by the act to be readmitted to the Union.

President Johnson's Impeachment and the Tenure of Office Act

As you now know, President Andrew Johnson clashed with the Republican-controlled Congress over Reconstruction policies. But what led to his impeachment? (Impeachment is the process by which a legislative body charges a public official with misconduct.)

Johnson was accused by the House of disobeying the Tenure of Office Act. This law had been passed to prevent the president from being able to dismiss people in certain posts without the Senate's approval. The president vetoed the bill, but Congress overrode his veto.

In 1868, Johnson ejected US Secretary of War Edwin M. Stanton without the Senate's permission, leading to him being put on trial. *High crimes* (major wrongdoings) and *misdemeanors* (minor rule-breaking) were used as reasons for his impeachment.

The resolution was passed on February 24th, 1868. On March 5th, the proceedings were underway in the Senate. At the time, Republicans held more seats than the two-thirds majority needed to relieve Johnson of his duties.

Johnson's defense team argued that the act was unlawful and that Johnson was not guilty of any impeachable offenses. The House managers, who acted as prosecutors, argued that Johnson's actions were a direct challenge to the authority of Congress and the Constitution.

A sketch depicting President Johnson's impeachment trial.[107]

On May 16th, 1868, the Senate voted on Article XI, with thirty-five senators voting "guilty" and nineteen voting "not guilty." The Senate was one vote of the two-thirds majority needed for conviction. Two more votes were held, but they all had the same results. Johnson was acquitted. He remained in office until the end of his term. He was politically weakened, though. Johnson did not seek reelection in 1868.

After leaving office, Johnson returned to Tennessee and remained politically active. Johnson was the only former president to serve in the Senate. He was elected to serve there in 1875, and he stayed until his death on July 31st of that year. He was vacationing when he suffered a stroke in Carter's Station, Tennessee.

Congress changed the Tenure of Office Act drastically on April 5th, 1869, under President Ulysses S. Grant. In 1887, the law was canceled. The Tenure of Office Act was later declared unconstitutional by the Supreme Court in 1926. This decision held that the president's powers were greatly diminished by the act.

The Fifteenth Amendment

On February 26th, 1869, the Fifteenth Amendment was introduced by Congress. The amendment declares, "The right of citizens of the United

States to vote shall not be denied or abridged by the United States or by any State on account of race, color, or previous condition of servitude." This means that African American men could not be denied the right to vote based on their race, color, or past enslavement.

This amendment officially became part of the Constitution on February 3rd, 1870. Nevada was the first state to ratify it.

To understand the context of voting rights before the Civil War and the ratification of the Fifteenth Amendment, it's important to note that some African American men already had voting rights. However, they had to meet certain conditions, making it difficult, if not impossible, for them to actually exercise these rights. For example, most states required African American men to own property to be eligible to vote, a condition that most did not meet.

Some Southern states granted African American men the right to vote before the Fifteenth Amendment was ratified. Some African American men could vote in certain Louisiana parishes, especially where there were many African Americans. After the Civil War, South Carolina's new constitution allowed all male citizens to vote, regardless of race. However, this right was later limited by discriminatory practices like poll taxes and literacy tests. In some areas of Florida, African Americans could vote, mostly in places with large African American populations. These were exceptions rather than the norm, though.

There was an increase in African American voters after the Fifteenth Amendment was ratified. Some progress had certainly been made. However, the Southern states had a few tricks up their sleeves to prevent this ratification from fully taking effect.

African Americans were required to overcome several obstacles before they could vote. They had to pay a fee, pass a reading and writing exam, and prove that their ancestors had the right to vote before a specific date.

On March 31st, 1870, Thomas Mundy Peterson of New Jersey broke this barrier by becoming the first African American to vote under this amendment.

African American Politicians

Before the ratification of the Fifteenth Amendment, some African Americans were appointed to government roles. These appointments came from sympathetic white politicians.

After the Fifteenth Amendment was ratified, African American men were elected to government positions all over the US, especially in the South. Several African American male politicians were elected during the Reconstruction era. However, these politicians faced racial discrimination, violence, and political opposition. The political power of African American politicians dwindled when Reconstruction came to an end and white supremacist forces took back control.

Women's Right to Vote

Before and after the Fifteenth Amendment's ratification, women of all races were still denied the right to vote. Groups like the National Women's Suffrage Association fought for women's right to vote, using various means such as lobbying, protests, and civil disobedience.

In 1920, the Nineteenth Amendment finally granted women the right to vote. However, women, especially women of color, still faced obstacles to voting, including literacy tests, poll taxes, and intimidation.

The Amnesty Act

The Amnesty Act removed penalties imposed on former Confederates by the Fourteenth Amendment. The act was introduced by Benjamin Butler. It was passed by the House and the Senate on May 22nd, 1872. President Grant signed the act into law. He directed district attorneys to dismiss prosecutions against Confederates who were disqualified from holding office according to the Fourteenth Amendment.

However, some people were excluded from this, including certain high-ranking officials, such as senators and representatives; officers in the judicial, military, and naval service; heads of departments; and foreign ministers.

Vital Institutions Formed during the Reconstruction Era

Many institutions were formed during the Reconstruction era to aid with the nation's rebuilding. Here's a breakdown of five important organizations.

- **Freedmen's Bureau**: Officially known as the Bureau of Refugees, Freedmen, and Abandoned Lands, this agency was created in 1865. It provided essential services, such as food, housing, medical care, education, and legal aid, to former slaves and impoverished whites in the South.

Office of the Freedmen's Bureau, Memphis, Tennessee. (1866) From Harper's Weekly: A Journal of Civilization.[108]

- **Fisk University**: Fisk University was set up in 1866 in Nashville, Tennessee. It was one of the first historically African American colleges and universities (HBCUs). It aimed to offer higher education opportunities to African Americans during and after Reconstruction.

- **Howard University**: Howard University was founded in 1867 in Washington, DC. It is another historically African American university. It was named after General Oliver Otis Howard, who led the Freedmen's Bureau.

- **Morehouse College**: Morehouse College was founded in 1867 in Atlanta, Georgia. It focused on educating African American men and played a crucial role in their academic and professional development during the Reconstruction era.

- **Hampton University**: Originally set up as Hampton Normal and Agricultural Institute in 1868 in Virginia, this institution focused on educating freedmen and preparing them for careers in teaching and other professions.

The End of the Black Codes

With that understanding of what happened after the Black Codes started being enforced, let's return to see what happened next.

With Reconstruction ending with the Compromise of 1877, Southern states asserted their control after the federal troops withdrew. The Jim Crow laws were a set of rules created to keep African American people separate and unequal in the Southern and Northern states. African Americans and white people had to use separate facilities. White people had access to far better services. The Jim Crow laws restored many Black Code provisions.

Southern states began passing the Jim Crow laws in 1877. In 1881, Tennessee enacted the first Jim Crow law requiring segregation on railroads. In 1887, Florida passed similar laws for public transportation. In 1890, Mississippi passed laws to segregate schools and public facilities. In the North, similar discriminatory practices were enforced through local laws and social customs.

In 1896, the Supreme Court's decision in *Plessy v. Ferguson* upheld the constitutionality of racial segregation under the "separate but equal" doctrine. There was more widespread implementation of Jim Crow laws in the Southern states after this ruling. In the early 1900s, other Southern states, including Alabama, Georgia, Louisiana, and South Carolina, passed extensive Jim Crow laws. In the North, segregation in schools and public places became more common in the late 1800s and early 1900s.

It was only in 1954 that the Jim Crow laws were challenged. The Supreme Court ruled separate schools for white and African American students were unconstitutional. This ruling came in *Brown v. Board of Education*. Eventually, the Jim Crow laws were dismantled. Discrimination based on race, color, religion, gender, or national origin was outlawed through the Civil Rights Act of 1964.

A year later, the Voting Rights Act removed legal barriers that stopped African Americans from casting their vote.

Other Opposition to the Reconstruction Process

Several groups wanted to undermine the Reconstruction efforts. The Ku Klux Klan, a white supremacist group, gained significant power during this period.

Former Confederate soldiers were angry and bitter after the war ended. In 1865, in Pulaski, Tennessee, some soldiers decided to act on their anger. They formed an organized group. It really began as a social club where Confederate veterans could share their concerns and frustration over the war's outcome.

However, the Klan soon became a terrorist organization. Its members used violent and intimidating methods to restore white supremacy. The Klan's main goals included preventing African Americans from taking part in politics. The Klan used lynchings, beatings, and arson to terrorize African Americans and their allies.

The Klan's first leader, a former Confederate general named Nathan Bedford Forrest, was appointed in 1867. The group held clandestine meetings to plan their activities. The men also used public displays of power, such as parades and rallies. Members took secret oaths and participated in rituals to show their loyalty.

By 1870, the Klan had spread to nearly every Southern state. Congress needed to act. It passed the Enforcement Acts in the early 1870s to protect African American voters and suppress the Klan. The Klan's influence declined in the late 1870s, but its presence was still a dark force that undermined Reconstruction efforts.

In the 20th century, the Ku Klux Klan began targeting immigrants, Catholics, Jews, and labor unions in addition to African Americans. In the 1910s, its members started to burn crosses. In the 1960s, bombings, murders, and other violent acts spiraled out of control.

Unfortunately, as chilling as it may seem, the Ku Klux Klan still exists today.

And on that serious note, it's time to move on to this chapter's activity.

Chapter 8 Activity

This activity requires you to imagine yourself as a teenager in the 1860s. Write a 350 to 400-word essay explaining how you feel the Thirteenth, Fourteenth, and Fifteenth Amendments would impact the community you live in and your own life.

Here are some questions for you to answer to guide you as you complete the activity:

1. What do you think each amendment means? Refer back to the chapter to understand what each amendment says.
2. Will these amendments make any changes to your life? Why or why not?
3. What do you hope will happen now that these amendments have been ratified?
4. Do you think these amendments will have any impact on your education or job opportunities?
5. How do you think future generations will view these amendments? Here, you should answer by looking at yourself in the present and writing about what you think of these amendments.

Here are some helpful pointers for you as you write your essay:

- Plan your essay by outlining your main points before you begin.
- Remember to check your spelling and grammar.
- Take the time to revise and edit your essay.
- Reread this book's content about the topic of your essay to make sure your facts are correct.
- Read and reread your essay to make sure everything flows.

And also remember, the more you practice writing, the better you'll get at it!

Chapter 9: The Faces of the War

Throughout this book, we've mentioned several key figures of the war. However, there are many more exciting stories about these heroes. Let's check out some short biographies of some of the most prominent figures of this period.

Clara Barton

On December 25th, 1821, Clara Barton came into the world. She was the youngest of five children. Raised in North Oxford, Massachusetts, she grew up in a family of abolitionists. Her first taste of life as a nurse happened when she was eleven. A tragic accident left her brother bedridden and in need of extensive care. Barton looked after him for the next two years.

Her schooling was done at home. She later attended the Liberal Institute in Clinton, New York. At seventeen, she became an educator and founded a free school in New Jersey.

At the start of the war, Barton was part of the US Patent Office team. However, she realized that her gift of caring for others could be better used in the war. She chose to quit her job and go to Washington, DC. Once there, she started collecting supplies for the frontline and hospitalized soldiers. Throughout the war, she raised funds and gathered supplies.

A photograph of Clara Barton.[109]

Barton was also approved to take provisions to troops on the battlefields where mobile hospitals were in place. Her first in-field journey was to the Battle of Cedar Mountain in 1862. Even as bullets flew around her, Barton continued her work. She aided doctors during operations in several battles, including the Second Battle of Bull Run, the Battle of Antietam, and the Battle of Fredericksburg.

Her exceptional work earned her the nickname "Angel of the Battlefield."[i] She wrote many details about the soldiers she came across. She also penned messages filled with news from the troops to their loved ones back home.

After the war, she named and marked the graves of dead soldiers. She notably did this work at Andersonville Prison. This prison, officially known as Camp Sumter, was a Confederate prisoner-of-war camp set up in February 1864. Found near Andersonville, Georgia, it was commanded by Captain Henry Wirz.

---

[i] Oates, S. B. (1995). *Woman of Valor: Clara Barton and the Civil War*. Free Press.

The facility was only designed to hold ten thousand prisoners. However, numbers reached over thirty thousand at its peak. Conditions were poor, with inadequate shelter, food, and water. Out of the roughly forty-five thousand prisoners held there, nearly thirteen thousand died due to the harsh conditions. Wirz was later tried and executed for war crimes because of the inhumane conditions at the prison.

Barton formed an office to contribute to finding and naming Union soldiers who were missing. Raising funds and awareness after the war was a priority for her. She traveled and gave lectures about her wartime experiences.

By 1869, she was exhausted. Barton set off for Europe to rest. In Switzerland, she discovered the International Red Cross, a humanitarian organization dedicated to helping all soldiers, regardless of which side they were fighting on. She also became aware of the work of the Geneva Convention, which was set up in 1864. The Geneva Convention is a series of international treaties that set rules for the protection of wounded soldiers, medical personnel, and civilians.

After returning to the US in 1873, she launched the American Red Cross on May 21st, 1881. As its first president, she led the Red Cross to provide disaster relief in areas affected by floods and hurricanes. She strongly pushed for the US to sign the Geneva Convention, which it did in 1882.

Barton's support for other causes like a woman's right to vote and other civil rights issues remained unwavering. Even after retiring from the Red Cross in 1904, she stayed active in humanitarian causes. *The Story of My Childhood*, her autobiography, was published in 1907. She died of pneumonia in 1912 in Glen Echo, Maryland.

Ulysses S. Grant

On April 27th, 1822, Hannah Simpson Grant gave birth to Hiram Ulysses. His father, Jesse Root Grant, was a tanner, and the family lived in Georgetown, Ohio. Ulysses developed a strong skill in handling horses. When he was seventeen, he went to West Point.

A photograph of Ulysses S. Grant.[110]

A simple clerical error at the academy changed his name to Ulysses S. Grant. While filling out the nomination for West Point, Congressman Thomas L. Hamer incorrectly listed Grant's name as "Ulysses S. Grant" on the papers. He was under the impression that Grant's middle name was his mother's maiden name, Simpson.

Grant tried to fix this, but he was told it would be too complicated to change the records. The "S" does not stand for anything, but he was often called "Sam" by his friends at West Point, a nod to his new initials, "U. S." Grant accepted this name and used it for the rest of his life.

He graduated in 1843 and went on to be a *quartermaster* (responsible for supplies and logistics). He earned promotions for bravery in the Mexican-American War. Grant met Julia Dent when he was stationed in Missouri, and the two married in 1848. After the Mexican-American War, he was stationed at various frontier posts, including Fort Vancouver in the Pacific Northwest.

Due to accusations of drunkenness, Grant resigned from the army in 1854. Civilian life was not what he was cut out for, leading him to hop from job to job. In 1857, the economic downturn placed more of a financial burden on him. In 1859, he took a job working at his father's leather goods store, moving back to Galena, Illinois. When the Civil War broke out, Grant rejoined the military.

Initially, he was appointed colonel of the 21st Illinois Volunteer Infantry. His talent and skill ensured he was quickly promoted to brigadier general of volunteers.

In 1862, he earned the nickname "Unconditional Surrender" at Fort Donelson. When the Confederate forces requested terms of surrender, Grant insisted on their unconditional and immediate surrender. This firm demand led to the surrender of about twelve thousand Confederate troops, solidifying his reputation as a determined and uncompromising leader. Despite his successes, Grant was criticized for the high casualties under his command.

Throughout the war, Grant kept strong ties with Lincoln. After the war, Grant was promoted to general of the US Army in 1866. In 1867, President Johnson appointed him as the secretary of war. In 1868, Grant became the country's eighteenth president. He focused on Reconstruction efforts and civil rights for freed slaves. Despite many scandals and corruption during his administration, Grant was reelected in 1872.

In 1877, after he finished his term, he embarked on a world tour, which boosted his image locally and abroad. He returned to the US in 1879 as a respected national hero. It's believed he even considered running for a third term in 1880, but he ultimately decided against it.

He invested in the brokerage firm of Grant & Ward. He did not own the firm, but he held a large stake in it. Unfortunately, fraudulent activities by his partner caused the firm to crumble in 1884. Grant faced financial difficulties, so he penned his memoirs. During this period, he struggled with health problems, including throat cancer. He died of this disease in 1885 in New York.

He is buried in Grant's Tomb in New York City. His wife, who died in 1902, is buried there beside him. It's the largest mausoleum in North America. His memoirs were printed after his death, and they achieved great success critically and financially.

A sketch depicting a bird's eye view of Grant's Tomb in New York City.[111]

Robert E. Lee

Ann Hill Carter gave birth to Robert E. Lee on January 19th, 1807. He grew up in Alexandria, Virginia. He was the proud son of Henry "Light Horse Harry" Lee, a respected and well-known fighter for American independence during the American Revolution. Lee went to West Point, where he finished second in 1829. He wed Mary Anna Randolph Custis in 1831. Interestingly, Mary was George Washington's step-granddaughter.

With his studies completed, Lee went on to be an engineer in the nation's army. During America's war with Mexico, he advanced through the ranks due to his bravery and exceptional

A photograph of Robert E. Lee.[112]

military skills. West Point Military Academy employed him as a superintendent from 1852 to 1855. Lee was in charge of the 2nd Cavalry in the frontiers of Texas from March 1856 to October 1857. He held this post again from February 1860 to February 1861. During this time, he dealt with conflicts involving Native American tribes.

By 1861, Lee was regarded as one of the most capable officers in the US Army. However, his strong attachment and bond to his family and Virginia sealed his decision to join the Confederacy. Virginia's secession caused Lee to resign from the army, even though he had been offered a senior command.

During the first year of the nation's war, Lee took part in minor operations. He was the senior military advisor to Jefferson Davis. He tackled engineering projects, including fortifying coastal defenses in the Carolinas and Georgia.

In June 1862, Lee took command of the Army of Northern Virginia. Under his guidance, this army became the most successful and renowned in the Confederacy. Later in the war, Lee was appointed general in chief of all Confederate forces. His ability to hold off larger Union armies for extended periods showcased his brilliant defensive strategies. Lee's leadership and personal conduct earned him the respect of his troops and his rivals.

After his final surrender and the war's conclusion, he went back to join his family in Richmond after his pardon. Washington College in Lexington offered him a post, and in 1865, he became the college's president. Today, the education center is named in his honor: Washington and Lee University. Lee worked hard to reform education standards by expanding the college's curriculum. His successful fundraising allowed the college to recover financially.

As a devoted educator, Lee took an interest in his students, which pushed them to excel. He was immensely dedicated to his students and work. His tendency to overwork was possibly the reason his health declined. He developed a heart condition, but he continued to work.

Lee was admired and respected for his post-war efforts. He promoted reconciliation. He had a stroke in September 1870, and he passed away on October 12th, 1870. He was laid to rest in the chapel at the same college where he had changed so many students' lives.

Controversy surrounds Lee's legacy. He played a very active role in the Civil War on the side of the Confederacy. His views on slavery are also questionable today. Nevertheless, throughout the South, many statues and memorials have been erected to honor him as a leader who made remarkable strides during the post-war era.

Jefferson Davis

Jefferson Davis was the youngest of ten children. He was born on June 3rd, 1808. He grew up in Christian County, Kentucky. He initially attended Kentucky's Transylvania University but later went to West Point. He graduated in 1828. His early military service included a period as a lieutenant in the Wisconsin Territory.

In 1835, Davis resigned from the army. He also took Sarah Knox Taylor to be his wife that same year. Only three months later, tragedy struck when she lost her life to malaria. Davis took on work as a planter in Mississippi at Brierfield Plantation.

A photograph of Jefferson Davis.[118]

In 1845, Varina Howell became his new wife. The couple had six children together. That same year, he was elected to office in the House of Representatives. During the Mexican-American War, he was a colonel in the 1st Mississippi Rifles. From 1847 to 1851, he served in the Senate.

Under President Franklin Pierce, Davis held the office of secretary of war from 1853 to 1857. After this term, he returned to the Senate, where he was a leading supporter of states' rights and slavery.

Davis was the chief commander of the Confederate Army. During the war, he was involved in the relocation of the Confederate capital from Montgomery, Alabama, to Richmond, Virginia. Davis focused on gaining support and recognition from European nations. He even ordered the creation of a Confederate currency.

After the war, Davis was put in jail. He was set free in 1867 after his bond was paid. He was never tried for treason. Davis traveled to many places, including Canada, Cuba, and Europe. In 1869, the federal charges against him were dropped. However, his citizenship was not restored until 1878. In 1869, he became the Carolina Life Insurance Company's president. Its headquarters were in Memphis, Tennessee.

He wrote his memoir, *The Rise and Fall of the Confederate Government*, which was published in 1881. Davis spent a lot of time traveling and speaking publicly to promote the book. It was a tragic time for him too, as he lost several of his children. His wife was a wonderful source of comfort for him during the post-war years.

Davis wrote and published several articles and letters defending the Southern cause throughout the rest of his life. He faced many legal battles over his property and finances. He lived in various places, including Tennessee, Mississippi, and Louisiana. Davis also struggled with his health in his later years.

He spent his final years at Beauvoir, a plantation in Biloxi, Mississippi. He eventually died from a severe bronchial infection. Davis took his last breath on December 6th, 1889, in New Orleans, Louisiana, and was buried in Hollywood Cemetery in Richmond, Virginia.

Despite initially being blamed for the Confederacy's defeat, Davis later became a hero to many Southerners.

William Tecumseh Sherman

On February 8th, 1820, Tecumseh Sherman was born. He was raised in Lancaster, Ohio. His father, Charles, made a good name for himself in the legal profession. Charles died when Sherman was only nine. A family friend named Thomas Ewing, who was very well connected politically, took Sherman in as a foster child.

A photograph of William Tecumseh Sherman.[114]

Sherman's name was originally Tecumseh (*teh-koom-seh*) after the famous Shawnee leader. His foster mother later added "William" to his name.

Ewing pulled some strings and got Sherman into West Point. He finished his schooling in 1840. He then served in Florida in the Second Seminole War. This conflict lasted from 1835 to 1842. It was between the US and the Native American Seminole tribe. During his time serving in the Mexican-American War, he worked in a clerical role in California. He did not see combat.

In 1850, Sherman wed Ewing's daughter, Ellen. He resigned from the military in 1853 to focus on a career in banking. However, the Panic of 1857 created economic difficulties. The Panic of 1857 was a financial crisis in America that caused widespread business failures, a decline in the railroad industry, and increased unemployment.

In 1858, Sherman moved to Kansas, where he worked for a short time as a lawyer. In 1859, he took a post as the superintendent of the Louisiana State Seminary of Learning & Military Academy, which is now Louisiana State University. When Louisiana left the Union, he resigned from this job.

After the war broke out, Sherman enlisted with the Union military in May 1861. He took the role of colonel and was promoted to brigadier general after the First Battle of Bull Run. In late 1861, he left his post due to mental health problems.

In early 1862, he was back reporting to Ulysses S. Grant. The men formed a close working relationship, which bolstered Sherman's career. He kept close communication with other Union leaders. He was viewed by some as *erratic (unreliable and unpredictable)* and brilliant by others. During the war, he lost two of his sons, which affected him deeply.

After the war, Sherman was elevated to commanding general of the US Army in 1869. He oversaw military operations during the American Indian Wars in the West. He stuck to his policy of total warfare. He also played a significant role in the military aspects of Reconstruction in the South.

In 1875, his memoirs were printed and released. They were highly praised. Sherman was a popular public speaker. He often told crowds stories of his war experiences. In 1884, after being urged to seek the presidency, Sherman rejected this idea, famously saying, "If nominated, I will not run; if elected, I will not serve."

Sherman spent his retirement with his wife and surviving children. He stayed busy by traveling extensively in the US and Europe. He was very interested in art and literature, which kept him in contact with notable writers and artists. He also kept himself busy by taking part in various veteran causes.

A photograph of the William Tecumseh Sherman Monument in New York.[116]

Sherman's health declined as he grew older. He developed asthma and *rheumatism (roo-muh-tiz-uhm)* (a joint and muscle inflammation disease). In 1888, his beloved wife died. He spent his final years in New York City. On February 14th, 1891, he took his last breath. His burial took place in St. Louis, Missouri, where he was laid to rest in Calvary Cemetery.

Controversy surrounds his legacy. Some consider him a hero, while others think he was cruel due to his harsh wartime tactics.

What do you think about these individuals? It's time to test your knowledge with this chapter's engaging activity!

Chapter 9 Activity

For each key figure mentioned below, list five important facts about that person's life. Refer to the content in Chapter 9 to verify the information you provide is accurate.

1. Clara Barton

---

2. Ulysses S. Grant

---

3. Robert E. Lee

Chapter 10: Honoring the Past

Remembering the Civil War is important in the modern era. This chapter highlights the memorials, museums, parks, and even the holiday dedicated to *commemorating* (remembering) this war.

The Lincoln Memorial

The statue of Lincoln at the memorial site in Washington, DC, is breathtaking. It measures nineteen feet tall from head to foot. It is about the height of a two-story building! It was crafted from Georgia white marble. Daniel Chester French gets the credit for designing the Piccirilli brothers' carved masterpiece.

A photograph of the imposing Lincoln statue at the Lincoln Memorial. [116]

The entire building's exterior was the careful work of Henry Bacon. He created it in the style of the Parthenon in Greece. It's made of Colorado Yule marble. There are thirty-six Doric columns for the thirty-six states in the Union when Lincoln was killed. Each was made up of multiple individual *drums* (the cylindrical sections that make up the columns). The memorial's *frieze* (border) lists the thirty-six states in the Union when Lincoln died.

The *cornice* (uppermost section of the building exterior) is decorated with *palmetto* (decorations that look like the fan-shaped leaves of a palmetto palm tree). It features lion's heads decorating a sculpted scroll. A reflecting pool is near the statue. Steps lead up from the pool to the memorial's plaza. The plaza is flanked by limestone buttresses topped with an eleven-foot-tall *tripod* (three-legged structure). These are carved from pink Tennessee marble.

A stunning aerial view of the Lincoln Memorial.[117]

The murals show themes of emancipation and unity. They were painted by Jules Guerin. There's a written engraving done by Royal Cortissoz. The interior space is divided into three distinct sections: north, south, and central. Each section boasts two rows of four fifty-foot columns.

The ceilings are adorned with bronze girders featuring decorative touches of laurel and oak leaf designs. The ceilings feature panels crafted from Alabama marble. These have been treated with paraffin to enhance their translucency. The south wall features the Second Inaugural Address, while the north wall showcases the Gettysburg Address.

The site is always open to the public, and it is incredibly well lit at night. This space is used as a gathering spot for visitors and is a popular venue for important occasions. It's where the well-known speech "I Have a Dream" was delivered by Martin Luther King Jr. This site attracts more than seven million people from around the globe.

Memorial Day

A national American public holiday began as a way to honor soldiers who died in the Civil War. It was initially called Decoration Day, and it commemorated Union soldiers who had fallen during the war. General John A. Logan, a Union general, issued an official statement leading to the first celebration of the event on May 30th, 1868.

In 1971, Congress passed the Uniform Monday Holiday Act. This officially made Memorial Day a federal holiday. Memorial Day is observed on the last Monday in May. The holiday also honors fallen soldiers from all wars.

On this day, people visit cemeteries and memorials to pay their respects to those who died while serving in the military. A moment of silence is observed at 3 p.m. local time. Many cities host parades featuring military personnel, veterans, and marching bands. Volunteers place American flags on the graves of military personnel in national cemeteries. Families also gather for barbecues and picnics. It is also seen as a celebration of the unofficial start of summer.

People attend national ceremonies, speeches, religious services, and community events. There's a wreath-laying ceremony at the Tomb of the Unknown Soldier at Arlington Cemetery. This tomb is a memorial dedicated to the unidentified soldiers who died in service.

The Gettysburg National Military Park

In Gettysburg, a park was created in 1895 to commemorate the important battle that took place there in July 1863. Lincoln's famous speech, which was given there after the battle, is also honored. Since 1933, the park has been under the management of the National Park Service. It was later added to the National Register of Historic Places on October 15th, 1966.

The park is extremely popular. Around 900,500 visitors from all over the world flock to this site each year.

A photograph of a Gettysburg battlefield cannon at the Gettysburg National Military Park. [118]

- The park houses the Gettysburg Museum and Visitor Center, which boasts forty-three thousand artifacts from the war. The grounds include 1,300 monuments, markers, and memorials, as well as Gettysburg National Cemetery. Many of the park's historic buildings have been restored to their 19th-century appearance. The buildings vary from modest farmhouses to larger, more detailed structures.

Here is a list of some of the park's buildings:

- **David Wills House**: This historic house is a museum in the park. It was where Lincoln stayed before delivering his famous speech.
- **Jennie Wade House**: This house is preserved as a museum in memory of Jennie Wade, the only civilian killed during the Battle of Gettysburg. She was visiting her sister's home, which is now known as the Jennie Wade House, when a stray bullet tragically ended her life.
- **Schmucker Hall**: This building is the Seminary Ridge Museum. A Lutheran seminary was transformed into a field hospital during the battle.
- **Dobbin House Tavern**: This house was built in 1776 and was used as a hospital during the battle. Today, it is used as a bed and breakfast in the park.

- **Lydia Leister House:** Restored to its 1863 appearance, this house was used as General Meade's headquarters during the battle.
- **Brian Farm:** This farm on Cemetery Ridge was heavily damaged during the battle. It has since been restored to its original state.
- **Bushman House:** This house was built in 1808 and used by the Confederates as a staging ground for attacks and a field hospital during the Battle of Gettysburg.

There are several ongoing projects to restore the battlefield to its 1863 appearance.

Activities at the Gettysburg National Military Park

The park is bursting with exciting and educational activities for visitors to take part in. Think of these as ways to experience history in the modern world! Reenactments of significant battles are presented at the park. Visitors are free to explore reconstructed encampments that show the conditions the soldiers lived through.

Demonstrations of musket-firing, artillery drills, and medical practices bring the war to life for visitors and scholars. There are also many interactive exhibits that provide visitors with hands-on learning experiences.

There are also actors dressed in period clothing. They interact with park visitors and answer questions about life during the war. Visitors can enjoy workshops on topics like war photography and battlefield archaeology and talks given by park rangers and historians.

Anniversary commemorations, themed weekends, and different seasonal programs are offered throughout the year. Special children's scavenger hunts and junior ranger activities make the park popular for younger visitors.

Licensed and certified battlefield guides take people on group tours. Visitors can also enjoy personalized tours, bus tours, walking tours, cycling tours, and car tours.

If you can't visit in person, there are online resources, such as virtual tours and educational materials.

The National Civil War Museum

The National Civil War Museum was planned to offer a balanced view of the war with perspectives from the Union and the Confederacy. It opened its doors in 2001 in Harrisburg, Pennsylvania. It runs as a private, nonprofit organization.

The museum boasts an enormous collection of more than twenty-five thousand artifacts, manuscripts, documents, and photographs. The museum has been linked to the famous Smithsonian Institution since 2009. There are seventeen permanent exhibits, although there are temporary exhibits as well. The museum has a famous memorial walkway known as the Walk of Valor, which includes bricks engraved with the names of the veterans of the Civil War.

Interactive exhibits, multimedia presentations, educational field trips, workshops, and lectures for visitors are all part of this museum's experience. Educational films and presentations are available in the museum's theater. A key attraction is the museum's research library, which is available by appointment only. The museum also hosts book signings, lectures, and reenactments of the war.

Arlington National Cemetery

Arlington National Cemetery is a famous burial place. It receives over four million visitors yearly. It was founded on May 13th, 1864. The cemetery was created during the war to provide burial space for the fallen Union soldiers. There's quite a story attached to the 639 acres of estate land on which the cemetery is found.

A photograph of hundreds of graves at Arlington National Cemetery.[119]

Originally, George Washington's step-grandson, George Washington Parke Custis, owned the estate. The estate's mansion, Arlington House, was set to be used as a memorial for George Washington.

In 1831, Lee married Washington Parke Custis's daughter, Mary Anna, and the land became their property. Lee and his wife lived at Arlington House until the war started. During the war, the property was confiscated by the Union due to a tax dispute. The house was converted into a village for free and escaped slaves.

On May 13th, 1864, Private William Christman was the first soldier to be buried at this site. On June 15th, 1864, it was officially declared a national cemetery. In 1920, an amphitheater was built to host grand ceremonies, including Memorial Day and Veterans Day.

In 1932, the iconic monument known as the Tomb of the Unknown Soldier was completed. It was dedicated to unidentified US service members. Since July 1937, the tomb has been guarded twenty-four hours a day, seven days a week, come rain or shine, by the 3rd US Infantry Regiment.

Until 1948, the cemetery was segregated by race and rank. Memorial Drive is lined with trees and memorials, and Memorial Bridge links the cemetery to Washington, DC. At the cemetery's entrance stands a memorial honoring women who have served in the US military.

There are over 400,000 graves at Arlington National Cemetery. Some of the famous burials include President John F. Kennedy, Supreme Court Justice Thurgood Marshall, and astronaut John Glenn.

Antietam National Battlefield

A very popular Civil War trail is Antietam National Battlefield, which is found near Sharpsburg, Maryland. The site was set up as a national park in 1890. It covers around 3,230 acres of land. The site offers stunning panoramic views of the battlefield. Hundreds of thousands of visitors go to the battlefield annually.

Its visitor center features exhibits, a theater, and a bookstore. Dunker Church has been restored. Burnside Bridge and Bloody Lane offer visitors a look at where brutal fighting happened during the war. There's also a cemetery with over 4,700 Union graves. Visitors are able to take a self-guided driving tour with eleven stops highlighting key battles.

Park rangers take visitors on guided tours featuring educational programs. There are reenactments and living history demonstrations available. Over one hundred monuments and markers honor the battle and its participants. The field hospital used during the battle has been converted into the Pry House Field Hospital Museum. Farmhouses and barns are also preserved within the park.

A photograph of the American Civil War Memorial.[190]

Modern Perceptions of the American Civil War

Is the Civil War still relevant, or is it just history? This war continues to be a hot topic. It stirs up a mix of emotions and opinions even today. More than half of Americans, around 56 percent, feel issues like race relations, states' rights, and national unity keep the conversations about the Civil War alive. For the other 39 percent of people, this war is viewed as not being relevant to current affairs.

Opinions are splintered over whether this war was worth it or not. Some argue that the war was essential to end slavery and preserve the

Union. They view it as a painful but necessary chapter in the history of the country. Others focus on the devastating loss of life and the long-lasting scars the conflict left on the nation.

As for whether key figures are viewed as heroes or villains, debates continue over their complex legacies. Some are celebrated for their leadership and vision. Others are viewed through a more controversial lens.

There's an ongoing controversy surrounding Confederate symbols in modern America. In recent years, states and cities have taken bold steps to remove Confederate symbols from public spaces, including renaming schools, streets, and military bases that were originally named after Confederate leaders. The removal of statues has sparked discussions and demonstrations.

Confederate symbols have a cultural footprint, influencing everything from fashion to music. However, this has gradually changed, with schools updating curricula to provide a more balanced and inclusive point of view. Many companies have taken a stand on using these symbols, with some retailers choosing to stop selling merchandise featuring the Confederate flag.

Conclusion

It's argued that the Civil War was a wake-up call that led to a stronger federal government. This curbed the power of individual states and unified the nation. The Thirteenth, Fourteenth, and Fifteenth Amendments were what the country needed to launch onto the global stage. The US would become a global powerhouse some seventy to eighty years later.

We hope you've enjoyed this fascinating exploration of one of America's most important historical periods. To finish the book, all that is left is for you to complete this chapter's activity.

We leave you with this note: There are so many remarkable stories from the past just waiting to be explored by a young historian like yourself. Until we meet again for another exciting, fun-filled historical adventure, we wish you happy learning and bid you farewell!

Chapter 10 Activity

Find the following words in the word search below:

- Memorial
- Decoration
- Gettysburg
- Military
- Museum
- Cemetery
- Battlefield
- Arlington
- Ranger
- Washington

A	M	S	D	A	W	E	N	M	H	G	F	D	V	T
Y	U	D	X	C	J	F	H	B	G	F	D	S	X	E
A	S	O	O	P	L	M	N	D	V	C	H	G	H	G
S	E	F	D	C	E	M	E	T	E	R	Y	G	E	G
G	U	S	X	C	A	H	N	G	C	V	F	T	N	E
O	M	F	S	N	X	Z	Y	U	I	O	E	R	T	T
G	S	M	L	P	W	S	Q	Q	S	X	C	G	R	T
V	P	D	E	C	O	R	A	T	I	O	N	S	D	Y
O	U	Y	N	B	V	G	F	V	C	H	J	N	B	S
M	A	R	L	I	N	G	T	O	N	E	D	F	S	B
X	J	W	S	A	X	Z	Z	S	E	R	T	F	C	U
E	H	J	H	J	N	G	B	M	R	A	N	G	E	R
M	I	L	I	T	A	R	Y	G	B	N	M	C	X	G
E	X	D	R	T	G	N	B	F	J	K	O	P	L	M
M	F	G	H	J	K	V	B	N	E	W	Q	R	T	D
O	D	C	S	B	A	T	T	L	E	F	I	E	L	D
R	A	S	D	F	G	H	J	U	Y	T	V	C	X	Z
I	W	W	A	S	H	I	N	G	T	O	N	N	M	V
A	T	U	I	E	R	F	V	D	Y	Z	N	D	S	O
L	Z	C	Z	B	I	M	F	O	T	E	A	P	Q	X

Chapter 10 Activity Answers

	M									
	U									
	S									
	E			C	E	M	E	T	E	R	Y			G
	U													E
	M													T
														T
		D	E	C	O	R	A	T	I	O	N			Y
														S
	A	R	L	I	N	G	T	O	N					B
														U
						R	A	N	G	E	R
M	I	L	I	T	A	R	Y							G
E											
M											
O			B	A	T	T	L	E	F	I	E	L	D
R											
I		W	A	S	H	I	N	G	T	O	N
A											
L											

Here's another book by Enthralling History that you might like

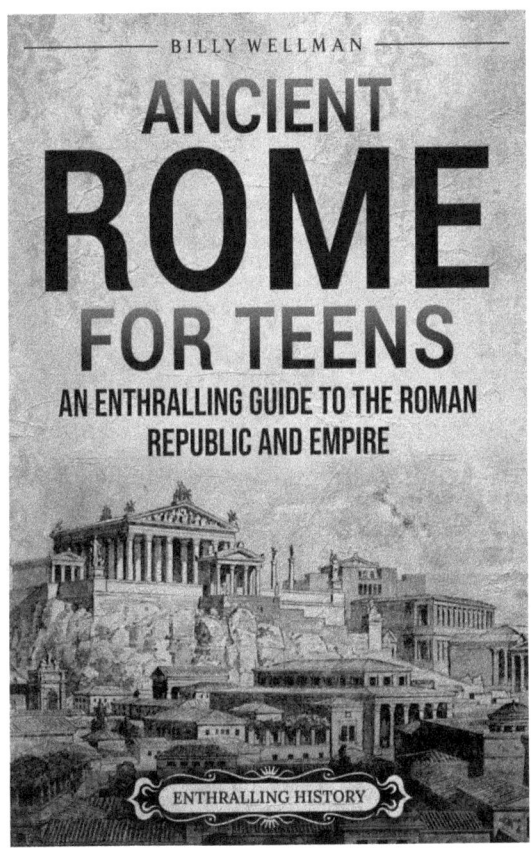

Free limited time bonus

Stop for a moment. We have a free bonus set up for you. The problem is this: we forget 90% of everything that we read after 7 days. Crazy fact, right? Here's the solution: we've created a printable, 1-page pdf summary for this book that you're reading now. All you have to do to get your free pdf summary is to go to the following website: **https://livetolearn.lpages.co/enthrallinghistory/**

Or, Scan the QR code!

Once you do, it will be intuitive. Enjoy, and thank you!

Bibliography

Part 1:

"Americans and the Holocaust." United States Holocaust Memorial Museum. Accessed January 4, 2025. https://exhibitions.ushmm.org/americans-and-the-holocaust/main/state-department-obstruction-1#:~:text=In%20early%201943%2C%20US%20State,from%20reaching%20the%20United%20States.

Barton, David, and Tim Barton. *The American Story: The Beginnings.* WallBuilders Press, 2020.

Bower, Bruce. "American Democracy Arrived Long Before Columbus Did." *Science News Explores: Archaeology,* February 23, 2023. https://www.snexplores.org/article/american-democracy-indigenous-native-people-government#:~:text=The%20peoples%20were%20governed%20through,glue%20holding%20these%20peoples%20together.6.

Bush, George W. "Global War on Terror." George W. Bush Presidential Library. Accessed January 4, 2025. *https://www.georgewbushlibrary.gov/research/topic-guides/global-war-terror.*

Chernow, Ron. *Grant.* Penguin Press, 2017.

Darwin, Charles. *The Descent of Man and Selection in Relation to Sex.*1781. The Project Gutenberg eBook, updated December 27, 2021. https://www.gutenberg.org/cache/epub/2300/pg2300-images.html#link2HCH0005.

Foner, Eric. "Reconstruction." *The Civil War Remembered.* National Park Service. Accessed January 4, 2025. https://www.nps.gov/articles/reconstruction.htm.

Franchi, Rodd. *19th Century American History for Teens: Understanding the Themes, Ideologies, and Conflicts that Inform Our Present.* Rockridge Press, 2021.

Guanghua, Li. "The Influence of Puritanism on the Shaping of Traditional American Values." *International Journal of English Literature and Social Sciences* 6, no. 4 (July-August 2021). https://doi.org/10.22161/ijels.

Keegan, John. *The Second World War.* Penguin Press, 2005.

Kennedy, Randall. "Martin Luther King's Constitution: A Legal History of the Montgomery Bus Boycott." *The Yale Law Journal* 98, no. 6 (April 1989):999-1067. https://www.jstor.org/stable/j232693.

Kidd, Thomas S. *American History, Combined Edition: 1492-Present.* B&H Academic, 2019.

Kidd, Thomas S. *Patrick Henry: First Among Patriots.* Basic Books, 2011.

King, David C. *American History: A Visual Encyclopedia.* Penguin Random House, 2023.

King, Jr., Martin Luther. "'I Have a Dream' Speech." *History*, updated December 19, 2023. https://www.history.com/topics/black-history/i-have-a-dream-speech.

Neely, Mark E. Jr., *The Abraham Lincoln Encyclopedia* (Da Capo Press, Inc., 1982). "Fourth Debate: Charleston, Illinois, September 18, 1858." National Park Service. Accessed January 4, 2025. https://www.nps.gov/liho/learn/historyculture/debate4.htm.

Nelson, Michael. "'America Is Under Attack': What the Morning of 9/11 Was Like for President Bush." *UVA Today,* September 8, 2022. https://news.virginia.edu/content/america-under-attack-what-morning-911-was-president-bush.

Paine, Thomas. *Common Sense.* W. & T. Bradford, 1776. The Project Gutenberg eBook. https://www.gutenberg.org/files/147/147-h/147-h.htm.

Payton, Bre. "Maya Angelou Explains Why She Decided Against An Abortion." *The Federalist,* June 29, 2016. https://thefederalist.com/2016/06/29/maya-angelou-explains-why-she-decided-against-an-abortion/.

Rafe, Jennifer. *Origin: A Genetic History of the Americas.* Twelve, 2022.

"Statement by the President on the Hydrogen Bomb." The American Presidency Project. Accessed January 4, 2025. https://www.presidency.ucsb.edu/documents/statement-the-president-the-hydrogen-bomb.

Taylor, Alan. *American Revolutions: A Continental History, 1750-1804.* W. W. Norton & Company, 2017.

"The Return of the Spirit: The Second Great Awakening." *Christianity Today*. Accessed January 4, 2025. https://www.christianitytoday.com/1989/07/return-of-spirit-second-great-awakening/.

"WW2 Stories: Five Compelling First-Hand Accounts from D-Day." Warfare History Network. Accessed January 4, 2025. https://warfarehistorynetwork.com/ww2-stories-5-compelling-first-hand-accounts-from-d-day/.

Part 2:

The following websites were accessed for relevant information in June, July, August, and September 2024:

- https://www.britannica.com/event/American-Civil-War
- https://www.thoughtco.com/the-lincoln-douglas-debates-of-1858-1773590
- https://www.encyclopedia.com/history/united-states-and-canada/us-history/american-civil-war
- https://www.encyclopedia.com/history/encyclopedias-almanacs-transcripts-and-maps/union
- https://www.thoughtco.com/civil-war-in-east-1863-1865-2360894
- https://www.britannica.com/search?query=stonewall+jackson
- https://www.britannica.com/topic/Confederate-States-of-America
- https://www.britannica.com/video/195131/Overview-role-Texas-American-Civil-War
- https://www.encyclopedia.com/social-sciences-and-law/law/law-divisions-and-codes/thirteenth-amendment
- https://www.encyclopedia.com/history/energy-government-and-defense-magazines/1857-1861-south-prepares-secede
- https://www.encyclopedia.com/history/energy-government-and-defense-magazines/northern-abolitionist-movement
- https://www.britannica.com/biography/Harriet-Tubman
- https://www.thoughtco.com/clara-barton-biography-3528482
- https://www.encyclopedia.com/history/united-states-and-canada/us-history/reconstruction
- https://www.encyclopedia.com/places/united-states-and-canada/miscellaneous-us-geography/arlington-national-cemetery
- https://www.encyclopedia.com/social-sciences/applied-and-social-

sciences-magazines/constitution-us
- https://www.encyclopedia.com/history/energy-government-and-defense-magazines/ulysses-s-grant
- https://www.britannica.com/topic/Army-of-Tennessee
- https://www.britannica.com/search?query=battle+of+gettysburg
- https://www.thoughtco.com/warships-of-the-civil-war-4063148
- https://www.britannica.com/question/What-was-Ulysses-S-Grants-policy-regarding-Reconstruction
- https://www.britannica.com/topic/Fifteenth-Amendment
- https://www.encyclopedia.com/history/dictionaries-thesauruses-pictures-and-press-releases/congress-debates-fourteenth-amendment-1866
- https://www.encyclopedia.com/politics/encyclopedias-almanacs-transcripts-and-maps/fourteenth-amendment-framing
- https://www.britannica.com/summary/Robert-E-Lee
- https://www.britannica.com/biography/Jefferson-Davis/Capture-and-imprisonment
- https://www.thoughtco.com/surrender-at-appomattox-2360931
- https://www.encyclopedia.com/politics/energy-government-and-defense-magazines/assassination-president-lincoln
- https://www.britannica.com/topic/Army-of-the-Potomac
- https://www.britannica.com/question/What-is-the-history-of-Memorial-Day
- https://www.britannica.com/topic/slavery-in-the-United-States
- https://www.encyclopedia.com/history/encyclopedias-almanacs-transcripts-and-maps/african-slavery-americas
- https://www.encyclopedia.com/science/encyclopedias-almanacs-transcripts-and-maps/history-exploration-ii-age-exploration
- https://www.encyclopedia.com/history/dictionaries-thesauruses-pictures-and-press-releases/jacksonian-democracy
- https://www.history.com/topics/american-civil-war/reconstruction
- https://www.thoughtco.com/the-whig-party-and-its-presidents-4160783
- https://www.britannica.com/topic/Free-Soil-Party
- https://www.britannica.com/topic/Whig-Party

- https://www.britannica.com/topic/Republican-Party
- https://www.encyclopedia.com/history/united-states-and-canada/us-history/tenure-office-act
- https://www.encyclopedia.com/reference/encyclopedias-almanacs-transcripts-and-maps/hamlin-hannibal
- https://www.encyclopedia.com/social-sciences-and-law/political-science-and-government/political-parties-and-movements/republican-party
- https://www.encyclopedia.com/history/dictionaries-thesauruses-pictures-and-press-releases/johnson-impeachment

Reference List
- United States. (1776). *Declaration of Independence*. Retrieved from National Archives.
- U.S. Const. art. VI, cl. 2.
- McPherson, J. M. (2003). *Battle Cry of Freedom: The Civil War Era*. Oxford University Press.
- O'Sullivan, J. L. (1845). Annexation. *The United States Magazine and Democratic Review*, 17, 5-10.
- Etcheson, N. (2004). *Bleeding Kansas: Contested Liberty in the Civil War Era*. Lawrence: University Press of Kansas.
- Larson, K. C. (2004). *Bound for the promised land: Harriet Tubman, portrait of an American hero*. New York, NY: Ballantine Books.
- Foner, E. (1995). *Free Soil, Free Labor, Free Men: The Ideology of the Republican Party before the Civil War*. Oxford University Press.
- United States Constitution. Amendment XIII.
- U.S. Const. amend. XIV, § 1, 1868.
- Oates, S. B. (1995). *Woman of Valor: Clara Barton and the Civil War*. Free Press.

If you're looking for additional information about the Civil War, check out these great resources:

Awesome Books for Teens about the Civil War:
- Hunt, I. (1964). *Across Five Aprils*. Follett.
- Keith, H. (1957). *Rifles for Watie*. Crowell.

Great Websites for Teens about the Civil War:
- https://www.history.com/news/harriet-tubman-facts-daring-raid

- https://www.history.com/this-day-in-history/states-meet-to-form-confederacy
- https://www.history.com/topics/us-presidents/abraham-lincoln
- https://www.nationalgeographic.com/premium/article/battle-of-gettysburg-day-maps
- https://www.nationalgeographic.com/history/article/how-mail-in-voting-began-on-civil-war-battlefields

Interesting Educational YouTube Videos for Teens about the Civil War:
- The Civil War - US History for Teens
  https://www.youtube.com/watch?v=N9gwt86Cazs
- Civil War 1862: The Civil War in Four Minutes
  https://www.youtube.com/watch?v=Dc0QETDv93I
- US Civil War Documentary - The Best Documentary Ever
  https://www.youtube.com/watch?v=avMU919vx8A

Image Sources

[1] User:Roblespepe, CC BY-SA 3.0 <https://creativecommons.org/licenses/by-sa/3.0>, via Wikimedia Commons: https://commons.wikimedia.org/wiki/File:Peopling_of_America_through_Beringia.png

[2] Garlan Miles, CC BY-SA 4.0 <https://creativecommons.org/licenses/by-sa/4.0>, via Wikimedia Commons: https://commons.wikimedia.org/wiki/File:Three_Sisters_4.jpg

[3] Herb Roe, CC BY-SA 3.0 <https://creativecommons.org/licenses/by-sa/3.0>, via Wikimedia Commons: https://commons.wikimedia.org/wiki/File:Braden_Style_Chunkey_player_St_Marys_Mound_Site_HRoe.jpg

[4] https://commons.wikimedia.org/wiki/File:Columbus_Taking_PossessionEXD.jpg

[5] https://commons.wikimedia.org/wiki/File:De_Soto_by_Telfer_%26_Sartain.jpg

[6] Bwickliffe, CC BY-SA 4.0 <https://creativecommons.org/licenses/by-sa/4.0>, via Wikimedia Commons: https://commons.wikimedia.org/wiki/File:The_Gonzalez-Alvarez_House_Oldest_Surviving_House_in_St_Augustine,_FL.jpg

[7] https://www.education.com/

[8] Photo zoomed in. https://commons.wikimedia.org/wiki/File:The-Lost-Colony_0.jpg

[9] https://commons.wikimedia.org/wiki/File:NPG_65_61_Pocahontas.tif

[10] Internet Archive Book Images, No restrictions, via Wikimedia Commons: https://commons.wikimedia.org/wiki/File:A_popular_history_of_the_United_States_-_from_the_first_discovery_of_the_western_hemisphere_by_the_Northmen,_to_the_end_of_the_first_century_of_the_union_of_the_states;_preceded_by_a_sketch_of_the_(14597125217).jpg

[11] https://commons.wikimedia.org/wiki/File:The_First_Thanksgiving_cph.3g04961.jpg

[12] https://commons.wikimedia.org/wiki/File:Jonathan_Edwards_engraving.jpg#file

[13] AlexiusHoratius, CC BY-SA 3.0 <https://creativecommons.org/licenses/by-sa/3.0>, via Wikimedia Commons: https://commons.wikimedia.org/wiki/File:NorthAmerica1763-A.png

[14] https://commons.wikimedia.org/wiki/File:Joseph_Siffrein_Duplessis_-_Benjamin_Franklin_-_Google_Art_Project.jpg
[15] https://commons.wikimedia.org/wiki/File:Paul_Revere%27s_ride_-_NARA_-_535721.tif
[16] https://commons.wikimedia.org/wiki/File:Washington_Crossing_the_Delaware_by_Emanuel_Leutze,_MMA-NYC,_1851.jpg
[17] https://commons.wikimedia.org/wiki/File:George_Washington_MET_DT220048.jpg
[18] https://commons.wikimedia.org/wiki/File:Frederick_Douglass_(circa_1879).jpg
[19] William Morris, CC BY-SA 4.0 <https://creativecommons.org/licenses/by-sa/4.0>, via Wikimedia Commons: https://commons.wikimedia.org/wiki/File:Louisiana_Purchase.png
[20] Made by User:Golbez, CC BY-SA 3.0 <http://creativecommons.org/licenses/by-sa/3.0/>, via Wikimedia Commons: https://commons.wikimedia.org/wiki/File:United_States_1861-08-1862.png
[21] https://commons.wikimedia.org/wiki/File:Clara_Barton_1865.jpg
[22] https://commons.wikimedia.org/wiki/File:Oil_on_Canvas_Portrait_of_Dred_Scott_(cropped).jpg
[23] https://commons.wikimedia.org/wiki/File:Freedmen%27s_Schoolhouse_Burns_in_1866_Memphis_Riot.jpg
[24] https://commons.wikimedia.org/wiki/File:Ku_Klux_Klan_demonstration_in_Tampa.jpg
[25] https://commons.wikimedia.org/wiki/File:Rosa_Parks_being_fingerprinted_by_Deputy_Sheriff_D.H._Lackey_after_being_arrested_on_February_22,_1956,_during_the_Montgomery_bus_boycott.jpg
[26] David Erickson, CC BY 2.0 <https://creativecommons.org/licenses/by/2.0>, via Wikimedia Commons: https://commons.wikimedia.org/wiki/File:Martin_Luther_King_Jr._-_I_Have_A_Dream_Speech.jpg
[27] Fluteflute & User:Bibi Saint-Pol (English translation), CC BY-SA 4.0 <https://creativecommons.org/licenses/by-sa/4.0>, via Wikimedia Commons: https://commons.wikimedia.org/wiki/File:Beginning_of_WWI_in_Europe_(belligerents_in_1914-1915).gif
[28] https://commons.wikimedia.org/wiki/File:Sinking_of_the_Lusitania_London_Illus_News.jpg
[29] Egrim21Egrim21, CC BY-SA 4.0 <https://creativecommons.org/licenses/by-sa/4.0>, via Wikimedia Commons: https://commons.wikimedia.org/wiki/File:Women_Navy_Recruit_Poster.jpg
[30] Michael Kassube, CC BY-SA 3.0 <https://creativecommons.org/licenses/by-sa/3.0>, via Wikimedia Commons: https://commons.wikimedia.org/wiki/File:WWI_postcard_trench.JPG
[31] https://commons.wikimedia.org/wiki/File:USS_SHAW_exploding_Pearl_Harbor_Nara_80-G-16871_2.jpg
[32] https://commons.wikimedia.org/wiki/File:We_Can_Do_It!_NARA_535413_-_Restoration_2.jpg
[33] SHAEF [Supreme Headquarters Allied Expeditionary Forces] Public Relations Division, Public domain, via Wikimedia Commons: https://commons.wikimedia.org/wiki/File:Normandy_landings_D_Day_to_D_plus_3_Supreme_Allied_Command_footage_(Signal_Corps_catalog_reel_nos_111-ADC-1319,_111-ADC-1318,_111-ADC-2093,_and_111-ADC-1336)_35.png

[34] *Photo zoomed in. J Malan Heslop, colorized by Julius Jääskeläinen, CC BY 2.0* <https://creativecommons.org/licenses/by/2.0>, *via Wikimedia Commons;* https://commons.wikimedia.org/wiki/File:Liberated_prisoner_of_the_Ebensee_concentration_camp_in_Austria,_8_May_1945._(4589900357.5).jpg

[35] https://commons.wikimedia.org/wiki/File:Nagasakibomb.jpg

[36] https://www.education.com/

[37] *Photo zoomed in.* https://commons.wikimedia.org/wiki/File:L_to_R_British_Prime_Minister_Winston_Churchill_President_Harry_S._Truman_and_Soviet_leader_Josef_Stalin_in_the..._-_NARA_-_198958_myhritage.jpg

[38] https://commons.wikimedia.org/wiki/File:P.S._58_-_Carroll_%26_Smith_Sts._Bklyn._hold_a_take_cover_drill_01489v.jpg

[39] *Photo zoomed in.* https://commons.wikimedia.org/wiki/File:LeMay_Cuban_Missile_Crisis.jpg

[40] *Mos.ru, CC BY 4.0* <https://creativecommons.org/licenses/by/4.0>, *via Wikimedia Commons:* https://commons.wikimedia.org/wiki/File:Laika_in_1957.jpg

[41] https://commons.wikimedia.org/wiki/File:Aldrin_Apollo_11.jpg

[42] https://commons.wikimedia.org/wiki/File:National_Park_Service_9-11_Statue_of_Liberty_and_WTC_fire.jpg

[43] https://commons.wikimedia.org/wiki/File:President_George_W._Bush_with_the_National_Security_Council.jpg

[44] *Hamid Mir, CC BY-SA 3.0* <https://creativecommons.org/licenses/by-sa/3.0>, *via Wikimedia Commons:* https://commons.wikimedia.org/wiki/File:Hamid_Mir_interviewing_Osama_bin_Laden_and_Ayman_al-Zawahiri_2001.jpg

[45] https://commons.wikimedia.org/wiki/File:United_States_Armed_Forces_in_the_Gulf_War_1991_GLF1058.jpg

[46] *justgrimes, CC BY-SA 2.0* <https://creativecommons.org/licenses/by-sa/2.0>, *via Wikimedia Commons:* https://commons.wikimedia.org/wiki/File:Bin_laden_death_washington_post.jpg

[47] https://commons.wikimedia.org/wiki/File:Gilbert_Stuart,_George_Washington_Lansdowne_portrait,_1796).jpg

[48] https://commons.wikimedia.org/wiki/File:Thomas_Jefferson_1805_Portrait_3x4_Crop.jpg

[49] https://commons.wikimedia.org/wiki/File:Abraham_Lincoln_circa_1860.png

[50] https://commons.wikimedia.org/wiki/File:Theodore_Rooseveltnewtry.jpg

[51] *Photo zoomed in.* https://commons.wikimedia.org/wiki/File:Yalta_summit_1945_with_Churchill,_Roosevelt,_Stalin.jpg

[52] *Photo zoomed in.:* https://commons.wikimedia.org/wiki/File:President_John_F._Kennedy_with_Robert_F._Kennedy,_Jr._(02).jpg

[53] https://commons.wikimedia.org/wiki/File:President_Ronald_Reagan_and_Prince_Charles.jpg

[54] https://commons.wikimedia.org/wiki/File:Mathew_Brady_-_Franklin_Pierce_(cropped).jpg

[55] https://commons.wikimedia.org/wiki/File:James_Buchanan_(cropped).jpg

[56] https://commons.wikimedia.org/wiki/File:Andrew_johnson2.png
[57] https://commons.wikimedia.org/wiki/File:Benedict_Arnold_1color_(crop).jpg
[58] https://commons.wikimedia.org/wiki/File:Susan_B_Anthony_c1855.png
[59] https://commons.wikimedia.org/wiki/File:Geronimo_(Goyathlay),_a_Chiricahua_Apache,_full-length,_kneeling_with_rifle,_1887_-_NARA_-_530880.jpg
[60] https://commons.wikimedia.org/wiki/File:Henry_Ford_and_Barney_Oldfield_with_Old_999,_1902.jpg
[61] Photo zoomed in. https://commons.wikimedia.org/wiki/File:Wright_First_Flight_1903Dec17_(restore_115).tif?page=1
[62] https://commons.wikimedia.org/wiki/File:Jesse_Owens_%C3%A0_Berlin,_JO_de_1936.jpg
[63] https://commons.wikimedia.org/wiki/File:Portrait_photograph_of_Maya_Angelou_with_a_copy_of_I_Know_Why_the_Caged_Bird_Sings_in_Los_Angeles,_November_3,_1971.jpg
[64] https://www.education.com/
[65] https://www.education.com/
[66] https://commons.wikimedia.org/wiki/File:American_Civil_War_Montage.jpg
[67] https://commons.wikimedia.org/wiki/File:Signing_of_the_Declaration_of_Independence_4K.jpg
[68] https://commons.wikimedia.org/wiki/File:Cotton_gin_EWM_2007.jpg
[69] Benutzer:ErnstA (Ernst Schütte), CC BY-SA 3.0 <http://creativecommons.org/licenses/by-sa/3.0/>, via Wikimedia Commons; https://commons.wikimedia.org/wiki/File:LouisianaPurchase.png
[70] https://commons.wikimedia.org/wiki/File:American_Progress_(John_Gast_painting).jpg
[71] https://commons.wikimedia.org/wiki/File:Main_deck_of_a_slave_ship-P6280084.JPG
[72] https://commons.wikimedia.org/wiki/File:Prince_hall_portrait.jpg
[73] Billy Hathorn, CC0, via Wikimedia Commons
https://commons.wikimedia.org/wiki/File:William_Lloyd_Garrison_at_National_Portrait_Gallery_IMG_4392.JPG
[74] https://commons.wikimedia.org/wiki/File:Harriet_Beecher_Stowe_c1852.jpg
[75] https://commons.wikimedia.org/wiki/File:Frederick_Douglass_(1840s).jpg
[76] CC BY-SA 4.0 <https://creativecommons.org/licenses/by-sa/4.0>, via Wikimedia Commons; https://commons.wikimedia.org/wiki/File:Tubman,_Harriet_Ross_(c._1821-1913).png
[77] https://commons.wikimedia.org/wiki/File:Undergroundrailroadsmall2.jpg
[78] https://commons.wikimedia.org/wiki/File:Andrew_jackson_head.jpg
[79] https://commons.wikimedia.org/wiki/File:Abrahamlincoln.jpg
[80] https://commons.wikimedia.org/wiki/File:Hannibal_Hamlin,_photo_portrait_seated,_c1860-65-retouched-crop_(cropped).jpg
[81] https://commons.wikimedia.org/wiki/File:Abraham_Lincoln%27s_return_home_after_his_successful_campaign_for_the_Presidency_of_the_United_States,_in_October,_1860_LCCN2003677696.jpg)

[82] Rakeem Abdiel Gunawan, CC BY-SA 4.0 <https://creativecommons.org/licenses/by-sa/4.0>, via Wikimedia Commons; https://commons.wikimedia.org/wiki/File:The_United_states_and_the_confederate_states_of_America_with_its_states.jpg

[83] https://commons.wikimedia.org/wiki/File:Flag_of_the_Confederate_States_(1861%E2%80%931863).svg

[84] https://commons.wikimedia.org/wiki/File:Bombardment_of_Fort_Sumter.jpg

[85] https://commons.wikimedia.org/wiki/File:Confederate_uniforms_(13147922734).jpg

[86] https://commons.wikimedia.org/wiki/File:James_Hope_-_The_Army_of_the_Potomac_-_45.890_-_Museum_of_Fine_Arts.jpg

[87] https://commons.wikimedia.org/wiki/File:First_Battle_of_Bull_Run_Kurz_%26_Allison.jpg

[88] https://commons.wikimedia.org/wiki/File:Stonewall_Jackson_portrait_by_William_D._Washington.jpg

[89] https://commons.wikimedia.org/wiki/File:Terrific_combat_between_the_%22Monitor%22_2_guns_%26_%22Merrimac%22_10_guns_The_first_fight_between_iron_clad_ships_of_war,_in_Hampton_Roads,_March_9th_1862,_in_which_the_little_%22Monitor%22_whipped_the_LCCN90710608.jpg

[90] https://commons.wikimedia.org/wiki/File:Kurz_%26_Allison_-_Battle_of_Antietam.jpg

[91] https://commons.wikimedia.org/wiki/File:Thure_de_Thulstrup_-_L._Prang_and_Co._-_Battle_of_Gettysburg_-_Restoration_by_Adam_Cuerden_(cropped).jpg

[92] https://commons.wikimedia.org/wiki/File:Picketts_charge_confederates_by_Edwin_Forbes.jpg

[93] https://commons.wikimedia.org/wiki/File:Gettysburg_Address_(poster).jpg

[94] https://commons.wikimedia.org/wiki/File:Fall_of_Petersburg_LCCN2003656875.jpg

[95] Stratton, Ella (Hines), Mrs. [from old catalog], No restrictions, via Wikimedia Commons https://commons.wikimedia.org/wiki/File:Surrender_of_General_Robert_E._Lee,_9_April_1865.jpg

[96] https://commons.wikimedia.org/wiki/File:Battle_of_Fort_Donelson.png

[97] https://commons.wikimedia.org/wiki/File:The_Great_Naval_Battle_Opposite_the_City_of_Memphis,_June_6,_1862_-_Alexander_Simplot.jpg

[98] https://commons.wikimedia.org/wiki/File:Chickamauga.jpg

[99] https://commons.wikimedia.org/wiki/File:Battle_of_Atlanta_Kurz_%26_Allison.jpg

[100] https://commons.wikimedia.org/wiki/File:Sherman%27s_March_to_the_Sea_-_Project_Gutenberg_eText_21566.jpg?20120301074300

[101] https://commons.wikimedia.org/wiki/File:BattleofFortBlakely1.png

[102] https://commons.wikimedia.org/wiki/File:Lincoln_assassination_slide_c1900_-_Restoration.jpg

[103] https://commons.wikimedia.org/wiki/File:President_Andrew_Johnson.jpg

[104] https://commons.wikimedia.org/wiki/File:The_surrender_of_Genl._Joe_Johnston_near_Greensboro_N.C.,_April_26th_1865_LCCN90714979.jpg

[105] Txsurfgirl1, CC BY-SA 4.0 <https://creativecommons.org/licenses/by-sa/4.0>, via Wikimedia Commons;

https://commons.wikimedia.org/wiki/File:Battle_of_Palmito_Ranch_marker_South_Texas.jpg
[106] https://commons.wikimedia.org/wiki/File:13th_Amendment_Pg1of1_AC.jpg
[107] https://commons.wikimedia.org/wiki/File:Chambers_of_the_Senate_during_the_impeachment_trial_of_Andrew_Johnson_(1).gif
[108] https://commons.wikimedia.org/wiki/File:Freedmens_Bureau_1866.jpg
[109] https://commons.wikimedia.org/wiki/File:Clara_Barton_1860s.jpg
[110] https://commons.wikimedia.org/wiki/File:President_Ulysses_S._Grant_by_Mathew_Brady_3.jpg
[111] https://commons.wikimedia.org/wiki/File:Bird%27s-eye_view_of_Grant%27s_Tomb,_New_York_LCCN97506556.jpg
[112] https://commons.wikimedia.org/wiki/File:Robert_Edward_Lee.jpg
[113] https://commons.wikimedia.org/wiki/File:Jefferson_Davis_1862.jpg
[114] https://commons.wikimedia.org/wiki/File:William_tecumseh_sherman.jpg
[115] By King of Hearts, CC BY-SA 4.0 <https://creativecommons.org/licenses/by-sa/4.0>, via Wikimedia Commons; https://commons.wikimedia.org/wiki/File:William_Tecumseh_Sherman_Monument_New_York_January_2016_002.jpg
[116] ys, CC BY-SA 2.0 <https://creativecommons.org/licenses/by-sa/2.0>, via Wikimedia Commons; https://commons.wikimedia.org/wiki/File:Lincoln_Memorial_EB.jpg
[117] https://commons.wikimedia.org/wiki/File:Aerial_view_of_Lincoln_Memorial_-_east_side_EDIT.jpeg
[118] Jlmachlin, CC BY-SA 4.0 <https://creativecommons.org/licenses/by-sa/4.0>, via Wikimedia Commons; https://commons.wikimedia.org/wiki/File:Gettysburg_Battlefield_Cannon,_Gettysburg_National_Military_Park,_PA.jpg
[119] Dudva, CC BY-SA 4.0 <https://creativecommons.org/licenses/by-sa/4.0>, via Wikimedia Commons; https://commons.wikimedia.org/wiki/File:Arlington_National_Cemetery.jpg
[120] https://commons.wikimedia.org/wiki/File:Antietam_National_Battlefield_Memorial_-_memorial_(Bloodylane)_18.JPG

www.ingramcontent.com/pod-product-compliance
Lightning Source LLC
Chambersburg PA
CBHW072104050526
44107CB00099B/429